GERMAN SEA-POWER

ITS RISE, PROGRESS, AND ECONOMIC BASIS

GERMAN SEA-POWER

ITS RISE, PROGRESS, AND ECONOMIC
BASIS

BY ARCHIBALD HURD AND
HENRY CASTLE

WITH MAPS AND APPENDICES GIVING THE
FLEET LAWS, ETC.

GREENWOOD PRESS, PUBLISHERS
WESTPORT, CONNECTICUT

VA
513
H82
1971

Originally published in 1913
by John Murray, London

Reprinted from an original copy in the collections
of the Brooklyn Public Library

First Greenwood Reprinting 1971

Library of Congress Catalogue Card Number 71-110846

SBN 8371-4513-9

Printed in the United States of America

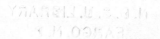

CONTENTS

Map of the World, showing Cables, Coaling Stations, etc., and
the possessions of the British and German peoples.

Map of the North Sea, showing Naval Bases, Distances, etc.

INTRODUCTION

ANGLO-GERMAN rivalry is definitely shaping under our very eyes the political conceptions and the defensive machinery of all the peoples within the British Empire. Already this hardly concealed antagonism between the world's greatest naval Power and the world's most formidable military Power, and all that it connotes, has completely changed the course of British foreign policy and led to a regrouping of the nations of Europe on the one hand, while on the other it is the determining factor in the policy of Japan and the United States. To many political prophets we appear to have reached the opening phase of a long struggle which will decide whether British or German civilization is to dominate the world in future. This Anglo-German antagonism finds its most acute expression in naval policy, and it is believed in many quarters that the struggle will eventually be decided by naval conflict. Whether this anticipation is well based or is merely the unfounded belief of politicians and philosophers who are prone to believe in war as the only solution of international difficulties time alone can show.

Whatever may be the outcome of the naval problem which is now so frequently the subject of controversy in both countries, it is of paramount importance that the people, not only of the United Kingdom, but of the whole British Empire, should comprehend at any rate the main factors underlying the remarkable expansion of the German Fleet which has occurred since the Navy Act of 1900 was adopted. These are the matters examined in the present volume with a completeness which it is believed has not been attempted before. There could be no more opportune moment for a study of the maritime development of Germany. This year the Emperor will celebrate the twenty-fifth year of his accession, and 1913 happens to be the centenary of the freedom of Germany, secured at a heavy cost on the battlefield of Leipzig on October 18 and 19, 1813.

In the course of the study of Germany's political and economic conditions and her maritime develop-ment, not a few popular conceptions firmly rooted in the English mind must be challenged, while it may be that Germans themselves will obtain from these pages a juster comprehension of the British position. The book has been written without any political object in view, but with an honest desire to set forth the truth. If it succeeds in dispelling some of the misconceptions which exist in both countries, this examination of the rise and progress of German sea-power, and its economic and political bases, will not have been undertaken in vain.

The present antagonism between the two countries and, in particular, the anxiety with which the British people watch the development of German naval arma-ments, rest upon no inherent antipathy between the two peoples. As Mr. Balfour pointed out recently in his article in *Nord und Süd*, the German nation has never been the enemy of the British nation. In the long series of wars in which Britain has been involved between the revolution of 1688 and the peace of 1815, German States were our allies, and on many Con-tinental battlefields English and German soldiers have fought in the same cause. Moreover, Englishmen do not forget the debt which the world owes to German genius and German learning, and down to a compara-tively recent period the two nations were united in their political policy. When the present Emperor came to the throne, and for many years afterwards,

England and Germany were on terms of closest friendship.

It is only during the past fifteen years, a period marked by the rapid growth of the German Fleet, that the relations between the two countries have become strained and even embittered. No responsible statesman on either side of the North Sea can desire that the present animosity should be perpetuated, and nothing can tend to eliminate occasions of misunderstanding better than an impartial review of Germany's maritime history and development in the effort to discover the real causes which have led to the growth of her war fleet.

If the expansion of Germany's naval power were purely an artificial expression of her desire to dominate the seas, if behind it lay no economic justification, then, indeed, the future of the two countries would be dark, and those who believe a war to be inevitable could be doubly sure that this was the only solution of the present controversy. But the growth of the German Navy, if it is not completely explained and justified by the development of German maritime interests, is at any rate not an exotic policy. If Englishmen desire to understand the standpoint of the German people they must recognize historical facts. The belief that Germany has no maritime past and no spontaneous maritime instincts is completely disposed of by the remarkable record of the Hanseatic League, which achieved a moral and economic victory in the only war in which we engaged with it. Moreover, Englishmen would do well to disabuse their minds of the idea that until recent times there has been no movement in Germany to possess what may be described as a political navy for the purpose of acquiring colonies— places of settlement in which German emigrants may preserve their German nationality and their distinctive German habits and customs. It is only necessary to recall the days of the Great Elector to comprehend that this belief is unfounded.

On the other hand, an examination of the course which German history has run during the past quarter of a century reveals the fact that, however keenly the Emperor William II. may have sympathized with and encouraged the movement for naval expansion, he cannot be regarded as its creator. In the early days of the naval agitation the Emperor took a prominent part in educating politicians and the public, but in recent years the direction of naval policy has passed largely beyond his control under the influence of a campaign engineered by the Navy League, which is, it is true, kept closely informed of the Imperial point of view, and—perhaps more important—by those newspapers which reflect the views and ends of the real creator of the modern German Fleet, Grand-Admiral von Tirpitz. This sailor, who until a dozen years or so ago was almost as unknown to the German people as to Englishmen generally, has for some considerable time controlled the development of German naval policy, and also in no small measure Germany's foreign policy, keeping the latter in just those channels calculated to feed the special interests which he has made it his life's work to create. Chancellors, Foreign Secretaries, and other Ministers may come and go— and have come and gone—but the Naval Secretary has remained in office, and still remains, as the personal embodiment of the aims and ambitions of the school of thought which dominates the Admiralstab in Berlin.

Admitting the domination of German naval policy by this sailor-statesman, admitting also that naval policy has outrun Germany's present economic development, and far exceeds the needs of German maritime interests, it yet remains a fact that Germany has a great stake on the seas, and therefore that the development of the German Fleet cannot be condemned as an exotic policy prompted solely by ambitions of aggrandizement and greed. Nothing will conduce better to an understanding between the two

peoples than the realization by Englishmen that
Germany has great and valuable interests afloat which
justify the accumulation of considerable naval armaments, though they cannot excuse the Anglophobe
tendency of German public opinion and the final and
aggressive expression of German policy embodied in
the Navy Act of 1912.

There is complete assurance that German naval
expansion is not a type of hypertrophy, in a financial
sense, and that the existence of a strong German Fleet
must be regarded as a permanent factor in world
politics, because it is, in some measure at least, the
expression of a natural and legitimate need. An
examination of German economic development reveals
the fact that, though German expenditure on military
and naval, and particularly naval, armaments in recent
years has been in excess of her financial resources, it
has not seriously affected her economic strength. If
the political conditions remain unchanged, she will
before long be able to bear much heavier burdens
than she bears to-day without suffering economic
injury.

But will those conditions remain unchanged? The
present naval policy of the German Empire rests
upon a state of unstable political equilibrium. If
that equilibrium is disturbed, as it well may be within
the next few years, German naval policy can hardly
remain unaffected. But for the present it is well to
recognize that that policy—embodied in definite legislation, which can be checked only by other legislation
—holds the field, and that, until a radical change occurs
in the political conditions, and this finds expression in
constitutional change, it will continue to operate from
year to year with unfaltering persistency until the naval
legislation has been translated into ships and men co-
ordinated for the purposes of war in accordance with
the principle repeatedly enunciated by Grand-Admiral
von Tirpitz and those who have supported him in the
Press and on the platform. We have to assume that in

1920 Germany will possess 61 capital ships—battleships or battle-cruisers—40 unarmoured cruisers, 144 destroyers, and 72 submarines, representing an accumulation of naval armament which in the days of their greatest pride the British people never possessed.

Is it surprising to the German people that this development of naval policy by the most formidable military Power in Europe should occasion acute anxiety, not only in the United Kingdom, but in all the Dominions overseas? It is only necessary to compare the relative strength of the two Empires, their populations, and geographical distribution,* to appreciate the British standpoint, and to understand the development of British policy which has occurred within the past few years. The world has witnessed a strengthening of the ties hitherto existing between England and her oversea Dominions, and a determination on the part of those young States to help bear the burdens of Empire which it has appeared to them might in a few years' time, owing to the acute pressure in Europe, prove too much even for the Old Country's broad shoulders. The armament movement on the continent of Europe, in which Germany has been in the forefront, bids fair to cement the British Empire into a close-knit confederation for defensive purposes. Not only have the Dominions adopted measures for defending their territories by adequately drilled citizen soldiers, but they have not hesitated to lend their aid to the defence of British interests afloat. Australia has founded a navy which it is intended shall be a branch of the ancient fleet of the United Kingdom; the Canadian Government has decided to present three large capital ships to the Royal Navy as an emergency contribution, and is about to elaborate a permanent policy of co-operation with the Mother Country in naval defence. The Dominion of New Zealand has given to the

* See Appendix VIII.

Mother Country a battle-cruiser of the Dreadnought type, and a yet more costly armoured ship has been voted by the Federated Malay States, which are not even part of the British Empire, but which, nevertheless, in recognition of British protection in the past, have shown that they share in the feeling of anxiety as to the future which casts its shadow over the British Empire.

It may be said that this anxiety is exaggerated, but what are the conditions which exist and which will continue? We cannot do better than quote the following passage from Mr. Balfour's admirable study of the Anglo-German problem to which reference has already been made:

"The external facts of the situation appear to be as follows: The greatest military Power and the second greatest naval Power in the world is adding both to her Army and to her Navy. She is increasing the strategic railways which lead to frontier States—not merely to frontier States which themselves possess powerful armies, but to small States which can have no desire but to remain neutral if their formidable neighbours should unhappily become belligerents. She is in like manner modifying her naval arrangements so as to make her naval strength instantly effective. It is conceivable that all this may be only in order to render herself impregnable against attack. Such an object would certainly be commendable, though the efforts undergone to secure it might (to outside observers) seem in excess of any possible danger. If all nations could be made impregnable to the same extent, peace would doubtless be costly, but at least it would be secure. Unfortunately, no mere analysis of the German preparations for war will show for what purpose they are designed. A tremendous weapon has been forged; every year adds something to its efficiency and power; it is as formidable for purposes of aggression as for purposes of defence. But to what end it was originally designed, and in what cause it will ultimately be used, can only be determined, if determined at all, by extraneous considerations.

" I here approach the most difficult and delicate part of my task. Let me preface it by saying that ordinary Englishmen do not believe, and certainly I do not believe, either that the great body of the German people wish to make an attack on their neighbours or that the German Government intend it. A war in which the armed manhood of half Europe would take part can be no object of deliberate desire either for nations or for statesmen. The danger lies elsewhere. It lies in the coexistence of that marvellous instrument of warfare which embraces the German Army and Navy, with the assiduous, I had almost said the organized, advocacy of a policy which it seems impossible to reconcile with the peace of the world or the rights of nations. For those who accept this policy German development means German territorial expansion. All countries which hinder, though it be only in self-defence, the realization of this ideal, are regarded as hostile ; and war, or the threat of war, is deemed the natural and fitting method by which the ideal itself is to be accomplished."

These decisive words reflect with perfect accuracy the British point of view. Great Britain is the centre of a vast maritime Empire of which the seas are the lines of communication. If the people of the United Kingdom were not dependent for almost all their food and raw material upon the free passage of merchant ships to and from their shores, if the Dominions overseas had no oversea commerce growing from year to year, still the necessity would exist for the maintenance by the British people of an unchallengeable supremacy. It is the most natural thing that they should regard with jealous anxiety the growth of a great war fleet, when that war fleet has behind it vast land forces to which the ships can give transport and a policy which is too frequently represented by leading Germans as being aimed at British security. The only hope for the disappearance of the antagonism between the two peoples lies in a comprehension of each other's economic and strategical necessities ; and if this volume succeeds in giving to Englishmen a truer conception of German policy and German economic and maritime development, and to Germans a better appreciation of the position of the British people as the guardians of an Empire to which un-challengeable sea-power is a necessity, it will have done something to dispel those dark clouds which still hang menacingly on the political horizon.

GERMAN SEA-POWER

ITS RISE AND PROGRESS AND ECONOMIC BASIS

CHAPTER I

GERMAN MARITIME ASCENDANCY IN THE PAST

AMONG the many popular errors which exist with regard to Germany, none is farther from the truth than the belief that her fleet is the arbitrary and artificial creation of the Emperor William II., and but for him would never have attained formidable dimensions. This idea is not only erroneous, but exceedingly mischievous, for it is likely to lead to false conclusions as to the probable development of Germany's position in the world and her future relations to other naval Powers. If Germany's naval expansion depended entirely, or even mainly, on the conviction or caprice of a single man, it might reasonably be expected to cease or slacken with the passing of his stimulating will. But, much as William II. has done to accelerate the pace of his country's naval progress, the German Fleet has its tap-roots in the soil of history, and has drawn sustenance from geographical, economic, and political conditions, of which it is the natural and inevitable product. It is, in fact, but the deferred logical outcome of a slow secular process, and will have a tendency to increase so long as that process continues.

Like the foundation of the Empire in 1870, the formation of the modern German Fleet is the result of a movement that had its origin among the people and not among the Princes of the country. And this naval movement sprang up and reached its greatest vigour in those sea-board districts that still sedulously keep alive the splendid tradition of the Hanseatic League, which, as the strongest maritime Power of its day, for centuries almost monopolized the trade of Northern and Western Europe, and, with the word "sterling," a corruption of "Easterling," the name popularly given to its members, has left on Great Britain the indelible stamp of its former mercantile domination. For the coin of the Hanse towns, by reason of its unimpeachable quality, was once universally sought after in England, and thus became the standard of monetary excellence.

The memories of the Hansa are the "historical foundation" on which are based Germany's present claims to a leading place among the maritime nations, and they have played a prominent part in every agitation for the increase of her fleet. Why, it is asked, should she not again assume upon the seas that dominating position which she once undoubtedly held? Why, with her expanding population, trade, and wealth, should she not reclaim that maritime ascendancy which she forfeited to Holland in the seventeenth century, and which a hundred years later passed to Great Britain? Why should she not realize that dream which was in the mind of Friedrich List when he wrote: "How easy it would have been for the Hanse towns, in the epoch of their rule over the sea, to attain national unity through the instrumentality of the imperial power, to unite the whole littoral from Dunkirk to Riga under one nationality, and thus to win and maintain for the German nation supremacy in industry, trade, and sea-power!"

It is, moreover, not without significance that the Hansa itself was, in a sense, democratic, and that, at a time when Germany, as a national unit, was rendered impotent in the world by her superabundance of

Princes, her citizens were able, on their own initiative, and by their own energies, to assert their power and capacity as a maritime people.

When that portion of Central Europe which is to-day inhabited by the German-speaking races emerged from the Dark Ages, it was as a complex and chaotic mosaic of principalities, spiritual and temporal, loosely held together by that grandiose figment the Holy Roman Empire, of which Voltaire very aptly said that it was neither holy, Roman, nor an empire. No other form of misgovernment which has ever existed in the Western world did so much as this venerable imposture to retard the development of the peoples living under its rule. It was only after Napoleon had freed the ground of its tottering ruins that the erection of Modern Germany became possible. He was no less necessary to clear the site than Bismarck was to raise the structure. To this extent Napoleon may be looked upon as the founder of the German Empire.

When the conqueror's legions marched across Europe, sweeping away unnatural and injurious frontiers, the German people had for a millennium incessantly been called upon to pay the price of the selfish feuds of its ruling dynasties. In the earlier phases of these devastating quarrels, the towns gradually acquired a position of actual or qualified independence. With their ramparts and bastions, they were like rocks rising out of a raging sea. Within their defences industry and trade progressed, while without all was storm and strife. By adroit bargaining with the impoverished Princes in whose territories they were situated, they little by little enlarged their immemorial liberties, till they eventually became—in fact, where not in law—independent municipal republics. Many of them were admitted to the rank of "imperial cities," and owed allegiance to none but the Emperor. Of these, three—Hamburg, Bremen, and Lübeck—which were also among the most prominent members of the

Hansa, and are still called the "Hanse Towns," even now retain that measure of independence which is left to the federated States known in their entirety as the German Empire. When the Hanseatic League was at its zenith, the towns which stood at its head and directed its policy would suffer little interference with their management of their own affairs, external as well as internal. The eleventh century witnessed the rise of the German towns, the twelfth the development of their spirit of independence, the thirteenth their first serious attempts at combination for mutual defence, the fourteenth the final triumph of the principle of federation in the ascendancy of the Hanseatic League.

It was the natural ideal of the German towns of the early Middle Ages to be self-sufficing in all things, for in that epoch of violence and tumult it was an obvious disadvantage to be dependent upon the outside world for any of the necessities of existence, and they accordingly inclined strongly to a policy of exclusive protection. There were, however, many commodities, which, for climatic or other reasons, they were unable to produce within the compass of their own walls. For the raw materials of their handicrafts, the silks and spices of the East, the woollen fabrics of Flanders, the furs of Russia and Scandinavia, the dried or salted fish prescribed for fast days by the Church, the towns were compelled to rely upon external trade, which increased in volume with the growth of their prosperity and the rise of their standard of life. But the journeys which their merchants undertook to adjacent States, or across the seas to distant countries that had a natural or acquired monopoly in the commodities which they sought, were perilous adventures. Even when not actually in the anarchical conditions which medieval warfare brought in its train, the trade routes were infested by robbers of every kind, whether gangs of outlaws evading in the forests the retribution for earlier crimes, disbanded soldiery awaiting enrolment by a new master, or predatory nobles who, in large numbers, provided for the carousals in their strongholds by plundering transports of merchandise, or levying heavy duties upon them for the right of passage through their domains. On the ocean a very similar state of affairs obtained. Not only did the seas swarm with veritable pirates, but a naval war was inevitably accompanied by innumerable gross outrages on neutral vessels by both belligerents.

In such circumstances a single traveller with a rich baggage had but little chance of reaching a distant destination in safety, and it became the custom for the merchants of every town to make their journeys, by land or sea, in large parties, under the protection of an escort of armed retainers. The fellowship engendered by the companionship of the journey, and the experience of common perils and adventures, as well as the uses of mutual support in a strange land, kept them together when they reached their foreign destinations, and in this way grew up those settlements known as " guild-halls," " hanses," " factories," or " counting-houses," which, at the close of the Middle Ages, were the head-quarters of German trade in other countries. By degrees this principle of co-operation was extended from individual citizens of a single town to the towns themselves, and culminated in the Hanseatic League, upholding with its fleets and armies a practical mon-opoly of the trade of Northern and Western Europe.

The story of the Hansa is full of strange anomalies and antitheses. Historians differ by centuries as to the date at which the existence of the League com-menced, and just as it never had a definite beginning, so it has never had a formal end, for to this day two of the Hanse towns—Hamburg and Bremen—have certain institutions in common, such as their supreme law courts and their diplomatic representation in Prussia. For hundreds of years the Confederation acted, and was treated by foreign Governments, as an independent State and a great Power, but its composi-tion was never certain and always fluctuating. From first to last the names of no fewer than ninety cities and towns were entered upon its rolls, but it is impossible to say of each of them how often and when it joined or left the League.   Foreign rulers, and especially the English monarchs, made repeated attempts to obtain from the Hansa an official list of its members, but compliance with their demands was systematically evaded on one pretext or another.   The League's policy was, as far as possible, to assert the claims of its members, and to disown responsibility for those made against them.   This policy is pretty clearly expressed in the following answer returned by the League in 1473 to complaints put forward on behalf of English merchantmen who had suffered through the depredations of the Dantzic privateer or pirate, Paul Beneke: " The towns of the Hansa are a corpus in the possession of the privileges they hold in any realms, lands, or lordships, and when their privileges are infringed, they are accustomed to meet and consult, and then to issue for all of them ordinances against all goods from the countries in which their privileges have been infringed, that they shall not be suffered in the commonalty of towns.   But they were not making war against England ; only some of the towns of the Hansa, which had been injured by England, had determined upon it at their own venture, win or lose, which did not take place in the name of the Hanse commonalty." The theory of the Federation was, in fact, that it existed for the purpose only of taking, and not of giving, and it refused to imply a corporate responsibility by publishing its membership rolls.   Fifteenth and sixteenth century lists of Hanse towns are extant in considerable numbers, but none of them can claim an official character, and they present many discrepancies.   The most complete of them contains seventy names.   It would appear that membership of the Hansa was synonymous with participation in the rights of its guildhalls and factories abroad, and that these privileges were often acquired, though no doubt irregularly, by individuals as well as by municipalities. Among the Hanse towns themselves two distinct classes seem to have existed —namely, those which were entitled to take part in the League's conventions, or "Tagfahrten," and those which, without themselves possessing this right, were permitted to make their wishes known at these assemblies through the delegate of one of the fully qualified municipalities.

The League had, apart from its establishments abroad, no definite constitution or set of statutes, no fixed headquarters, no permanent body of officials or system of finance. Its legislative procedure was governed by customs and traditions which had gradually established themselves, but which never acquired the binding force of law. For example, it became the rule at the height of the League's power to hold the Tagfahrten once every three years, but the practice was soon broken with, and these gatherings took place very irregularly. They were, in fact, seldom convened unless some special circumstances had arisen on which it was desirable to take the opinion of the members of the Federation; and during the second half of the fifteenth century a period of eleven years was allowed to elapse without a Hanse parliament coming together. The legislation—if it may be called so—of the League took the form of resolutions, or "recesses," which were adopted at the close of the deliberations of the Tagfahrten. Of these decisions large numbers are still extant, and they constitute the most important source of our knowledge of Hanse history. The earliest of them that has come down to us embodies the Greifswald Agreement of 1361, of which more hereafter. No regular meeting-place was appointed for the Tagfahrten, though they were generally held in Lübeck. The delegates, however, always assembled in a seaport town, which was never west of Bremen or east of Stralsund. Perhaps the nearest approach to a common headquarters permanently possessed by the Hansa was the "Trese," a vault beneath St. Mary's Church at Lübeck, where its charters were deposited, and where they still repose. Only once in the course of its history did the League boast of a permanent staff. That was in the years following 1552, when a legal official, called the "Syndic," was appointed to look after certain of its affairs. The innovation does not seem to have been a success, for the first occupant of the post was also the last. Nor had the Hansa a permanent common treasury and system of finance. It is true that, towards the end of the fifteenth century, efforts were made to establish the principle of regular matricular contributions from the partners in the League, but they met with only partial success, and appear to have been soon abandoned. The fact is that, as the foreign agencies of the Hansa were self-supporting, it had little need of a permanent administrative machine.

While the Hansa declared war and concluded peace, there never was an occasion on which all its members took the field simultaneously. The actual fighting was generally confined to a few towns specially qualified to equip fleets or raise bodies of mercenaries, and the others participated in the campaign only by a monetary contribution, which they levied by an imposition of tonnage or poundage dues on the commerce of their citizens. It was also by no means an uncommon thing for one or more of the Hansa towns to be separately involved in hostilities in which none of the others had either share or interest of any sort. Lübeck, while regarded by Europe as the head of the Confederation, waged war single-handed in pursuance of its own private and special ambitions. And though the differences of the Hanse towns never degenerated into formal armed conflict among themselves, there were cases in which some of them, as neutrals, suffered severely at the hands of others who happened for the moment to be belligerents.

The power of the Hansa seems all the more remarkable when we consider the territorial diffusion of the towns united by its loose organization. Though they were for the most part situated either on the sea-coast or the banks of the Rhine, the Weser, the Elbe, or the Oder, the League's ramifications extended to Dinant in the south-west and to Cracow in the south-east, and took in places of such thoroughly inland character as Dortmund, Paderborn, and Göttingen. While it was throughout essentially German, and all its establishments in foreign States displayed the imperial eagle in their coats of arms, it included, at various epochs, towns lying altogether outside the frontiers of the Empire. Both the Order of the Teutonic Knights and the inhabitants of the extensive regions which it had wrested from the Slavs during its advance in the twelfth and thirteenth centuries into what is now the north-east of Germany, enjoyed the privileges and prerogatives of Hanse membership. The Order itself has been called "the biggest capitalist of Europe" in the fourteenth century. It built ships, and freighted them to destinations as remote as Spain and Portugal, and it traded in almost every article of commerce that was either produced or consumed in the territories under its sway. Moreover, it had arrogated to itself proprietary rights over all the amber found on the shores of its dominions, and thus possessed in Europe a practical monopoly of this valuable commodity.

The appearances of the Hansa as a "great Power" marked only the supreme crises in its fortunes. Its normal and enduring activity was the promotion of the commercial interests of its members through the instrumentality of the guildhalls and factories which it maintained in foreign lands. Of these establishments by far the oldest and most important was the Steelyard in London.

Just as obscure as the derivation of the name is the origin of the Steelyard itself. It is thought not improbable that a co-operative settlement of German merchants, trading the wines of the Rhine for the wool and tin of England, existed at London in the latter days of the Roman occupation. At the time of Ethelred (979-1016) "the people of the Emperor" were granted in London the same trading rights as were enjoyed by natives, for the slight consideration of a gift at Christmas and Easter of two pieces of grey and one of brown cloth, ten pounds of "pepper" (a word then applied to spices of all kinds), two pairs of men's gloves, and two kegs of vinegar. A century and a half later the merchants of Cologne, which has been called "the only seaport of the early German Empire," received a pledge for the protection of their "house in London," and for the maintenance of the privileges it had been endowed with in the past.

In one sense this "house in London" may be regarded as the authentic germ from which the Hanseatic League developed. It was apparently in England that the word "Hanse" was first used to designate an association or guild of merchants, and with this meaning it was also applied to the community of German merchants regularly trading in London. They, in their turn, seem to have adopted it and carried it to their own country. The term, "the merchants of the Hanse of the Germans," appears in contemporary English records as early as 1282, and it was not till more than half a century later that it had passed into general currency on the Continent. Until the reign of Henry III., Cologne alone of the German towns had the right to maintain a "Hanse" in England, but the privilege was extended to "the merchants of Gothland" in 1237, to Hamburg in 1266, and to Lübeck in 1267. Towards the close of the thirteenth century, the four establishments were united to form what was afterwards known as the Steelyard.

When the Hanseatic League was at the height of its power—from the last quarter of the fourteenth to the first half of the sixteenth century—the Steelyard constituted in England little less than a State within the State. It occupied a site now covered by the Cannon Street Station, extending from Thames Street to the

river, and bounded to the east and west respectively
by All Hallows and Cousins Lanes. Strong walls, like
those of a fortress, surrounded it, and were more than
once necessary to protect the inmates from the fury
of the London mob. In the sixteenth century the
principal structure within the ramparts was a building
of several stories, with three large doorways upon the
street, two of which had been walled up, while the
third was kept jealously guarded to prevent the entrance of undesirable visitors. Carved upon the lintels
were Latin inscriptions from the pen of Sir Thomas
More. One of these made the announcement: "Glad
is this house and always filled with good; here dwell
peace, tranquillity, and honest joy." The second was
to this effect: "Gold is the father of happiness and
the child of pain; to do without it is hard, to possess
it brings fear." The third ran: "Whoever refuses to
obey the good avoids the smoke but falls into the fire."
Behind the main building was a garden, in which vines
and fruit-trees were cultivated. An important feature
of the settlement was the "Rhenish wine house," where
ministers, nobles, and men of fashion were accustomed
to assemble to sip the choicest vintages of the Rhine,
and try the flavours of caviare and other delicacies
of Eastern Europe. That this tavern was a favourite
rendezvous would appear from an allusion in Webster's
"Westward Ho," where a servant bids one of the
characters "meet his master at the Rhenish wine
house in the Stilyard." Possibly it was here that
Shakespeare first discovered that caviare is not for
"the general."

The commercial community that dwelt within the
precincts of the Steelyard, and in the neighbouring
houses, which, in course of time, it was found necessary
to rent for the accommodation of its growing numbers,
was governed with monastic severity. No married man
was allowed to reside on the premises, nor was any
woman to enter them; the gates were shut regularly at
nine o'clock in the evening; heavy fines were imposed

for breaches of morals and good manners ; brawling, gambling, and even "games of ball" were rigorously repressed. The brotherhood dined at a common table in the great hall, which was adorned with a rich display of plate, and in its latter days hung with the pictures of Holbein representing the triumphs of wealth and poverty.

The Steelyard was administered by an alderman, with the assistance of two adjuncts and nine councillors. All the members of this governing body were elected annually on New Year's Eve, and they met for consultation every Wednesday evening. The community also acquired the right to choose an alderman of the City of London, whose duty it was to safeguard their interests, and whose services were recognized every Christmas by a present of a pair of gloves and fifteen gold nobles. Some uncertainty exists as to the duration of his tenure of office, but it was held without interruption by one occupant for a period of eighteen years. Not infrequently the Lord Mayor himself accepted the position, and this was regarded by the Steelyard as of great benefit to its interests. Both the English and the German alderman seem to have possessed certain rights of jurisdiction over the members of the settlement in criminal as well as in civil cases, but there is some doubt as to the limits of their powers in this respect. Even in cases that came before the Royal Courts, a member of the Steelyard could, except when indicted for a capital offence, claim that half the jury should be of German speech. The current business of the settlement was transacted by paid officials, called " secretaries " or " clerks," whose experience and knowledge of the details of Hanse relations to England lent considerable importance to their position. They were often entrusted with weighty diplomatic negotiations. The Steelyard exercised supervision, and to some extent also control, over the subsidiary colonies of Hanse merchants in England, which are known to have existed at Hull, Boston, Lynn, Yarmouth, and

Ipswich, and which, in all probability, were also to be found, at one time or another, in Newcastle-on-Tyne, York, Norwich, Colchester, Sandwich, Southampton, and Bristol, since German merchants had extensive dealings with all these places. These branch establishments contributed to the upkeep of the Steelyard, and occasionally sent delegates to London for joint deliberation on matters of interest to all of them. The expenses of both the headquarters and the provincial " Kontors " were defrayed by dues levied on all Hanse merchandise entering or leaving England.

In State and civic pageants, the alderman, councillors, and merchants of the Steelyard took part as a corporation, marching in the processions immediately behind the representatives of the City of London. At such times, too, it was no unusual thing for thirsty citizens to be regaled with a largesse of wine and beer from the cellars of the Rhenish Tavern, and for the settlement to be brilliantly illuminated in the evenings by flaming tar-barrels and hundreds of candles, made from that Russian or Polish wax which was one of the principal articles of the Hanse trade.

The quite exceptional nature of the position occupied by the Easterlings in London is evident from the fact that they were burdened with the obligation of maintaining and, in case of need, assisting to defend, the Bishop's Gate. The origin of this custom also seems lost in the obscurity of antiquity, but a suit which came up for decision in the last quarter of the thirteenth century showed that it had the validity of law. In 1275 the Gate had fallen into a ruinous condition, and the civic authorities demanded that the inhabitants of the Steelyard should restore it. This they refused to do, and some years elapsed before the dispute was settled, before the Court of Exchequer, by a compromise, under which the Steelyard, in return for one of the innumerable confirmations of its privileges, covenanted to pay the sum of £240 for the necessary repairs to the Gate, and thereafter to maintain it in a proper state, besides contributing one-third of the cost and of the guard required for its defence. Weapons for this purpose were stored in the settlement, and every member was bound by the statutes to keep in his private apartment a full equipment of arms and armour for his own use. When the City walls were renewed in 1477, it was German money that rebuilt the Bishop's Gate, and it was only in the reign of Edward VI. that the Easterlings were relieved of the duty of defending it.

The Steelyard itself was consumed in the Great Fire of 1666, and though it was subsequently re-erected, the new premises were, in consonance with the diminished prestige and business of its owners, of a much less imposing character than the old ones. They were finally sold in 1853 for the sum of £72,500. Ten years later the " House of the Easterlings " at Antwerp was also disposed of, and with it disappeared the last possession of the Hansa on foreign soil.

Before further reference is made to the political and commercial dealings of the Hanseatic League with England, it will be as well to cast a glance at the events in Northern Europe which raised the Confederacy to the status of a great sea-power. The development of the Hanse navy was as gradual as that of its trading establishments abroad, and likewise extends back to the age of historical darkness. But while it was Cologne that took the lead in the movement which culminated in the Steelyard, it was Lübeck that showed the way in the building up of the Hanse fleet, and so gained a political predominance in the League which it maintained for centuries.

The old town on the Trave, with its thirteenth and fourteenth century brick churches and its quaint, timbered houses, has, at the present day, little more than an antiquarian importance ; but five hundred years ago it was not merely the chief seaport and the first ship-building centre of Northern Europe, but, to all intents and purposes, the veritable mistress of the Baltic. The mere number of its inhabitants shows the leading position it had then attained to. Even after the ravages of the Black Death, which struck it with particular severity, so that its ships were often found drifting before the wind and wave manned only by the dead bodies of their crews, its population was 80,000, or very nearly as large as it is at the present time; whereas at the very height of the Hanse power the now mighty mercantile metropolis of Hamburg was a town of not more than 21,000 inhabitants.

Lübeck first acquired the independence of an imperial city in the year 1226, and at once entered on that sempiternal struggle with the Scandinavian kingdoms which at first brought it power and glory, but ultimately contributed largely to the acceleration of its decay. Eight years later the ships of its citizens burst through a boom laid across the entrance to their harbour by the Count of Holstein, and, sailing round to the mouth of the Warnow, won "the first victory of a German fleet," capturing or burning five large vessels, one of which, we are told, had 400 armed men on board.

It has been said that Amsterdam was "built on herrings," and the remark might with equal truth be applied to Lübeck. Indeed, the herring was a very essential element in the prosperity and significance of the entire Hanseatic Federation. In the thirteenth and fourteenth centuries, the west coast of Scania (the southerly projection of what is now Sweden) was the chief centre of the herring fishing and curing industries of Europe. Late in the summer the fish appeared in the Sound in vast shoals, which sometimes extended in every direction without a break as far as the eye could reach, and which were so dense that they "raised boats out of the water." The herrings were caught by Danish fishermen, and landed at places along the shore of Scania, where they were salted and packed. The curing and wholesale trade were almost

exclusively in the hands of merchants from the German
Baltic and North Sea towns, who eventually succeeded
in driving away their English, French, and Flemish
rivals, and in erecting a legal bulwark round the
monopoly which they had gradually built up on a
prescriptive basis. The headquarters of the herring
industry was the triangular peninsula on which stand
the towns of Skanör and Falsterbo, and in the season
this patch of land was one of the busiest spots in
Europe. Rude huts on an island close to the shore
afforded shelter to the numerous assemblage of fishers,
and a special site on the mainland was allotted to each
of the towns engaged in the trade, for the accommodation of the temporary dwellings, offices, packing-rooms,
and warehouses of its citizens. The merchants of
Lübeck alone owned a group of as many as fifty
wooden buildings, which were situated between Falsterbo and the sea. In the train of those immediately
engaged in the catching, curing, and marketing of the
herrings, came handicraftsmen and traders of every
description—coopers, shoemakers, butchers, bakers,
and publicans—to minister to their various wants;
and one summer it was estimated that no fewer than
20,000 of these season visitors were congregated in the
vicinity.

It was mainly for the sake of the Sound herrings
that the Hansa undertook against the Scandinavian
States the numerous campaigns by which it won the
keys of the Baltic, and kept them in its possession
for so many generations. As early as 1248, Lübeck
entered upon a war against Denmark in defence of its
Scanian privileges, plundering Copenhagen, and wreak-
ing its vengeance with so little discrimination that, on
the complaints of the Church, whose property had
suffered in the sack, it was compelled to submit to
a temporary diminution of its franchises. English
merchants at Copenhagen were also despoiled by the
reckless looters, and their grievances led to temporary
difficulties for the German traders in London.

An alliance between Lübeck and Hamburg in 1255, under which the two towns pledged themselves to stand by one another against all who should do injury to either of them, is regarded by many as the real foundation of the Hansa, and was perhaps more intimate in its nature, and more far-reaching in its scope, than any of the similar coalitions that had preceded it. Half a century later, a defensive and offensive alliance was contracted by Lübeck, Wismar, Rostock, and Greifswald, the signatories undertaking to support one another in the protection of their rights on sea and land, and to begin no war without consultation with their confederates. Though the compact was at first made for a term of only three years, the community of interests which existed between these towns remained the groundwork of all the more extensive subsequent operations of the Hansa.

It was, however, by the war which culminated with the Peace of Stralsund in 1370 that the League raised itself to the rank of a first-class sea-power. This conflict was of so high an importance for the subsequent position of the Hansa and for its relations to the rest of Europe, that the circumstances under which it arose and was decided deserve to be considered in some detail. And, first, it will be advisable to take note of the general situation in Europe at that time, and of the preoccupations which then absorbed the attention and energies of what are now its leading States.

At the date of the signature of the Treaty of Stralsund, England and France were deeply involved in the throes of the Hundred Years' War. The recent bright memories of Crecy and Poitiers were in a few years' time to be blurred by the loss of all the French dominions of the English Crown, with the exception of Calais, Bordeaux, and Bayonne. " It was," says Green, "a time of shame and suffering such as England had never known. Her conquests were lost, her shores insulted, her fleets annihilated, her commerce

swept from the seas ; while within she was exhausted
by the long and costly war, as well as by the ravages
of pestilence." The regions which now form Germany
and Austria were in a state of well-nigh hopeless
chaos. The Holy Roman Empire was so far from
representing a national unity that Edward III. was
actually chosen as its head by the electors, anxious
above all things that no strong and energetic authority,
ever present on the spot, should curtail their prerogatives and repress their licence. It was only after the
English monarch, acceding to the protest of Parliament, had refused the ambiguous honour, that the
King of Bohemia was able to ascend the German
throne as Charles IV. Generations of anarchy were
soon to culminate in a fierce war between federations
of towns and leagues of nobles that filled all Central
Germany with turmoil and devastation. Russia was
still but a congeries of mutually hostile States, paying
tribute to the Tartar Khans of the Golden Horde, and
the process by which the Empire of the Tsars crystallized round the principality of Moscow was only in its
earliest stages. Such was the general European background to the great conflict between the Hansa and
the Scandinavian States.

In Scandinavia itself, something like order had been
re-established by Valdemar IV., who had been elected
to the Danish throne by a Congress of Princes held at
Lübeck in 1340. For twenty years he had applied
himself with great energy and astuteness to the
restoration of the former frontiers of his kingdom, and
among the regions which he won back were the
Scanian provinces beyond the Sound, which had been
acquired by Magnus of Sweden in 1332. In his work
of consolidation, he had received material assistance
from the Hanse towns, whose herring merchants had
not received from the Swedish master of Scania the
benevolent treatment which they considered to be
their due. Denmark was once more a powerful and
respected State when the events occurred which were

to reduce it almost to the level of a dependency of the
Hanseatic League.

The trouble arose in the first instance out of the
betrothal of Magnus's son Hakon, King of Norway, to
Valdemar's eight-year-old daughter Margaret. This
match was opposed by the nobility of Sweden, who
feared that in the union of the three Scandinavian
kingdoms, in which it seemed likely to result, they
would be overshadowed by the more cultured and
influential aristocracy of Denmark, and they were successful in forcing Magnus to repudiate the agreement,
and to promise his son's hand to Elizabeth, the daughter
of Count Gerhard of Holstein.

Valdemar sought to avenge himself for this rebuff by
overrunning the island of Gothland with fire and
sword. The island itself was a dependency of Sweden,
but its chief town, Visby, had acquired the very considerable importance that it then possessed solely as
the central point of the Baltic trade of the Hanseatic
towns, which were supreme within its walls.

To trace the rise of Visby as a commercial centre, it
is necessary to go back to the earliest days of navigation, when Gothland was the beacon by which trading
vessels felt their way across the Baltic. From a
harbour of refuge and a port of call, Visby became
in the Baltic very much what a coaling station in the
Pacific is to the Oriental merchantmen of to-day. It
might, indeed, not unfitly be compared with Shanghai,
for it was virtually ruled by the Hanse merchants who
resided there, and who must have been very numerous,
since even in the thirteenth century no fewer than thirty
towns, from Reval in the east to Cologne in the west,
were represented in its German guild. With its 20,000
inhabitants and its massive ramparts, Visby was a seaport and fortress of absolutely first rank, which gave
its name to a code of maritime tradition—it could hardly
be called law—that for some time was recognized
throughout Northern Europe. To-day the town is
shrunk to less than half its former size, but the ancient

walls, with their forty-eight square towers—many in an excellent state of preservation—and the impressive ruins that remain of its eighteen medieval churches, still tell a tale of its earlier glory. How high its repute stood among the contemporaries of its prosperity is indicated by an old rhyme, according to which its citizens weighed gold by the hundredweight, while their children played games with precious stones, their wives spun with spindles of gold, and their swine ate out of silver troughs.

Valdemar seems to have had no immediate quarrel with the Hansa at that time, but in the blind fury of his vengeance he confounded the Germanized town in a common doom with the Swedish island. Possibly Visby would have escaped his wrath if its citizens had awaited his attack behind their lofty walls, but they rashly ventured out into the open field against him, and the stone cross which commemorates the slaughter that overtook them is to be seen to this day. The town was burnt and sacked, and was never able to recover from the blow. Tradition says that the ships in which the Danish King was carrying his rich booty home were sunk on the passage, and that two enormous carbuncles, which, blazing from the summit of the tower of St. Nicholas's Church, had for generations lighted seamen to the harbour, can still be seen on dark nights sparkling beneath the waves.

The news of the pillage of Visby found the burgomasters of the chief Hanse towns assembled in conference at Greifswald, and before they dispersed they entered into an agreement with Magnus and Hakon, both of whom came to the place of their meeting in person, to make common cause against Valdemar. The compact was signed by Lübeck, the so-called Wendish towns (Wismar, Rostock, Stralsund, and Greifswald), Stettin, Kolberg, and Anklam, but the alliance was afterwards strengthened by the adhesion of Hamburg, Bremen, and Kiel, as well as of the Duke of Schleswig and the Counts of Holstein. Moreover, the Prussian towns undertook to contribute to the costs of the campaign by levying special poundage dues.

A fleet of fifty-two ships, manned by 2,740 fighters, was fitted out by the Hanse towns, and put to sea under the chief command of the Burgomaster of Lübeck, Johann Wittenborg. After once more burning Copenhagen, it proceeded to Helsingborg to reinforce the Norwegian and Swedish armies engaged in the siege of that fortress. Here, to give more vigour to the land operations, the ships were incautiously denuded of their crews, and while they were in a defenceless condition, they were attacked by Valdemar's fleet, and, almost without exception, captured or destroyed. Numerous prisoners fell into the hands of the Danish King, who is said to have derisively adorned with the golden figure of a goose the tower in which the bulk of them were confined.

Immediately after the disaster to his fleet, Wittenborg had concluded a truce with Valdemar, and it was in expiation of this act, no less than of his defective generalship, that his head fell on the block in the Lübeck market-place. Possibly, if the terms of the arrangement had been carried out, his life would not have been forfeited, for he had secured an undertaking that the Hanse merchants should be allowed to pursue their occupation unmolested within Valdemar's dominions; but the King was not the man to trouble himself about his pledged word when it stood in the way of his ambitions, and a lucky chance placed him, as he thought, in a position to break his promise with complete impunity. While on the voyage to Sweden, Elizabeth of Holstein, the bride-elect of Hakon, was driven ashore on the coast of Scania and fell into the hands of Valdemar, who used his power over her to effect a reconciliation with his two royal enemies. The upshot of the incident was that his daughter Margaret was married to the Norwegian monarch at Copenhagen on April 9, 1363, and the bride, then only

eleven years old, lived to bring about the amalgamation
of the three Scandinavian kingdoms by the Union of
Calmar, and so earn the title of the "Semiramis of the
North."

The Swedish nobles, however, were not prepared
to submit to the dreaded fusion without a struggle,
and, taking up arms against Magnus, they called upon
his nephew Albert, son of the Duke of Mecklenburg,
to assume the Crown in his stead. Magnus was
deposed in 1364, and was completely defeated and
captured when he attempted to regain the throne in
the following year. Valdemar now determined to
take advantage of Sweden's exhaustion to extend his
own dominions at her expense, and, after a successful
invasion, he extorted from the Duke of Mecklenburg a
treaty, in which the latter, on behalf of his son, undertook to cede the island of Gothland, the provinces of
Halland and Blekinge, and considerable portions of the
provinces of Smaaland and West Gothland. Albert,
however, refused to surrender the regions which his
father had signed away, and before Valdemar could
take effective steps to enforce his rights, a quite
different complexion was given to the struggle by the
intervention of the Hanse towns, which thought that
the time had come to wipe out the stain of Helsingborg.

On November 19, 1367, the most celebrated of all
Tagfahrten assembled in the chamber of the Cologne
Rathaus, which is still known as the "Hanse Hall,"
and solemnly declared war against Valdemar. The
treaty which the delegates of the towns subscribed is
known as the "Cologne Confederation," and is regarded
as the most momentous decision in Hanse history.
The towns which were actually represented at the
gathering were only eleven in number, but they
pledged themselves to furnish forty-one ships and 1,950
armed men. Between thirty and forty other towns
were invited to join in the operations, but most of
them were compelled by their inland situation to confine their participation to a money contribution. It is

a curious fact that Hamburg and Bremen, later the Hanse towns *par excellence*, took no active share in the most important campaign in the history of the League, the municipality in each case excusing itself on the ground of some special circumstances.

Valdemar was now threatened by a very formidable coalition, for Sweden, Mecklenburg, and the Hansa were joined by Count Heinrich of Holstein, and at this critical juncture he was taken in the rear by a rising of the nobles of Jutland. Losing heart, he fled to Pomerania, and the allies, following a carefully pre-arranged plan of campaign, carried all before them. Having yet again possessed themselves of Copenhagen, the forces of the Baltic Hanse towns united with the Swedish army in Scania, where all the fortresses were besieged, and, one by one, compelled to surrender. Recrossing the Sound, the allies seized the islands of Möen, Falster, and Laaland, which were ravaged from end to end. Against Norway the North Sea members of the League were equally successful, reducing the Royal Court at Bergen to a heap of ashes. The Hansa had taken the lead throughout the war, and the towns now found themselves for the moment masters of Scandinavia.

In the negotiations which were concluded by the Peace of Stralsund (May 24, 1370), the League imposed on Denmark crushing and humiliating conditions. In addition to insisting on the restoration of all privileges and facilities its members had ever possessed in Scania, it demanded and secured, as an indemnification for the expense it had been put to, half the revenues of Malmö, Helsingborg, Skanör, and Falsterbo, and of seven neighbouring bailiwicks, for a term of fifteen years. As a guarantee for payment, it was stipulated that the fortresses at the places named should in the meantime be garrisoned by the League. It was further agreed that, on the death of Valdemar, a successor to the Danish throne should not be appointed till he had received the approval of the Hansa

It is impossible here to consider in detail the subsequent relations of the Federation to the Scandinavian kingdoms, but one further development of them must be recorded, if only on account of its importance as a source of strife between the Hansa and England. On the death of Valdemar, in 1375, commenced the forty years' domination of his daughter Margaret, who, nominally as the guardian of her son Olaf, and, later, of her grand-nephew, Eric of Pomerania, became the autocratic ruler of all Scandinavia, which was legally consolidated by the Union of Calmar. A necessary step towards this consummation was the expulsion of Albert of Mecklenburg from Sweden, and he was crushingly defeated and taken prisoner at the Battle of Falköping in 1389. But for some years afterwards, Stockholm, which had been prominent in offering him the throne, held out in his behalf, and the attempts made to relieve the besieged town resulted in a recrudescence of piracy that for generations to come was to prove a terrible scourge to the Baltic and North Sea. The Hanse towns Rostock and Wismar were mainly responsible for this outcome. For once in a way espousing the dynastic cause of the duchy in which they were situated, they struck out on a line of policy distinct from that of the Hansa as a whole, and issued letters of marque, known as "charters of robbery," to all who would undertake the task of supplying Stockholm with provisions and munitions of war. The prospects of plunder opened out by these licences called to the sea a motley rabble of adventurers and soldiers of fortune, who, however, numbered in their ranks the owners of such now illustrious names as Moltke and Manteuffel.

Under the specious titles of the "Victualling Brothers" and the "Equal Sharers," which were respectively derived from their supposititious mission and their manner of disposing of their booty, these buccaneers fell upon every defenceless merchantman that came their way and stripped it to the ribs. By degrees they organized themselves into a formidable piratical community, which for some time had a regular fortified capital in Visby, where they had established themselves. From this stronghold they were ultimately ejected by an expedition led against them by the Grand Master of the Teutonic Order, and they thereupon transferred the scene of their operations to the North Sea, where they could always take refuge from pursuit among the shoals and islands off the Frisian coast. They made Emden their new headquarters, and their depredations were not effectively checked till 1433, when Hamburg captured the town, which it kept in its possession for twenty years. Contemporary ideas of the fabulous treasures amassed by the Victualling Brotherhood may be gathered from the tradition that Claus Stortebeker, one of the most redoubtable of these freebooters, when captured off Heligoland by a fleet belonging to merchants of Hamburg, offered to lay a chain of solid gold right round their town if they would allow him his life. The legend must not be taken too literally, for it continues that, though this bargain was refused, Stortebeker was granted his further petition, that as many of his followers as he could run past after he had been decapitated should be spared, and that he had already saved five of his men in this way, when the executioner flung a stick between his legs and brought his headless corpse to the ground.

Since the Victualling Brothers had been called into existence by two of the leading Hanse towns, it is not surprising that in England the League itself was blamed for the innumerable outrages committed by these corsairs on English shipping. It was largely to the misdeeds of this piratical sodality that were due the quarrels between the English Government and the Hansa, which continued almost without intermission from the signature of the Treaty of Stralsund till Queen Elizabeth shut up the Steelyard and expelled its inmates from the country. At the same time, it must be admitted that, with the exception of Rostock and Wismar, whither the privateers repaired to dispose of their spoils, the Hanse towns themselves probably suffered nearly as much as anyone else through this plague of piracy.

By its triumph over Valdemar the Hansa secured a practical monopoly of the shipping and trade of the Baltic and North Sea, which it held almost unimpaired for nearly two hundred years. In the words of Gustav Wasa, "the three good (Scandinavian) Crowns remained small wares of the Hansa up to the sixteenth century," and as long as this was so the commercial and maritime supremacy of the League was practically unchallengeable. The manner in which the Easterlings availed themselves of the ascendancy they had now acquired is a classic example of the ruthless and unscrupulous exploitation of political power for the purposes of purely material gain, for they were actuated by no national or ideal aims, but solely by the desire to enrich themselves. Favoured by the confusion and chaos prevailing in the lands of their potential rivals, they became the exclusive brokers through whose mediation the spices of the Orient, the wines of France, the cloth of Flanders, the tin, wool, hides, and tallow of England, were exchanged for the dried cod of Norway, the ores of Sweden, the wheat of Prussia, the honey and wax of Poland, the furs of Russia, and the myriads of herrings which every summer were caught in the Sound, and salted and packed on the coast of Scania. What they aimed at, and what for long years they substantially obtained, was the disappearance of all flags but their own from the North Sea and the Baltic. Moreover, a great part of the carrying trade between England and France also fell to their lot.

The Hanseatic League had sprung from the need of mutual protection and support, and at the outset had had a purely defensive character. By its early efforts for the suppression of piracy, highway robbery, and the infamous "beach law," under which a wrecked ship became the property of the owner of the foreshore where it stranded, it had incidentally performed valuable services to humanity. Unfortunately, wherever and whenever it became sufficiently powerful to do so, it adopted aggressive tactics, and established a commercial tyranny which could be upheld only by violence or fraud. Its methods were in principle exceedingly simple: they consisted in the extortion of exclusive privileges from others, and in absolute refusal to reciprocate; and the League not only determined the commercial policy of its own members, but, through its establishments at Bruges, Bergen, and Novgorod, exercised a decisive influence on that of other countries. The Sound was repeatedly closed to all but Hanse ships; foreigners other than Germans were forbidden to reside in Russia, even with the object of learning the language; and, while the Easterlings were amassing in their hands the whole of England's trade with Northern and Western Europe, English merchants were, by their servants or at their instance, expelled from Bergen, Dantzic, and other emporia of the Baltic, if they were not actually plundered and massacred. Recesses passed by the Tagfahrten at various times forbade the citizens of Hanse towns to sell ships to foreigners, to enter into partnership with an Englishman, to consign goods to a merchant in England who was not affiliated to the Steelyard, to export British manufactured wares.

The Hanseatics were neither the first nor the last to profit from the quarrels of others, but they played the part of *tertius gaudens* with a persistency for which it would be hard to find a parallel, and nowhere was their policy more successful than in England, whose foreign wars and internal embarrassments they turned to account with equal promptitude and skill. From the earliest days of their settlement in London, we find them shrewdly exploiting the predicaments of the English Crown. When, for example, Richard Cœur de Lion was returning from his Austrian captivity, the merchants of Cologne rendered him valuable assistance in the raising of the ransom which was the price of his liberty, and in recompense they received a charter acquitting them of the rent of their guildhall, and of all royal dues on their persons and wares in England. It was apparently Hanseatic influence which gained for Richard of Cornwall, brother of Henry III., the doubtful dignity of "German King"; and a couple of years after his coronation at Aix, "the merchants of Alemannia, who own in London the house which is usually called the 'Guildhall of the Germans'" obtained the confirmation of all the "freedoms and usages" they had enjoyed in the reigns of the English monarch and his predecessors. From Edward III. Hanse citizens took the Crown jewels into pawn, being allotted the revenues of the wool duties and the royal tin-mines in Cornwall till the pledges had been redeemed; and the King, in gratitude for their help, extended their privileges, so that by the middle of the fourteenth century they were actually trading in England on more favourable terms than the native merchant.

It was, however, only after the Peace of Stralsund that the Federation entered into regular diplomatic relations with England. Till that event changed the international status of the League, the Steelyard had been left to make for itself the best terms it could as a mere association of foreign traders, dependent on their own resources for the securing of favours. Now a radical alteration took place in the conditions, and the Hanse settlement in London became an important political mission as well as a commercial agency. The adoption of fresh methods was the necessary expression of a modification of policy, which was undoubtedly the direct outcome of the success of the League in the Scandinavian campaign. So far the Hanseatics had gained their ends chiefly by guile, but they now felt themselves strong enough to bully, and the unintermittent controversies and quarrels between

England and the League, which, almost exactly a hundred years after the signature of the Stralsund Treaty, culminated in open warfare, were but a natural sequel of the humbling of Valdemar.

It was characteristic of these disputes that grievances were invariably brought forward by both sides. The ultimate basis of the Hanse complaints was, in nearly all cases, the Carta Mercatoria, which had been issued to the Steelyard by Edward I. in 1303. By this charter the King, in consideration of the acquiescence of the foreign merchants trading in England in a substantial increase of the export duties, which in the cases of wool and hides amounted to 50 per cent., granted them far-reaching liberties and privileges. In the succeeding reign it was confirmed to the Germans alone, and henceforth it formed the legal title to which the Easterlings always appealed in their differences with the English Government. What they claimed was that legally they could not be called upon to pay duties at higher rates than were fixed in the charter, and that consequently they were entitled to exemption from any additional taxation that might be imposed in England. Whenever fresh financial burdens were placed on the shoulders of the people of England, whether in the form of augmented export duties, poundage, tonnage, "subsidies," or poll-taxes, the merchants of the Steelyard raised protests, and sometimes flatly refused payment. Not infrequently their resistance was crowned with success, and, in so far as this occurred, they were given an advantage over the Englishman, which enabled them to crush his commercial competition.

On the other hand, the English merchant had much to complain of in addition to this favouring of the foreigner in his own country. One of the first acts of the Federation on entering on its fifteen-year tenancy of Scania, was the issue of a decree forbidding British subjects to salt herrings in that province. At the same time the bailiffs responsible for public order in

the Hanse settlement round Falsterbo and Skanör
were restrained by a penalty of fifty marks from allowing foreigners to reside within the areas under their
jurisdiction, while a few years later they were expressly
enjoined to afford such intruders no protection against
robbery, outrage, and murder. Similar measures were
enforced in Bergen, with the object of making residence
there intolerable to all aliens who did not rejoice in
the qualification of Hanse membership. It was at this
period, too, that Prussia first systematically placed
obstacles in the way of merchants from England.
Close commercial dealings between the two countries
had sprung out of the participation of English nobles
in the crusades of the Teutonic Knights against the
Lithuanians—Henry IV., as Prince of Wales, fought in
two of these campaigns—but the enterprising rivalry
of the English traders seems by degrees to have become
irksome to the citizens of the prosperous towns that
had arisen on the conquered territories. At any rate,
the Grand Master adopted a much less hospitable
attitude than heretofore towards his English visitors,
and Prussia occasionally took the lead in urging upon
the Hansa a ruthless and uncompromising policy
towards England. The commercial factors in the
antagonism were naturally less disturbing than the
wholesale piracies of the Victualling Brothers, and the
League, for its part, repeatedly raised the charge that
its merchantmen had been plundered by English warships engaged in the operations against France. That
unjustifiable accusations were made on both sides is
more than likely, for at that epoch the lines of de-
marcation which separated regular war vessels from
privateersmen, and these from pirate ships, were very
indefinite, and it was a common practice for neutrals
to hire out their craft for belligerent purposes. It is
also highly probable that the Hansa was sometimes
held responsible for the violence of those who had
been federated to it yesterday, and would be so again
to-morrow, but had no official connection with it on

the to-day of their transgressions. At the same time, it had none but itself to blame for the doubt that existed in the world as to the extent of its membership.

The visit of two Hansa envoys to London in 1373, as the spokesmen of a Tagfahrten which had met at Lübeck, seems to have been the first attempt to establish direct diplomatic relations between the League and England. The mission found on its arrival that its purpose had gone, for a truce had been arranged between England and France, and the subsidies from which it hoped to obtain exemption for the inmates of the Steelyard had been dropped. Five years later the League again found it advisable to despatch a couple of envoys to England. Their errand on this occasion, their manner of fulfilling it, and its issue, are very typical of Anglo-Hanse relationships at that time. On the accession of Richard II., as at the commencement of every fresh reign, the English merchants petitioned that the Hanse privileges should not be confirmed till their own grievances against the League had been redressed. In particular they demanded greater liberty for their commerce at Bergen and in Scania, and their case was supported by Parliament. Eventually the renewal of the Steelyard charters was promised on the acceptance of the following conditions: Freedom for English trade in Prussia and in the Hanse towns, repeal of the obnoxious regulations at Bergen and in Scania, exemption of Englishmen in the Hanseatic territories from liability for the debts and misdoings of their countrymen, and disclosure of the names of all the members of the League. With suspicious emphasis the representatives of the Federation flatly refused even to consider these conditions. Ultimately the stipulations with regard to Bergen and Scania were dropped altogether, and the English merchants had to be satisfied with a general undertaking that they would receive in Hanse lands like treatment to that accorded to the League's members in England.

With the exception that this provision of "like treatment" was subsequently altered to the still vaguer and more worthless promise of "treatment according to ancient usage," the negotiations were exemplary in occasion, course, and result, for many which succeeded them. For nearly two centuries not a year passed in which grievances were not being nursed, or discussed, or submitted for decision by one side or the other, or by both. As a rule, a period of retaliations and reprisals intervened between the occurrence which formed the original bone of contention and the actual negotiations; ships and goods were confiscated by complainant as by defendant; English merchants were expelled from German towns and German merchants were flung into prison in England ; spontaneous violence, born of hatred and the sense of wrong, burst out here as there, and outrage was often enough requited with outrage.

On neither side, it must be admitted, was there very much of either constancy of view or consistency of action. The policy of the English Crown varied with the vicissitudes of the long struggle with France and with those of its recurring internal troubles, of which the Wars of the Roses were only the most violent and prolonged. On the other hand, the Hansa was often crippled by its perpetual embroilment in Scandinavia; and by its very nature and the diversity of the interests which it represented it was prevented from pursuing a definite and fixed line of action. The towns of the West had not the same stake as those of the East in the exclusion of strangers from the Baltic; the Norwegian, the Scanian, and the Russian preserves were not of equal importance to all members of the League. More than once Hanse Parliaments decreed the suspension of all Baltic trade with England, but these measures proved so injurious to some of the confederates, that they were speedily either revoked, ignored, or evaded. While such prohibitions were in force, pitch, tar, and potash were smuggled westward

in beer barrels, and English cloth still penetrated to
Prussia in large quantities by way of Scandinavia.
The Hansa, in fact, suffered even more from the recoil
of such commercial blockades than England did from
the original blow. By taking advantage of dissensions arising from the lack of complete unity of aim
in the League, the English Government sometimes
succeeded in effecting separate settlements with its
main component parts.

Like England, the Federation was weakened by
internal troubles. The government of the Hanse
towns had by this time passed into the hands of a few
"patrician" families, which were exclusively engaged
in the business of buying and selling, and the rule laid
down by the Lübeck statute, that only "those who
do not earn their bread by the work of their hands"
should sit in the Council, was of almost universal
prevalence. As the councils were constituted by co-
optation by their own members, and not by popular
election, they had no difficulty in maintaining this rule
so long as it was not challenged by violence. But at
the beginning of the fifteenth century the growing
and intelligent class of handicraftsmen was in many
quarters asserting its right to a voice in the administration of the towns, and these movements often resulted
in long and sanguinary struggles that incapacitated
the municipalities from taking an active interest in the
foreign policy of the League. Lübeck, the diplomatic
and naval head of the Hansa, was for some time gravely
embarrassed by one of these constitutional conflicts.
Another event of sinister omen for the future of the
Federation that occurred at this epoch was the Battle
of Tannenberg (1410), in which the rising State of
Poland completely defeated the Teutonic Order, dealing it a blow fatal to its power and prestige. These
occurrences temporarily enfeebled the League to such
a degree that when, in 1417, an English fleet seized a
number of Hanse ships returning from the Bay of
Biscay, the aggrieved German merchants, distrusting

their own strength, appealed for mediation to their supreme sovereign, Sigismund, " King of the Romans," who had contracted an offensive and defensive alliance with England. It was characteristic of the attitude of the German Emperors towards the towns, that, when the conference of English and Hanse delegates, which was convened by Sigismund at Constance and presided over by him in person, failed to reach an agreement, the monarch turned on the envoys of the League with the rough exclamation that he regarded as an enemy anyone who attacked his ally. That the Hansa's powers of commercial resistance also flagged at this time is shown by the German complaints that in one season the English had bought up almost the entire supply of Russian wax brought to Prussia, and that in two separate years a Lynn merchant had penetrated into the interior of Poland and bought where they grew the yew-trees from which the famous long bows of England were made.

The negotiations between England and the Hansa took place sometimes in London, sometimes in Lübeck or another of the League towns, sometimes at Bruges or on other neutral ground. An important success was obtained for the Federation in 1437 by the Burgomasters of Lübeck, Hamburg, and Cologne, who visited London, and, according to German historians, bribed Cardinal Beaufort with the present of a handsome mansion, and so induced him to persuade Henry VI. that the demands of the English merchants for the limitation of the privileges of the Steelyard were illegal, and that the Hanse trade was indispensable to England. All the League's freedoms were on this occasion confirmed without restriction ; it was assured exemption from all dues not specified in the Carta Mercatoria, and an undertaking was given that certain compensations, the justice of which had been admitted in a treaty concluded at The Hague thirty years earlier, should at last be paid. The only satisfaction received by the English merchants was the familiar and absolutely valueless promise that they should be treated within Hanseatic jurisdiction "according to ancient custom."

It was because the spirit of this vague and elastic provision was never observed that the 1437 Treaty failed, like all its predecessors, to establish permanent friendly relationships between England and the Hanse towns. As they were interpreted, all the engagements between the two parties were quite one-sided; the give was all on the part of England, the take all on that of the Hansa. The treaty was succeeded by the usual period of complaints by English merchants and petitions by Parliament, Hanseatic countercharges, arbitrary attempts to execute justice for themselves by the aggrieved merchants on both sides, retaliations—private as well as governmental—and unsuccessful overtures for negotiation. At length it was agreed to confer at Deventer in June, 1451, but the arrangement was thwarted by the action of a privateering fleet fitted out by the English East Coast ports, which seized in the Channel an enormous convoy, said to have contained 108 vessels. Half of these belonged to members of the League, for the most part to merchants of Lübeck and Hamburg, and were carried off to be sold as prizes. At about the same time, a number of Hanse ships were plundered as they lay at anchor in the harbour of Boston.

These occurrences precipitated an acute crisis. The injured towns at once confiscated all the English goods discoverable within their boundaries, and Henry retaliated by giving the merchants thus despoiled permission to indemnify themselves from the wares accumulated in the Steelyard. The King attempted to ignore the existence of the League, and sent a mission to Prussia to conclude a partial settlement with the Grand Master, but his envoys were captured off Skagen by ships of Lübeck, and carried off as prisoners to that town. It was, however, again found impossible to reconcile the divergent views of the Hanseatics. While the Prussian and Rhenish towns advocated a conciliatory attitude, Lübeck was all for ruthless self-assertion, and, following a line of its own, sent out privateers to snap up the cargoes of cloth that attempted to evade the closure of the Baltic to English goods which had been declared by Christian of Denmark. Nevertheless, the moderation of the other members of the Federation ultimately prevailed, Lübeck recalled its privateers, and in 1456 a truce was concluded with England, now deeply preoccupied with the Wars of the Roses, for a period of eight years.

It is hardly possible to disentangle the intricate knot of Hanse dealings with England during the long struggle between the houses of York and Lancaster. Both parties were in turn, and sometimes simultaneously, helped by the League, or by its individual members, with ships or money. When fortune frowned upon them, neither hesitated to apply to the Hansa for assistance, promising in return the confirmation of the privileges of the Steelyard; and the federated towns were, as usual, guided in their policy solely by their anticipations of material benefit. But the most interesting incident of this period was that the Hansa, with the encouragement of England's domestic embarrassments, took heart to wage open war against her for the first and last time in its history, and, as the issue will show, came out of the conflict victorious.

The war was the outcome of a series of mutual aggravations and provocations, of which the first of any importance was the attack by Warwick on a convoy of eighteen large Hanse vessels putting up the Channel for Livonia, with wine and salt from France. After a stubborn fight for six hours the Kingmaker withdrew to Calais, of which port he was then Governor, with six prizes, and the remainder of the German flotilla continued its voyage claiming the victory. Warwick's action, which is said to have had no better justification than the refusal of the convoy to salute the English flag, was regarded by the Hansa as a flagrant breach of the truce of 1456, and Lübeck at once recommenced its naval guerilla. It was, however, unable to induce the other towns to follow the example, and seems to have decided to recall its ships and await the development of events in England, rather than carry on the operations alone.

The quarrel might have simmered down, especially as Edward IV. had provisionally confirmed the Steelyard privilege, had it not been complicated by an English grievance of a similar character. This was the seizure in the Sound of seven English vessels laden with cloth for Prussia. There seems no doubt that the ships which effected this coup belonged to Dantzic, but, according to the German case, they were at the time in the pay of Christian of Denmark, and were exacting reparation for the murder by Lynn sailors and fishermen of an Iceland bailiff. The Danish King, indeed, went so far as to certify that the Hansa was entirely devoid of guilt in the matter. In England, however, the League was blamed, and the Steelyard was accused of having notified it of the departure of the confiscated ships. The English Government in this case acted with great promptitude, the Privy Council ordering the imprisonment of all German merchants in London till satisfaction had been given for the outrage. It was decided by the Courts that the League was guilty, and that the property of the Steelyard members should be valued and divided among the aggrieved English merchants. In the meantime, the Cologne traders, who had long been drawing away from the League and pursuing a more accommodating policy of their own, were released from prison, and installed in the Steelyard as its sole masters and the exclusive beneficiaries of its privileges and freedoms. Feeling seems to have run very strongly against the foreigners in London, for the Steelyard was stormed by a mob and partially destroyed, and a courier from the Emperor, to whom the Hansa had appealed for mediation, was attacked in the streets and very seriously maltreated.

In April, 1469, delegates of twenty-three Hanse towns assembled to consider the situation thus created, and agreed to break off all relations with England unless the distrained goods were restored to their original owners by June 24. As this condition was not complied with, the merchants of the German colony at Bruges and the town of Dantzic sent out privateers into the North Sea to prey on British commerce. Two of these naval condottieri—Paul Beneke and Martin Bardewick —wrought great havoc among English shipping, and by the daring of their exploits won for themselves a place of fame in the sparse chronicle of German maritime history. It was not, however, till the following year that the Hansa as a whole, at an unusually well-attended Tagfahrt—the conflict with England had had the effect of healing the dissensions in the League— decided upon common measures in defence of its interests. The merchants of the Steelyard were instructed to return to their native towns, and it was agreed to urge the Kings of Denmark and Poland to join in a comprehensive boycott of English cloth. At the same time, the ban of "Verhansung" was pronounced against Cologne, which meant that the members of the Federation pledged themselves to have no further commercial dealings with that city.

Almost at the very moment at which the assembly was passing these recesses, Edward IV. was in imminent peril of falling into the hands of the Hansa as he fled across the North Sea to Flanders, after the landing of Warwick in England. The vessel in which the King and his brother, the Duke of Gloucester, afterwards Richard III., had taken passage, was so hotly chased by Hanseatic privateers, that, as the only method of escape, her captain ran her ashore on the Dutch coast, trusting that she would refloat on the turn of the tide, and that in the meanwhile the pursuers would have put out to sea again in search of readier booty. The Germans were, however, not so easy to choke off, for they, too, beached their ships; and had not partisans of the Duke of Burgundy succoured the distressed vessel from the land side, the royal party would certainly have become prisoners of the Hansa, and a decisive change might have been brought about in the course of English history. For Queen Margaret had already, in flattering terms, appealed to Lübeck for assistance, and made solemn promises that, if it were successfully granted, she would become an advocate of the Hanse cause in England. At an earlier date, it may be remarked, she had received substantial financial aid from Cologne. As things turned out, Edward, too, now became a suitor for Hanse favours, and, through the mediation of Duke Charles, effected a provisional and informal reconciliation with members of the League. It was on Dantzic ships, in Burgundian service, and manned by Shakespeare's "hasty Germans and blunt Hollanders," that the King and his adherents returned to England to win the Battle of Barnet.

It would be tedious and unprofitable to follow the details of the desultory hostilities between England and the Hansa which occupied the next two years. On neither side could the war be waged with vigour and determination. England was engrossed with her domestic feud, and the Hanse towns were at one neither on the broad lines of their policy nor on the measures expedient for carrying it out. Though Poland and Denmark had closed their frontiers to English cloth, the blockade against it could not be rendered effective, as that profitable article of commerce was still smuggled into the Baltic in large quantities. The League members aggravated their dissensions by mutually accusing one another of carrying on the contraband trade. The naval operations of the League were equally lacking in system, persistency, and vigour. At times a Hanse flotilla would descend upon the East Coast of England, and disembark a force to burn and plunder for miles inland. At other times the conduct of the war would be left to one or two particularly reckless and enterprising privateers, who strung up to the yard-arm all the English sailors who fell into their clutches, and had only the like treatment to expect if they were ever captured in their turn. During the last year of the struggle, the dashing Paul Beneke, in a large ship purchased from Dantzic by citizens of Hamburg, was practically the sole representative of the Hanse naval power in the North Sea, but his presence there was enough to keep the English mercantile marine in a state of trepidation.

In spite of the half-heartedness of its naval measures, however, the Hansa refused to agree to an armistice when overtures for negotiations were made in the spring of 1472 by the English Envoy at the Burgundian Court, and it was not until a conference had been definitely agreed upon, a year later, that the League's letters of marque were finally revoked. The peace envoys met at Utrecht in July, 1473. On the one side were delegates of the towns of Lübeck, Hamburg, Bremen, Dantzic, Dortmund, Münster, Deventer, and Kampen, as well as of the Hanseatic settlements at London, Bruges, and Bergen; on the other were representatives of the English King, the Dukes of Burgundy and Brittany, the rulers of Bergen-op-Zoom, Holland, Zeeland, and Friesland, and of the towns of Cologne, Antwerp, Mechlin, and Dinant. The congress lasted nearly a year, and three separate series of negotiations were necessary before the individual quarrel between England and the League could be composed. The English delegates declared at the end that they would rather negotiate with all the monarchs of the world than try another bout with such hard bargainers as the Hanse burgomasters.

As the sequel showed, the League either was better represented or played with stronger cards, for in all essentials it carried the day. It secured the unrestricted confirmation of its privileges, the annulment of the judgment pronounced against its citizens in 1468, and an indemnity of £10,000, without prejudice to private claims for compensation. Edward struggled hard before he consented to abandon Cologne to its fate, and refused to ratify the original treaty, in which that town was expressly mentioned by name as having forfeited its right to the franchises of the Steelyard. Eventually another version of the treaty, which provided merely that no town that had been excluded from the League should enjoy Hanse privileges in England, was ratified, and the ejection of Cologne from the Steelyard was stipulated in a separate instrument. Other benefits obtained by the League were the full freehold of its establishments in London, Boston, and Lynn, and the renewal of a series of agreements with the City of London extending back to the thirteenth century.

England once more did a great deal of giving and very little taking. All that Edward's envoys could obtain was a repetition of the worthless provisions with regard to English trade with Hanse lands that had been contained in the treaty of 1437. Even this slender concession almost broke up the peace conference, so obstinately was it contested by some of Hanseatics, and on its account Dantzic deferred the ratification of the treaty for two years, while some of the other towns chose to quit the League rather than undertake to comply with it. More than a year elapsed before Cologne, thoroughly humbled and penitent, was readmitted to the ranks of the Hansa.

Till the close of his reign, Edward, unlike the other contracting parties, faithfully observed the provisions of the treaty, and the Hanse trade with England advanced by leaps and bounds. The Easterlings' export of English cloth, which had been 4,464 pieces in 1423, and 6,159 in 1461, rose by 1500 to 21,389. But as soon as the battle of Bosworth put a final end to the Wars of the Roses, the outcry against the Hansa became louder and more insistent than ever. The preferential conditions which the League enjoyed in England could, in fact, be maintained only so long as the country was embarrassed by foreign campaigns or internecine strife. Immediately after the accession of Henry VII., another epoch of complaints, outrages, confiscations, and reprisals was commenced. The popular feeling in London against the Hansa showed itself in attacks on German merchants in the streets, and in a determined attempt by a large body of apprentices to storm the Steelyard and rifle its warehouses. Henry was by no means blind to the disadvantages under which the industry and the trade of his kingdom were labouring, and he struck hard blows at the predominance of the League by statutes prohibiting the export of unshorn cloth, and the import of certain commodities, except in British bottoms, as well as by subsidizing shipbuilding and granting a charter to the Corporation of Merchant Adventurers. He also negotiated a treaty with Denmark, which secured for British trade in that country what were practically most-favoured-nation terms. Notwithstanding these and other measures with the object of stimulating English industrial and commercial life, and his declaration that " our merchants must be as free in Prussia and all other places belonging to the Hanse towns as the merchants of the Hansa are in England," he seems to have been actuated by a sincere desire to give the members of the League their lawful due. A provisional prolongation of the Utrecht Treaty was agreed to by a conference at Antwerp in 1491, and the grievances on both sides for many years past were also discussed at Bruges in 1499, but no understanding promising a permanent settlement of the points at issue was reached. However, until the end of this reign, no further serious friction arose.

Nor had the Hansa much ground of complaint for the first few years after the crown fell to Henry VIII., who refused to listen to charges of piracy brought

against the League by English merchants, and also
turned a deaf ear to the proposals of John of Denmark,
that he should combine with him in crushing it. He also
confirmed the Peace of Utrecht, besides giving repeated
assurances that the Steelyard privileges should not be
impaired by Acts of Parliament. It was only on the
rise of Wolsey to power that a change in this respect
took place in English policy. The immediate pretext
was the seizure by Stralsund, then engaged in war
with Denmark, of an English ship, which was answered
by the imprisonment of the merchants of the Wendish
towns residing in London, and the confiscation of their
wares. The Hansa had so far fallen from its former
arrogance, that it induced Stralsund to consent to
make reparation, and to send to London a peacemaker,
who, however, achieved nothing. A couple of years
were wasted in futile efforts to agree to a rendezvous
for a conference, Wolsey refusing to send envoys to
the Continent, and the Federation rejecting, as humiliating, his proposal that the negotiations should take
place in London. Eventually a meeting was arranged
at Bruges in July, 1520, and this time the English delegates absolutely insisted on being supplied with a list
of the members of the Federation. After protracted
attempts at evasion, they were furnished with the
names of forty-five towns. The bulk of the time of
the congress was consumed in legal arguments as to
the validity of the Hanse privileges, and, in the end,
it was announced, that Wolsey had come to the conclusion that by law these were forfeit, and that the
Steelyard was dependent for exceptional treatment
entirely on the grace of the King. The negotiations
produced no definite result, the position of the Hansa
in England became more precarious than ever, and
the merchants of the Steelyard were secretly advised
by the heads of the League to remain in London as
long as possible, but to put their charters, jewels,
and plate in a place of safety. Nevertheless the
danger blew over once more, and in the later years

of his reign Henry VIII. found the friendship of the
Federation useful both in his ecclesiastical policy and
in his matrimonial projects.   For some time the most
cordial relations existed between him and Lübeck,
and it would indeed appear that a treaty, by which that
town was to have undertaken to make over to him
the Kingdom of Denmark and to furnish him with
warships, was actually drafted for signature.

Fresh bickerings arose soon after Henry's death,
and the Easterlings were cited before the Privy Council to answer the charges of a number of English merchants, whose agents had been subjected to ill-usage
at Dantzic and Stralsund.   The proceedings elicited
the interesting fact that in the previous year the Hansa
had exported 44,000 pieces of English cloth, whereas
the export of all other traders, native and foreign, had
amounted to no more than 1,100 pieces.   The decision
of the Council was to the effect that the Steelyard was
not a legal corporation, and had forfeited all the rights
and privileges conferred upon it.   The final execution
of a decree, placing its members on exactly the same
footing as other foreign merchants in England, was,
however, prevented by the death of Edward VI., and
the brief rule of Mary brought the Hansa yet another
respite.   The League did its utmost to deserve the
favour of the new ruler.   When Philip of Spain entered
London to lead her to the altar, the Steelyard spent
£1,000—no inconsiderable sum at that date—in celebration of the event, and not long after, Lübeck, to
gratify the Catholic Queen, drove from its gates in the
full rigour of winter the Protestant refugees from
England who had sought its protection.

The complete emancipation of England from the
Hansa yoke was the work of that virile woman, Queen
Elizabeth.   How blind the League was to the signs of
the times was shown by the events which occurred at
Hamburg in the opening years of her reign.   The
Elbe port had evidently realized that, in the changed
conditions of the world, the policy of unqualified exclu-

sion could not be upheld, and, in 1567, permitted the Merchant Adventurers to establish a factory within its walls. The concession was granted for a term of ten years, and before two of them had elapsed the turnover of the settlement had attained the sum ot three and a half million thalers. At the instigation of the Hansa, a prolongation of the concession was refused, and the League, no longer in a position to enforce its wishes by its own strength, appealed to the Emperor and Reichstag, who issued a decree prohibiting the settlement of the Merchant Adventurers in Germany.

The final catastrophe of the Steelyard was precipitated by England's war with Spain, to whom the Easterlings, in spite of Elizabeth's emphatic warnings, systematically furnished supplies. No sooner had the Armada been scattered, than Drake and Norris appeared in the mouth of the Tagus, and seized sixty German vessels, laden with ships' stores, which were lying at anchor there. The perplexity and vacillation which the Hansa displayed when confronted by this action are clear signs of the decay and impotence that had fallen upon it. Only Wismar seems to have advocated the use of force to obtain redress; the other towns were unable to agree as to the course to be followed, and many of them were now openly disregarding the order for the expulsion of Englishmen from their territories. While a suspension of the conveyance of grain to, and of cloth from, England was being debated, Philip II. himself intervened, and procured the issue of an imperial decree (August 1, 1597) ordering all Englishmen to leave German soil within three months.

With commendable promptitude, Elizabeth retaliated by expelling the Hanse merchants from England. The term for their departure, originally fixed at fourteen days, was prolonged to a few months, but on July 25, 1598, the Lord Mayor and Sheriffs were charged by the Privy Council to take possession of the Steelyard, and ten days later its members, headed by their Alderman, filed out of their premises in melancholy

procession. Though the Hansa's property in London
was restored to it under James I., its expulsion by
Elizabeth was the final doom of its power in England.

But for the Hundred Years' War with France and
the struggle between the houses of York and Lancaster,
the Hansa would never have been able to win and
maintain its mercantile ascendancy in England. As
soon as the island kingdom was at peace at home and
abroad, the exactions of the Easterlings were felt to
be intolerable. But while its position in England was
being undermined, the Hansa was steadily losing
ground elsewhere. The decline of the German orders,
whose conquests it had exploited commercially; the
extension of the Kingdom of Poland to the sea; the
rise in Sweden of that most capable of ruling families,
the Wasas; the independence of Holland; the suppression by the Princes of Moscow (1478) of the Republic
of Novgorod, which had been the centre of Hanseatic
trade in Russia, were all important factors in bringing
about the collapse of the League. Everywhere the
arrogance, selfishness, and unscrupulousness of its
commercial policy raised it up enemies, who seized
the first opportunity of throwing off its yoke. Many
of the towns which had once been members of the
League, and especially those of Brandenburg, now
under the Hohenzollerns, had lost their independence
as the German Princes waxed in power, and were no
longer allowed to send delegates to the Tagfahrten.
Those that remained free had been weakened by the
revolt of the handicraftsmen against the oligarchic
rule of the captains of commerce, and by religious
strife. Moreover, the diversity of interest that existed
among the Hanse towns in consequence of their
geographical diffusion and their commercial differentiation, had always tended to become acuter.

In its commercial policy in the narrower sense, the
Hansa showed an extraordinary inability to adapt itself
to a fresh set of conditions. Instead of recognizing
that the world had changed, and that the new wine

could not be put into the old bottles, it acted as if
the circumstances which had favoured its ascent had
remained unaltered, and wore itself out in futile
struggles to uphold the privileges it had extorted from
the weakness of rivals now become strong. The
discovery of America and the opening up of the
inexhaustible resources of the New World found it
incapable of grappling with that great opportunity.
Finally, that most fickle of fish, the herring, which had
done so much to promote the shipping and trade of the
Hansa, deserted it in the hour of its sorest need.
During the course of the sixteenth century, the shoals
gradually abandoned the track which had brought them
to the Sound, and appeared instead on the British and
Dutch coasts, thus favouring the two nations which
were successively to occupy the place so long held by
the League.

In conclusion, a word may be said as to the naval and
military forces of the Hansa. At the outset of its
career, its warships were manned by the burghers
themselves, but as the fleet increased in size—it was
quadrupled during the first half of the fifteenth
century—recourse to mercenaries became more and
more general. The commanders of the ships were
invariably citizens of the towns which had equipped
them, and were frequently members of the governing
council, while the admiral of a fleet was always a
councillor, and usually a burgomaster. The officers
of the land forces, which were raised as occasion
demanded, were principally drawn from the impoverished nobility, whose members welcomed any
opportunity of repairing their shattered fortunes by
martial adventure. Of the naval resources of the
League, some idea can be formed from the fact that,
in the war against the three Scandinavian Kingdoms
in 1426, it sent out a fleet of 260 ships, manned by
12,000 sailors and fighting men. For the exhausting,
if not inglorious, seven years' war against Gustav
Wasa's successor, Lübeck alone fitted out 18 men-of-

war, of which one, the *Adler* carried 400 sailors, 500 fighting men, and 150 "constables." Her armament consisted of 8 carthouns, 6 demi-carthouns, 26 culverins, and many smaller pieces of ordnance. Among her munitions were 6,000 cannon-balls and 300 hundred-weight of powder. Such was the type of vessel with which Germany "last armed for a naval war."

It is an interesting fact, in view of modern controversies, that, in its naval wars, the Hansa asserted the principle that hostile ships make hostile goods and that hostile goods make hostile ships.

CHAPTER II

THE FIRST HOHENZOLLERN FLEET AND COLONIES

In one of the window niches on the ground floor of the Military Museum (Zeughaus) at Berlin lies an old and dilapidated 8-pounder gun. In its deep and disfiguring coat of rust it is an inconspicuous object, and, amid that rich and varied collection of artillery from all the ages, the eye of the casual visitor will not rest upon it for more than a disparaging moment. And yet few of the treasures of the museum have a more interesting history to tell, for it is the sole remaining relic of the first serious experiment in naval and colonial policy ever made by a German ruler. On an elevation rising from the beach of Cape Three Points, on the Gold Coast, now British territory, are still to be seen the crumbling ruins of the fort of Gross-Friedrichsburg, built there by the Elector of Brandenburg in 1681, and when the German corvette *Sophie* visited the spot, with pious purpose, in 1884, this corroded gun was unearthed from beneath the weeds and brushwood that have overgrown the decayed ramparts.

Frederick William, the Great Elector, has been exemplary for many of his successors. Frederick the Great rightly considered him the most able of the previous Princes of the house of Hohenzollern, while the present German Emperor has made a special cult of his memory, and assuredly had a symbolic intention when he appeared at a fancy-dress ball disguised as the first of his ancestors who equipped a fleet and founded a colony.

49

When Frederick William was called to the Brandenburg throne in 1641 at the age of twenty, Germany was still in the throes of the Thirty Years' War, and no part of the Empire had suffered more than his Electorate from the consequences of that unspeakable calamity. Of all the causes which have contributed to impede the normal development of the painstaking and industrious German race, none had so malign an influence as that stupendous conflict. It not merely delayed civilization, but over vast tracts of country positively exterminated it. At the close of the war many once flourishing towns had absolutely disappeared from the face of the earth, and where formerly a numerous peasantry had tilled its fertile fields a howling wilderness extended in all directions as far as the eye could reach. In North Germany to-day an apparently purposeless pond, or a detached clump of venerable trees, still shows where once a village stood, and bears mute witness to the ruthless barbarity with which the religious partition of Central Europe was brought about.

When an end was put to the bloodshed and rapine by the Peace of Westphalia (1648), the population of Germany had been reduced to one half—in some districts to one tenth—of its former dimensions. Many portions of the Empire are even to-day not so thickly inhabited as they were before the war. Industry and commerce had migrated to England, France, and Holland; and Leipzig and Frankfort were the only German towns that had retained any trade worthy of mention. The Hansa, with its fleets of warships and merchantmen, was but a memory of the past. Königsberg had no longer a ship of its own; the trade of Dantzig and Stettin was almost entirely carried in foreign bottoms; and even Hamburg, which directly had been but comparatively little touched by the thirty years of chaos and turmoil, and had benefited from its exceptional connection with England, was left commercially crippled. At a Hanse Parliament held in 1630, only Hamburg, Lübeck, and Bremen were represented. Germany had been so drained of money that barter had generally taken the place of purchase by coin; wages were paid in the products of labour, grain, ore, and manufactured goods, and even state officials in some cases received their salaries in kind.

Even before the war broke out, Brandenburg, a country of barren soil and few natural resources, had stood far below the rest of Germany both materially and intellectually. In 1600 the twin towns, Berlin and Cöln, which faced one another from opposite banks of the Spree, and have since been merged to form the colossal capital of the new Empire, contained together no more than 14,000 souls. Brandenburg and Frankfort-on-Oder each had a population of 10,000. Only two other towns, Stendal and Salzwedel, could boast more than 5,000 inhabitants. And it was of the mere ruins of this country that Frederick William formed the foundation-stone of the Prussian Kingdom and of the German Empire of to-day.

If the Thirty Years' War had produced any form of national consolidation, if it had increased the authority of the Empire or resulted in the absorption of the smaller States by the larger, that would at least have been some compensation to Germany for its long and terrible ordeal. But exactly the opposite was the case. The war ceased simply because no one had the will or the strength to continue it, and a miserable compromise was the result. The only gainers were the Princes, who, as the wielders of the armed forces, had been able to enhance their power, and now acquired a larger measure of independence in their relationships to the Emperor. Their number remained legion. In the Germany mapped out by the Westphalian negotiators there were eight electors, sixty-nine spiritual and ninety-six temporal Princes, sixty-one imperial towns, and a multitude of Counts and Barons exercising various degrees of sovereign power.

Frederick William's claim to the title "Great," which was bestowed upon him by his own generation, has been contested, but may be allowed to pass. As military leader, diplomatist, organizer, and administrator, he certainly had unusual gifts. Above all, he excelled in duplicity and treachery. The most eminent living German historian has said of him that " both in internal and external politics he acted with an unscrupulousness so manifest that it cannot be palliated," and can find no better excuse for his many deeds of "faithlessness" and "double-dealing" than that, in this respect, he was merely " the master of the diplomatic art of his day." The Elector was actuated solely by his own personal and dynastic interests, and was utterly devoid of " German" patriotism, for in return for the liberal subsidies on which he prospered, he undertook, in a secret treaty, to support a candidature of the French King or Dauphin for the Imperial German throne, and he was mainly responsible for the truce which left Strasburg in French hands for nearly two centuries. During the incessant wars which filled up most of his reign he fought both with and against every other belligerent. His sword was always at the disposal of the highest bidder, either of hard cash or of territorial extension, and by adroit choice of the moment for changing sides he generally made a profitable bargain. True, he was obliged to restore the western portion of Pomerania which he had conquered from the Swedes, but he obtained a much more important acquisition—the recognition of his full sovereignty in what is now East Prussia.

That region had been wrested from the Slavs by the German orders of chivalry, founded at the time of the Crusades, and had subsequently become an evangelical duchy, ruled by a junior branch of the house of Hohenzollern, as a fief of the Kingdom of Poland. On the extinction of the Ducal line, it had reverted to the rulers of Brandenburg, and by a timely sale of his military assistance, first to the Swedes and then to the Poles, the Great Elector induced both to admit his unrestricted and unqualified rights of sovereignty in the duchy. His successor persuaded the Emperor to agree to his assumption of the kingly title for this territory, and it is an interesting fact—especially in view of the last development of the German Empire, which in its present constitutional form and in much else is dependent upon Catholic support—that this elevation was largely brought about by the intervention of two Jesuit fathers. It was from the Kingdom of Prussia, which was thus established, and which was a completely independent State, altogether outside the competencies of the Holy Roman Empire, that arose the Hohenzollern ascendancy in Germany, and round it that the new German Empire crystallized. For this reason the episode is quite germane to our present purpose.

The Germans excel as diligent pupils and patient imitators, and the Great Elector was no exception to this rule. From his fourteenth to his eighteenth year he had been educated under the care of Frederick Henry, the Statthalter of Holland, then the chief Sea-Power of the world, from whom he had imbibed many ideas as to the importance of navies, colonies, and sea-borne trade. His connection with the Netherlands was maintained and strengthened by his marriage with an Orange Princess, the aunt of William III. of England, and many Dutchmen entered his service. Among them was an ex-admiral, Gijsels by name, who assiduously kept alive the dreams of sea-power which the Elector had brought back with him from Holland. It was on his prompting that, in 1659, when Frederick William was embroiled with the Swedes, and found his operations hampered by the lack of a fleet, an enquiry as to the possibility of remedying this deficiency was ordered by the Elector. The investigation resulted, for the time being, only in the compilation of a memorandum as to a " Brandenburg-Imperial admiralty," and some fruitless attempts to obtain ships in the Netherlands.

But Gijsels' projects went far beyond a mere fleet.

All the world was then discussing the colonizing activity of the western European States, and Frederick William's predecessor on the Electoral throne had conceived abortive plans for founding an East Indian trading company. What the ex-admiral proposed to the Elector in 1660 was, that Brandenburg, Austria, and Spain should combine for the purpose of securing a colonial ascendancy, which was to be arrived at by playing off England, France, and Holland against one another. Negotiations to this end seem actually to have been commenced, but they broke down over the jealous suspicions of the diplomatists approached, and the perpetual turning of the European kaleidoscope.

During the next fifteen years the idea of a Brandenburg navy appears to have been allowed to sleep. In the meantime a very remarkable book had been published, which should be mentioned here because it contains the essential elements of the programme of the most modern naval agitation in Germany. The author was Johann Becher, by profession a chemist, but in his leisure a political seer of the type of Friedrich List, whose great forerunner he was. His work, " Political Discourse on the Causes of the Rise and Decline of Towns and Countries," was published in 1667. Becher had travelled much, and he wrote :

" In Germany there is hardly any longer trade or commerce ; all business is going to ruin ; no money is to be found with either great or small ; on the other hand look at Holland, how rich she is and how she grows richer every day ; that could not be if she feared the sea as much as our nation of High Germany."

Becher then addressed to his countrymen the following impassioned exhortation :

" Up, then, brave German ; act so that on the map, besides New Spain, New France, New England, there shall in the future be found also New Germany. You are as little lacking as other nations in the intelligence and resolution to do such things ; yea, you have all that is necessary ; you are soldiers and peasants, alert, laborious, diligent, and indefatigable."

Becher had held positions at various German Courts, and it is not improbable that his appeal fell upon sympathetic ears among the entourage of the Great Elector. But however that may be, the war of Denmark and Brandenburg against Sweden, which broke out in 1675, did actually, for the first time in history, witness a fleet at the disposal of a member of the dynasty that now occupies the imperial throne in Germany. True, it was not yet the actual property of the Elector, but of Benjamin Raule, an enterprising Dutch merchant, who had migrated to Denmark, and now laid a naval project before the Brandenburg sovereign. His proposals were readily acceded to, and he received permission to fit out a flotilla of two frigates and ten smaller vessels, and to operate with them under the Brandenburg flag against the Swedes. The Elector merely stipulated that he should receive 6 per cent. of the value of all prizes captured. Raule's vessels rendered substantial service in the capture of Stettin, and of that much-coveted strip of the Pomeranian coast which was so essential to the realization of Frederick William's maritime aspirations.

The Elector's hopes were disappointed by the Treaty of St. Germain, under which he was compelled to restore this precious booty to the intrusive Scandinavians, but in the meantime his naval plans had taken a wider scope in fresh contracts with the resourceful Dutchman. In the first of these, Raule undertook, for a monthly subsidy of 5,000 thalers,* to maintain a fleet of eight frigates and a fire-ship, mounting altogether 182 guns. Shortly afterwards the terms of the agreement were extended, and at the commencement of the year 1680, twenty-eight ships of war, with a total of 502 guns, were flying the red eagle of Brandenburg.

* Thaler then = about 4s. 6d.

Though robbed by the peace of the coast-line and seaports on which he had counted as the base of his maritime power and the recruiting ground for his fleet, the Elector did not allow himself to be discouraged, and he very soon found fresh work for his little flotilla to do. The greatest master of German mercenaries at that date, he had, a few years previously, hired a portion of his army to Spain for use against the French. As repeated applications for the price of this support had proved unavailing, he now determined to collect the debt, which amounted to 1,800,000 thalers, by forcible distraint.

Accordingly six ships, which were followed at an interval of some months by three others, were sent out to attempt to intercept the silver fleet on its way to the Spanish Netherlands. The vessels were almost without exception commanded by Dutchmen, but were mainly manned by Germans, though the crews included many English, Dutch, Danish and Norwegian sailors. Naturally the soldiers carried on board were drawn from the Brandenburg army; and orders were given that they should be trained in ship's work "because we are disposed to use the same permanently for the navy."

Though the flotilla did not fulfil either its immediate or its ultimate purpose, the expedition was notable for two reasons. In the first place, a large Spanish warship, the *Carolus Secundus*, with a valuable cargo of lace on board, was captured, and so became the first war vessel that was actually the property of a Hohenzollern State. In the second place, the quest of the Spanish silver resulted in a sea-fight, which, in respect both of the force engaged and the losses sustained, still heads the record of naval warfare under a Hohenzollern flag.

A detachment of four ships, cruising in the neighbourhood of Cape St. Vincent, sighted a fleet of a dozen Spanish frigates, which had put out for the special purpose of chasing the Germans from the sea. The

Brandenburg commander, thinking that this was the anxiously-expected silver flotilla, bore down upon it, and did not realize his mistake till it was too late to avoid something of a conflict. Before he could succeed in manœuvring his ships out of range of his over-whelmingly superior enemy, he had lost ten men killed and thirty wounded; and since that day Germany has fought no more terrible battle on the sea.

Another section of the Elector's fleet cruised for several months in West Indian waters without achiev-ing much result, while the retaliatory measures adopted by the Spaniards secured a safe passage for the silver ships and rendered it prudent for Frederick William to abandon his daring and risky enterprise.

Meanwhile the Elector had allotted his infant navy a task of a different character. Soon after entering the service of Brandenburg, Raule had drawn up plans of colonization, and in the same year in which the fruitless search for the silver convoy began, he obtained per-mission to try his luck on the Gold Coast, and got together a syndicate to finance the undertaking. The Elector was wary, and declined to risk pecuniary participation, but he ordered that "twenty good healthy musketeers, together with two non-commis-sioned officers," should be placed under Raule's com-mand. One of the principal objects of the expedition was to secure a share in the profitable trade in slaves which was then carried on between the West Coast of Africa and North America, but modern German historians for the most part ignore this feature of the enterprise.

The two vessels despatched on this errand reached the Gold Coast in safety, but aroused the resentment of the Dutch already settled there, who confiscated one of them, and compelled the other to quit African waters. However, the leader of the expedition had by that time managed to conclude what served the purposes of a treaty with certain native chiefs, who thereby placed themselves under the suzerainty of the

Elector, and consented to the erection of a fort in the district under their control.

On the strength of this questionable document, an "African Company" for the "improvement of shipping and commerce wherein the best prosperity of a country consists," was called into existence in the year 1682. In the charter of incorporation, the Elector promised to protect the Company against "all and everyone who may undertake to trouble, incommode, or to any extent injure the same in its actions in free places on the coasts of Guinea and Angola"; but both the naval and the military commanders were charged to keep at a respectful distance from "all Dutch Company fortresses, as well as those of other potentates, such as England, France, Denmark, etc." The capital of the Company was the modest sum of 50,000 thalers. Of this Frederick William contributed only 8,000, and the Electoral Prince 2,000 thalers, while almost half of the total was supplied by Raule, who had by now become "Director-General of the Brandenburg Navy."

The two frigates in which the second Gold Coast expedition shipped cast anchor off Cape Three Points on December 27, 1682, but some difficulty was experienced in finding the chiefs who had "signed" the provisional treaty and who were each to have received a ratification engrossed in letters of gold, "a silver-gilt cup, and a portrait of his Electoral Highness." Frederick William had also issued instructions that his black allies and their wives were to be entertained on board the warships.

After a great deal of trouble, some other chieftains of the "Moors," as they are called in the official correspondence relating to this matter, were hunted out and induced to contract a second and definitive treaty; and on January 1, 1683, with due ceremony and much beating of drums, blowing of trumpets, and firing of guns, the Brandenburg flag was hoisted over "the first German colony." The flagstaff had been planted on a little eminence, which was subsequently, with all

speed, transformed into the fort Gross-Friedrichsburg,
and no doubt the rusty cannon now in the Zeughaus
at Berlin is one of the half-dozen which had been
mounted on the hill on the previous day in preparation
for the great occasion.

In the following year the headquarters of the African
Company was removed from Pillau to Emden. This
latter town was not situated on Brandenburg soil, and
the manner in which the Elector secured a footing in
it is both instructive and characteristic of his easy
methods of intervening and making a good bargain
wherever an opportunity presented itself. It chanced
that at that time the Estates of East Frisia were at
loggerheads with their ruler, and they appealed to
Frederick William for assistance. Nothing loth, he
landed a force by night, and by a surprise attack seized
the castle of Greetsiel, which thus became his naval
base. By an agreement with the town of Emden he
subsequently acquired the right to station within its
walls a "compagnie de marine" for the service of the
African Corporation. This force, which was gradually
increased to three, and temporarily to four, companies,
and ultimately received the name of the "Marine
Battalion," was drawn upon to man both the ships and
the forts in Africa.

The transfer to Emden brought other advantages
besides an ice-free port, a base on the North Sea, and
an abbreviation of the route to Gross-Friedrichsburg
for the East Frisian Estates and the Elector of Cologne
were both persuaded to invest largely in the African
Company in consequence of the change.

In the year of the Emden agreement, the Brandenburg Navy was formally founded by the establishment
of an "Admiralty" at Berlin. The Cabinet order by
which this institution was created shows that the fleet
then in full possession of the State comprised 10 ships,
with 240 guns, while Raule was still under contract to
provide 17 further vessels. The permanent personnel
consisted of 1 vice-commodore, 5 naval captains,

3 officers of Marines, 12 mates, and 120 seamen. In 1686, the Elector took the Company entirely into his own hands, and simultaneously acquired a station on the island of St. Thomas, in the West Indies, as a place of call for the ships engaged in the slave traffic. He had also at that time made preparations for forming an East Indian trading company (at a much earlier date he had unsuccessfully attempted to acquire Tranquebar, on the Coromandel Coast, from the Danes) and for fitting out an expedition to China and Japan. These schemes, however, came to nothing.

The settlement at Cape Three Points had by no means an easy existence. Fever made fearful ravages among the garrison, which, when the first reliefs arrived, after an interval of nearly a year and three-quarters, had been reduced by sickness from ninety to sixteen men. Everything that was needed for the construction of the fort, even building-stone, had to be brought thousands of miles across the sea from Germany. The Dutch traders in the neighbourhood had at once raised objections to the new colony, and, as their protests were unheeded, stirred up the natives against its members. It was only after prolonged negotiations at The Hague that the Elector secured a full recognition of his right to the settlement. And none the less the Dutch West India Company continued to harass the German colonists, appropriating their ships, and turning them out of a couple of subsidiary fortifications which they had erected at other points along the coast. Gross-Friedrichsburg and Taccroma, another of the four Brandenburg stations on the Guinea littoral, for several years maintained themselves only by the menace of their guns. These untoward events are believed to have preyed upon the mind of the Great Elector, and to have hastened his end. At the time of his death, in April, 1688, Brandenburg and Holland were on the brink of war over the Gold Coast affair.

His successor on the Electoral throne in one very

important respect reaped what Frederick William had sown, for he obtained the title of King of Prussia, by virtue of which, far more than from any specifically imperial prerogatives, William II. holds his present power in Germany. Frederick I. was a vain man, who was more interested in appearances than in realities, and cared more for the pomp and ceremonies of Court life than for the solid business of colonization and slave-trading. As a source of revenue, with which to defray the cost of his empty extravagances, the African undertaking was feebly encouraged to continue its work; but, deprived of the directing brain and the stimulating enthusiasm of its founder, it soon sickened and languished. Accada and Taccarary, the two settlements which had been seized by the Dutch, were delivered up after a lengthy squabble, but the fortifications of the latter had been destroyed, and they were not rebuilt.

At first the trade of the colony, which had called into existence a flourishing shipyard at Havelberg, near the junction of the Havel and the Elbe, was fairly satisfactory, and the spirit of the Brandenburg Navy was raised by the successful operations of a couple of its frigates against French merchantmen, but in 1697 the Company fell upon evil days. It suffered pecuniary loss, both through the capture of some of its ships by the French and through the peculations of several officials, whose multiple dishonesty hints at a scandalous laxity of control. The invaluable Raule, too, fell into disfavour, and spent four years in gaol, though he was reinstated in his position on being liberated. At last the Company was no longer able to send out ships of its own, and for eight years, during the War of the Spanish Succession, the garrison of Gross-Friedrichsburg was left entirely to itself. For a considerable portion of that time five large Brandenburg ships of war were rotting in the harbours of Emden and Hamburg, when they might have been much more profitably employed in attempting to keep up communications with the perishing colonists. When at last reliefs reached Gross-Friedrichsburg only seven men out of an original force of 1,700 were fit for duty.

What little credit attaches to the last days of the first German colony is the due of Jan Cuny, a native chief, who had placed himself under Brandenburg protection, apparently for the purpose of obtaining support against the English and Dutch settlements of the vicinity, with both of which he was at feud. It is characteristic of the period that, while Prussians were fighting shoulder to shoulder with English and Dutch on the continent of Europe, they were in open conflict with them on the West Coast of Africa. Frederick I. at one time thought it necessary to protest, through his Minister at London, against the difficulties which the English were causing him on the Gold Coast.

All the trouble seems to have arisen out of the demand made by a Dutch official at Axim for the surrender of a female relative of Cuny whom he claimed as his slave. Jan was evidently a man of considerable parts. He led his army with great discretion and resourcefulness, and no doubt the Prussians at Gross-Friedrichsburg thought it to their advantage to be on good terms with so formidable a warrior, especially as he was the sworn foe of their jealous European neighbours. At any rate, the relations between Cuny and the fort became both cordial and confiding, and when the last Governor of Gross-Friedrichsburg, Du Bois, discouraged by the indifference and neglect of the home authorities, sailed for Emden to enter remonstrances, he entrusted the protection of the colony to his black ally.

Du Bois arrived in Europe only to find that the doom of Gross-Friedrichsburg was already irrevocably sealed. The parsimonious Frederick William I., the father of Frederick the Great, had ascended the Prussian throne, and his careful mind, completely absorbed by plans of immediate economy, was incapable of taking such flights into the distance and the future as were necessary for the appreciation of the value of colonial policy. The African settlements had been doing badly and had become unremunerative, and his only thought was to dispose of them as speedily as possible for hard cash, which could be either hoarded or spent on his solitary extravagance—seven-foot grenadiers. Immediately after his accession, he instructed his representative in London that he was prepared to "transfer his forts on the coast of Guinea to anyone else upon easy conditions." He was not long in finding a purchaser in that very Dutch West India Company which had from the outset been a thorn in the side of the Great Elector's colonial enterprise. On November 22, 1717, Gross-Friedrichsburg and its dependent territory passed from Hohenzollern rule for the sum of 6,000 ducats and twelve negro boys, of whom it was stipulated that six should be adorned with golden chains.

The signing of the contract and its execution were, however, two very different things. The redoubtable Jan Cuny had not been reckoned with, and when two Dutch vessels arrived to take over the fort they found him in possession and flying the Prussian flag. The order for the transfer of the fort was shown to his emissaries, who, after a good deal of delay, were sent on board the ships, but this he flatly refused to recognize, declaring that he would yield up his trust only to a vessel belonging to the King of Prussia. The commander of the Dutch expedition, Captain van der Hoeven, thought he would make short work of this insolent chieftain, and landed a body of fifty men to take the fort by storm. But Cuny once again showed the generalship which had raised him to the eminence of a Prussian deputy-governor. A force of 1,800 natives fusilladed the landing party from an ambuscade and killed nearly every one of them. Hoeven was only able to save himself by swimming back to his ship, with three bullets in his body, and retired to the nearest Dutch settlement to excogitate a fresh plan of campaign.

Cuny, however, was flushed by his success, and not at all inclined to give up the prestige which he derived from a fortress bristling with guns and well furnished with small arms and ammunition.   For seven long years he held out, repulsing the repeated attacks of the Dutch, and it was only when his supplies were exhausted and an overwhelming force had been put into the field against him, that he withdrew from his defences and vanished into the jungle from which he had come.

Simultaneously with Gross-Friedrichsburg, there was transferred from the Prussian King to the Dutch Company yet another African Colony, of which mention has yet to be made.   This was the island of Arguin, which lies off the coast of what is now French territory to the south of Cape Blanco, and in some maps is given the ominous name of Agadir.   The islet, which was one of the principal centres of the gum trade, had been first occupied by the Portuguese in 1441, but had passed by conquest to Holland, and from the latter to France. After the Peace of Nymegen, in 1678, however, the French Senegal Company found itself unable to maintain a garrison in Arguin, and obtained permission from Louis XIV. to blow up the fort which had been erected there.   The island then fell into the hands of the native ruler of Arguin, on the mainland, and remained subject to him till two ships of the Great Elector appeared off its coasts in October, 1685.

On the strength of a treaty concluded by the commander of the expedition with the King of Arguin, Frederick William seems to have claimed jurisdiction right along the coast of Africa from the Canary Isles to the Senegal River.   These pretensions were not allowed to pass undisputed, and, towards the end of 1687, a couple of French vessels appeared off the fort and demanded its evacuation by the Germans.   As this was refused they made an attempt to seize it by

force, but, meeting with a stubborn resistance, abandoned the attack, and, after an unsuccessful endeavour
to assert their rights during the peace negotiations
at Ryswick, the French seemed to reconcile themselves to the new situation, for they even proposed
commercial co-operation with the occupants of the
Arguin fort.

After the death of the Great Elector, Arguin suffered,
like Gross-Friedrichsburg, through the indifference
of his successor, and the difficulty of communication
arising from the War of the Spanish Succession.
When a relief ship arrived in 1714, it found that the
Governor had been captured by the natives, with
whom he had quarrelled; and the remnant of the
Arguin garrison was in so deplorable a condition,
that "in a few days they must have perished of
hunger."

The transfer of Arguin to the Dutch proved as
difficult as that of Gross-Friedrichsburg. In 1717
the French had renewed their claims to the island,
and, a few years later, the Senegal Company, landing
700 men and heavy guns, laid siege to the fort. After
holding out for a few weeks, the commander, Jan
Wynen, a Dutchman, withdrew secretly by night
with his force in order to escape the humiliation
of a formal surrender, and when its new owners
at last arrived to take possession of it the colony
was actually in French hands. It was in both
cases a foreigner who last kept the flag flying over
what were to be the only German colonies established
till the final quarter of the nineteenth century. With
the colonies disappeared the force with which they
had been won, the fleet, and it too had to wait long,
though not quite so long, before it experienced a
revival.

It is interesting to reflect how the history of the
world might have been changed if the Great Elector's
two immediate successors had united to his far-reaching schemes of "world-policy" his determination in

carrying them out, and had bequeathed to the greater Frederick prosperous colonial possessions and a formidable navy. As it was, the naval episodes of the reign of this gifted monarch only show how pitifully and completely the dawning sea-power of his grandfather had passed away.

In the Seven Years' War, the shores of Prussia were continually ravaged by Swedish frigates, and as nothing could be effected by the armed fishing boats and coasting vessels which were all that could be pitted against them, Field-Marshal Lehwald, to whom the protection of that part of Prussia had been entrusted, appealed for help to the corporation of merchants at Stettin. That body responded with energy and promptitude, and, with great haste, a flotilla of four galliots, four large fishing boats, and four coasting vessels were transformed into "ships of war." In August, 1759, this improvised fleet ventured out of the Oder to attack the Swedes, but it was so completely overthrown, after several days' fighting, that the experiment was never repeated.

In the meanwhile Frederick had been inveigled into another maritime adventure, which was to prove just as barren of positive results. Early in the war several Englishmen communicated to the King their readiness to fit out privateers to prey on the commerce of Austria and Sweden, both of which countries had seized Prussian merchantmen. They protested in all cases that their principal motive was a desire to serve the cause of a monarch whom they admired and revered, and who was, as a matter of fact, at that time the ally of England. But at the same time they promised him "prodigious profits" from the enterprise, and it was admittedly the latter consideration which induced the King to listen to their proposals. Though his own Ministers expressed strong doubts, and the English Government urged that he would run the risk of embroiling himself with neutral States, he issued a number of letters of marque. The advice which had been given him proved to have been only too well founded. Not only were there no "prodigious profits," but the blunders of the royal officials and the indiscretions of the ships under his flag involved the King in voluminous diplomatic correspondence and long and fruitless litigation.

To accelerate the process of destroying the enemy's trade, a number of blank letters of marque, ministerially signed and stamped with the royal seal, were sent out to the Prussian Minister in London, and he somewhat imprudently lent a couple of these to an interesting adventurer, named Erskine Douglas, who said that he wished to show them to shipowners with whom he was in treaty for the equipment of privateers. Douglas claimed to be a relative of the Prussian Field-Marshal Keith, who was of Scottish origin, and he brought letters of introduction from well-known members of the English nobility, so the Minister may perhaps be excused for entrusting the documents to him. But his confidence was gravely abused, for Douglas, having come to an agreement with the firm of Dunbar and Eyre, filled in the forms on his own responsibility, and two privateers were sent out with these fraudulent credentials.

Shortly afterwards, one of these ships, the *Lissa*, put into Emden with a rich Swedish prize. Lying in the harbour was an English man-of-war, and the captain of this ship, declaring that the English sailors on board the *Lissa* were all either deserters or men who had bound themselves to serve in the British Navy, required that they should be given up to him. As compliance was refused, he went on board the *Lissa* with an armed escort, and, disregarding all the protests of its captain, took away with him twenty-six members of the crew. This action was regarded by Frederick as an infraction of Prussian rights of sovereignty, and representations to that effect were made in London before it was discovered in how irregular a manner the *Lissa* had become possessed of her papers. The

matter was then discreetly allowed to drop.   The
Swedes, for their part, contested the legality of the
capture, but the Prussian Government ruled that the
letter of marque was valid, although it had not actually
been issued by royal authority.   At the same time
Prussia advanced the strange view that, in the event of
the owners of the *Lissa* having had cognizance of the
deception which had been practised, King Frederick
was entitled to the whole value of the prize.   Instructions were, however, given that the *Lissa* should be
deprived of her charter, but before they could be
executed she had sailed for England.

Another of Douglas's privateersmen, the *Prince
Ferdinand*, under a Captain Merryfield, had betaken
herself to the Mediterranean, where, in a nine-months'
cruise, she captured thirteen prizes, but caused so much
confusion that the King thought it wiser to put a stop
to the whole undertaking.   The immediate ground for
this step was the complaints of the Ottoman Government, with which Frederick was negotiating with a view
to obtaining its support in the prosecution of the war.
The appropriation of a couple of female negro slaves
belonging to a pasha, who were on board one of the
ships captured by Merryfield, seems to have had at least
as much weight in the Turkish grievance as the more
substantial losses of the merchants of Salonika.   As
Prussia had no territory and very little diplomatic
representation on the shores of the Mediterranean,
Merryfield was obliged to take his prizes into neutral
harbours and place them in the custody of the English
Consuls.   They were the subjects of endless law suits,
tedious international wrangling, and practically no
profits.   Merryfield's wild career was terminated by a
charge of secretly selling neutral goods from one of
his prizes to his own advantage.   At the instance of
the Prussian Government he was flung into gaol at
Malta.   He remained in prison five years, and even
at the end of that term would not have regained his
liberty if the Grand Master of the Maltese Knights

had not refused to pay for his maintenance any longer.

Hardly less chequered were the fortunes of Captain Wake, the only regularly accredited Prussian privateer of whom anything is known. The operations of his ship, the *Embden*, in the Mediterranean also resulted in ceaseless bickerings, and he was delayed in Cagliari for two years by disputes of one sort or another. At last, growing weary, he set off to Berlin to prosecute his claims to a Swedish ship which he had seized, but of which the authorities at Cagliari would not permit him to dispose. Four and a half years after the capture, she was adjudged his good prize; but before he could enter into possession of her she was sunk at her moorings by a violent storm.

The total gain of the Prussian Government from the activity of these three privateers was quite negligible; while, on the other hand, the trouble and annoyance caused by them was immeasurable. The anticipations that the seas would be swept of Austrian and Swedish commerce by a swarm of vessels under the Prussian flag proved to have been quite illusory, and it was a particular disappointment to Frederick that the German shipowners looked askance at the whole business, and in no single instance applied for letters of marque.

A noteworthy feature of the episode is that Frederick's Government, reversing the practice of the Hansa, laid down for its privateers the rule that a neutral flag covered the enemy's goods, and that neutral goods were safe from capture even when under the enemy's flag. This, it is maintained, has ever since been Prussian tradition.

A final word is due to the "Société de Commerce Maritime"—now under the name "Seehandlung," the State bank of the Kingdom of Prussia—which was established by Frederick the Great in 1772, "to carry on shipping under the Prussian flag, and trade with the ports of Spain and all other places where reasonable and certain prospects of substantial profits from imports and exports are to be found." It was vessels of this corporation which, towards the close of the first half of the nineteenth century, bore a German flag for the first time round the world, and its foundation shows that the Great Elector's ideas were only dormant and not dead.

Frederick's immediate purpose was to open up the markets of South America to Silesian linen, but, in consequence of the rigid protectionist policy of Spain, it was only possible to do this by transhipment at Spanish ports. The original capital of the company was 1,200,000 thalers, in shares of 500 thalers each, and of these 2,100 were the property of the King. The Société was granted the exclusive right of trading in English, French, and Spanish salt, and in Polish wax, and was also endowed with many other privileges. It did not at first prove a very profitable venture, and its early days were also clouded over by the defalcations of one of its managers. In course of time it became little more than a branch of the Royal Treasury and the negotiator of State loans, but in the thirties of last century it passed under the control of a man who determined to restore to it something of its original character, and laid out a considerable capital in English-built ships. At that period German merchantmen seldom ventured beyond Bordeaux and Lisbon; but the vessels of the Seehandlung repeatedly encircled the globe, showed their flag in the remotest harbours of Orient and Occident, and established directly that export to South America of the wares of the Riesengebirge which Frederick the Great had in his mind when he called the company into existence.

CHAPTER III

THE GERMAN NAVY IN THE NINETEENTH CENTURY

THOUGH the sword of Napoleon completed the destruction of the Holy Roman Empire, which had done so much to hamper the development of the Teutonic race, the Vienna Congress, rearranging the map of Europe after his overthrow, left Germany still divided into thirty-nine different states. There were four kingdoms, one electorate, seven grand duchies, ten duchies, ten principalities, one landgraviate, and the four free towns—Hamburg, Bremen, Lübeck, and Frankfort-on-Main. These states were loosely united in the German Confederacy.

The people of Germany, and especially those who had risen against Napoleon, had expected a more complete unity on a democratic basis, and the disappointment of their hopes was one of the chief causes of the revolution which, in 1848, broke out simultaneously in nearly every one of the federal capitals. This movement took the Governments by surprise, and so overwhelming was the popular demand for unity, that they offered but little opposition to the convening of a National Assembly, which met at Frankfort-on-Main on May 18, 1848, and appointed the Austrian Archduke Johann provisional "Administrator of the Empire." It is generally asserted that the failure of this serious attempt to weld Germany together was an inevitable consequence of the jealousy existing between Austria and Prussia, but none can say with certainty what the sequel might not have been, had not Frederick William IV., the grand-uncle of the present German

71

Emperor, refused the imperial crown when it was offered to him by the National Assembly. It is very well conceivable that, if that monarch had been less fully persuaded of the divine rights of Kings and of the incompetence of popular representatives to bestow crowns, the work which Bismarck did in the next twenty years, with so grievous an expenditure of blood and iron, might have been accomplished by peaceable means, and that the world might to-day have been confronted with the problem of a much larger, much richer, and much more united Germany. Possibly those who would not regard German domination in Europe as an unmixed blessing have reason to be thankful for Frederick William's archaic theories on the relationships of Princes to their peoples.

And those who care to amuse themselves by following up the grand alternatives of history must not forget that 1848 saw the birth of the modern German Fleet, which was the fruit of a purely popular movement. Indeed, the patriots of the Frankfort Parliament found in the "imperial fleet," which they actually founded, the necessary symbol of that national unity which was the goal of their aspirations.

Strong, spontaneous, and almost universal as was the German naval movement of 1848, it did not attain its actual dimensions without an effective external stimulus. In the very month in which the revolutionaries were defending their barricades in the streets of Berlin and other German capitals, Frederick VII. had declared his intention of incorporating Schleswig in Denmark; and, while an informal convention was arranging the preliminaries for the National Assembly, the Danish fleet was blockading the coasts of Prussia in retaliation for the military support afforded by that Kingdom, as the mandatory of the German Confederation, to the rebellious duchies. Nothing was better calculated than an incident of this sort to bring home to the German mind the importance of sea-power. That the ships of a little country like Denmark should be able, with impunity, to forbid the sea to a great military Power, seemed to every German who reflected upon it a grotesque inversion of the natural order of events.

Though the National Assembly, at one of its first sittings, appointed a permanent committee to grapple with the naval question, the impatient interest of the public displayed itself in schemes and suggestions which poured in from every side. In many places committees were formed to help to raise the funds necessary for the equipment of a fleet. It is significant of the widespread nature of the movement that the raftsmen of Gernsbach, in the Black Forest, offered to transport down the River Murg free of cost the timber required for the building of Germany's warships. The seaports, which felt most keenly the insulting pressure of the Danish blockade, took the leading part in the agitation. A congress of delegates from the German coast towns came together at Hamburg and nominated a "naval commission," on which, in addition to the Governments most immediately concerned, a number of private committees were represented. This body wasted no time in talk, but set to work with feverish activity. As warships were not to be had ready-made, several merchant vessels were purchased and hastily armed with guns, furnished by Hanover; and at the beginning of July, the Federal Government was notified that these extemporized men-of-war were ready to put out and attack the enemy. But at the moment the negotiations with Denmark for a truce had already begun, and for the time being the squadron remained peacefully at its moorings.

Meanwhile, even before an Imperial Executive had been got together, the Frankfort Parliament had voted for naval purposes a sum of 6,000,000 thalers,* half of which was to be spent immediately and the remainder

* Thaler = about 3s.

as necessity might arise. Part of the money was to be taken from the fortress fund of the old Confederacy, and the remainder raised by levies in due proportion on the various states of the union. The question of these "matricular contributions," which in some cases were altogether refused, and in others only paid after much hesitation and vacillation, was one of the chief reasons for the ultimate dissolution of the first "German" Navy.

In November an imperial naval authority was constituted under the control of the Minister of Commerce, who was at the same time deputy for Bremen. An advisory commission of experts was also appointed, and the chair in this body was, at the personal request of the Archduke-Administrator, taken by the man who, in one sense, may be regarded as the father of the present German Fleet, Prince Adalbert of Prussia, and to whom, for this reason, more detailed reference must be made hereafter. The commission submitted a scheme, in which it was recommended that Germany should, for the present, make no attempt to gain a place in the ranks of the first-class naval Powers, but content herself with the protection of her Baltic and North Sea coasts and her sea-borne trade. These purposes, it was held, could be fulfilled by a fleet of fifteen sixty-gun sailing frigates—if possible with auxiliary engines—five steam frigates, twenty steam corvettes, ten despatch-boats, five schooners, and thirty gun-sloops.

During the winter, officials were despatched to England to purchase and order ships, and to America to induce the United States Government to allow some of its naval officers to enter temporarily into the German service. These latter negotiations at first promised success, but in the end the Government at Washington declared itself unable to entertain the request. With the purchase of material the German emissaries had better luck, and when the truce with Denmark expired in the spring of 1849, the Navy List already contained the names of twelve vessels, though, it is true, hardly one of them was yet fit for action. A Commander-in-Chief had also been found in the person of Karl Bromme, a native of Leipzig, whose name had been permanently anglicized into " Brommy " while he was learning seafaring in the American merchant service. This man, " the first German Admiral," had followed Cochrane to Greece, where he was successively Flag Captain to Admiral Miaulis, organizer in the Ministry of Marine, and Commandant of the Military School at the Piræus. From there he was tempted away to become " Imperial Commissioner" to the incipient German Navy, and after taking part in the sittings of the commission of experts, he was sent in that capacity to Bremerhaven to supervise the formation of the fleet and to found a naval arsenal.

On June 4 Brommy, with a steam frigate and two steam corvettes, attacked a Danish frigate, which was lying becalmed off Heligoland. Hardly, however, had the engagement commenced before a signal shot from the island warned the belligerents that they were within British territorial waters, and must suspend hostilities. Soon afterwards the Danish blockading squadron approached the scene, and the German ships hurried back to their harbour. This was the only opportunity the German Fleet had of showing its quality. Brommy was promoted to Rear-Admiral later in the year.

Insignificant as the Heligoland skirmish was in itself, it had a sequel which has played a great part in all subsequent movements for increasing the German Fleet. Brommy's ships had fought under the black-red-and-gold that were to be the colours of the new Empire. But this Empire had then no legal existence, and, as a matter of fact, never did have one, and no doubt Palmerston was only giving expression to recognized principles of international law when he wrote that vessels committing acts of belligerency under the black - red - and - gold flag would render themselves liable to be treated as "pirates." The Frankfort Government, a product of excitement and inexperience, made many mistakes which the ripe tradition of an old-established administration would have avoided, and, in its haste to assert itself on the seas, doubtless did not give sufficient thought to the restrictions imposed upon it by its own anomalous status. The hoisting of the black-red-and-gold on a flotilla of warships was undeniably a questionable proceeding, and one which justified the view propounded by the British Foreign Minister. At the same time, his words belong to the category of things which had better have been left unsaid. The word "pirate" rankled then, and has ever since continued to rankle, and the Palmerstonian note has been cited ten thousand times, and is still cited, as the supreme example of the tyrannous arrogance with which Britain rules the waves. Much will have been gained when British politicians get to understand the German psychology, which is exceedingly sensitive, and realize how much depends, in dealing with Germans, on a careful choice of words.

A fortnight after Brommy's one exploit as a German naval commander, the remnant of the National Assembly was dispersed by military force at Stuttgart, where it had taken refuge, and Germany relapsed into the condition of a loosely-jointed federation of mutually jealous and suspicious Princes, whose rival claims had to be settled on the battlefield before the great work of unification could be accomplished. The infant navy, which had been the work of a popular movement and a popular Parliament, proved a source of dissension and embarrassment to the Confederacy Governments. Several of the inland states were altogether opposed to the idea that Germany needed a navy. A strong party advocated that one fleet should be provided by Austria for the Adriatic, a second by Prussia for the Baltic, and a third by the remaining German states for the North Sea. The last point of this project was the subject of special negotiations, and at one time there seemed some chance of Hanover assuming the office of "Federal Admiral."

In the end, however, divergent interests and irreconcilable rivalries produced the only possible result, and, in February, 1852, the Confederated Governments decided to cut the Gordian knot. The promising German Navy was dissolved, Admiral Brommy received his discharge (he was subsequently employed for some time as Chief of the Technical Department of the Austrian Admiralty), and an Oldenburg official, whose unforgettable name has helped to brand his memory with the whole infamy of a transaction for which he was in nowise responsible, was appointed "Commissioner of the Germanic Confederation charged with the regulation of naval affairs." This, at least, is the designation appended to his signature on the advertisement which, in the German, English, and French languages, announced to all the world that the German Navy was forthwith to be knocked down to the highest bidder. It is the form rather than the fact of the sale which is taken so ill in Privy Councillor Hannibal Fischer, but it is difficult to see what else he could have done. He made efforts to dispose of the ships by private treaty, and actually sold some of them to Prussia and others to English firms, but a residue remained for which no purchaser could be found in this way, and there was nothing for it but to put them up to public auction. There thus came under the hammer two steam frigates, six steam corvettes, a sailing frigate, and twenty-seven gunboats propelled by oars. Of the eight steamers three had been built at Bristol, and one each at Glasgow, Leith, New York, Hamburg, and Bremen. Except in the case of the American vessel, the engines were all of British make. It must be conceded that the progress which Germany made in this respect during the next half-century was nothing less than prodigious.

Concurrently with the abortive efforts to found a German Navy, Prussia had taken independent action, and laid the real foundation of the great fleet which now aspires to contest the British mastery of the seas. At that time there was not even the slenderest basis for the kingdom to work upon. The task had to be undertaken from the very beginning. During the first half of the nineteenth century, it is true, the advisability of building a navy had more than once been exhaustively discussed by the Prussian Government. In the general resettlement of 1815, the island of Rügen and the strip of Pomeranian coast opposite to it had passed from Sweden to Prussia, and included in the transfer were six gun-sloops and a Swedish officer, Captain Christian Lange, who was summoned to Berlin to report to the War Ministry on the utility of the little flotilla. As the result of his representations, he was commissioned to submit plans and estimates for a war schooner, and for an armed rowing boat for use on the rivers. These vessels were eventually built, with the express idea that they were to serve as experiments and models for the construction of a regular fleet. In great haste prescriptions as to a naval uniform were issued, and the questions of dockyards and harbour works were also deliberated. But the only issue of all this work was the conviction that the national resources were not yet equal to the financial strain which would have been entailed by the creation of a navy. Similar investigations and discussions in the years 1825 and 1832 were, for the same reason, equally fruitless. At the commencement of the revolutionary year, the only vessels in the possession of the Prussian Government were a corvette, which was employed as a Navigation School, a paddle steamer, which conveyed the mails between Stettin and St. Petersburg, and which, under the terms of the contract for its construction, was to be adaptable to the purposes of an " auxiliary cruiser," and a couple of armed yawls.

By the autumn of 1848 a Prussian flotilla of ten

sloops and yawls, three of which had been built with the funds collected by private committees, was ready for operations against the Danes. It was placed under the command of a Dutch ex-naval captain named Schröder. The crews provided for him—465 men in all —were a strange medley of active soldiers, reservists, and seamen from the merchant service. For various reasons, not the least weighty of which was the doubtful status of the black-red-and-gold flag, the squadron sailed under the Prussian colours. While it was fitting out, the first steps were taken towards the establishment of a naval organization and the training of a corps of officers.

By the following summer the Prussian fleet could already boast two steamers, one sailing corvette, and twenty-one gun sloops, with a total complement of thirty-seven officers and 1,521 men, and mounting in all sixty-seven guns. But only once did this primitive navy have the satisfaction of taking part in a pitched naval engagement. This was a duel between a Prussian steamer and a Danish brig, which fought for five hours off the island of Rügen. The encounter was terminated by the fall of darkness, and before day broke again another Danish corvette arrived on the scene and put the Prussians to flight. But, in spite of a lack of fighting, the presence of Commodore Schröder's force along the coast undoubtedly did much to relieve the pressure of the blockade.

The peace with Denmark in 1850 ushered in a period of assiduous and systematic labour at the task of building up a Prussian fleet. Throughout this important period, the moving spirit was the man who has already been described as the father of the German Navy, Prince Adalbert of Prussia. This enthusiastic and indefatigable sailor was a first cousin of King Frederick William IV., who refused the imperial crown as a democratic gift, and of the Emperor William I., who finally won it on the battlefields of France. In his boyhood, Prince Adalbert had had the doctrine of the vital importance of sea-power implanted in his mind by a veteran soldier, Field-Marshal Gneisenau, and he never forgot the lesson. At the age of twenty-one he paid a visit of two months' duration to England, where he was cordially welcomed into naval circles, and where his passion for the sea was inflamed by the conversation of men who had fought under Nelson at Trafalgar. He lost no opportunity of inspecting war vessels, shipyards, and docks, and returned to Germany with note-books crammed with information as to all he had seen and heard. A British admiral is said to have declared that the Prince knew more about the warships of Great Britain than many of their own officers, and one of the last acts of this sailor Hohenzollern was to pay a visit to the English dockyards to familiarize himself with the latest novelties in naval construction.

Four years after his first journey to England, one of those naval enquiries already alluded to was held at Berlin, and a commission was appointed to advise as to the type of vessel to be chosen for the fleet which the Prussian Government contemplated building at some indefinite future date. Prince Adalbert was a member of this body, but when asked for his views on the subject he satisfied himself with laying before his colleagues the opinion of his friend, Captain Mingaye, a British naval officer, who advised that the triumph of steam over sails and oars presented Prussia with a splendid opportunity to create sea-power which should be " mighty " from the outset. Curiously enough, the War Minister, von Rauch, inferred from this suggestion that naval construction was passing through a transition stage of doubtful issue, and it was used by him as a pretext for postponing the consideration of the whole question; for, he argued, Prussia could not afford to squander money on uncertain experiments. In the succeeding years, the Prince cruised the Mediterranean in an Austrian ship with his friend the Archduke Johann, afterwards the Imperial

Administrator, and made in Sardinian and British war vessels several longer voyages, during which he devoted himself with a whole heart to the study of seamanship and navigation. He also added materially to his knowledge while on board one of the ships of the British Mediterranean Squadron, which at the time was engaged in manœuvres. On his return home from these experiences, he secured the appointment of Schröder to the Navigation School ship *Amazon*, always with the idea that the vessel would be the training - ground of the officers' corps of a future Prussian Navy. As we have seen, the Prince was chosen as chairman of the Frankfort advisory committee on naval questions. Some months previously he had addressed to the National Assembly a "Memorandum as to the Formation of a German Fleet." This document, which was printed and published, not only is a remarkable testimony to the author's insight into the true nature of naval problems, but also contains a clear enunciation of the principles which guide Germany's naval policy at the present day. Pointing to the humiliation of the Danish blockade he wrote:

"And this Germany—united Germany—must calmly submit to, precisely at the great moment when, after long years, it once more feels itself a whole, a Power of forty millions of people. But the Fatherland recognizes the oppressive nature of its situation; it demands a remedy all the more speedy because, after these events, it foresees with certainty how much more painful its position might some day be if it were pitted against one of the great Sea-Powers, a Power against which the German ships would not be secure even in their own harbours, a fleet which could menace our coasts with debarkations on a much more extensive scale than is possible to our present foe. United Germany, however, wishes to see her territories energetically protected, her flag respected, her trade once more flourishing, and in the future to have some influence on the sea."

Prince Adalbert then weighed the three alternatives : (a) Defensive coast protection ; (b) offensive coast protection; and (c) an independent German sea-power; and finally reached the conclusion :

" Germany must either build no battleships or at once build so many that she can act towards her neighbours as an independent Sea-Power.   Anything intermediate would be a useless expense, an empty pretension, and would arouse in the nation expectations which, in the moment of danger, our sea-power would not be able to fulfil.

" If we now ask what would be the smallest number of battleships which would allow us to act in European waters as an independent fleet, especially against the ever-ready Russian Baltic fleet, I think we must take twenty battleships as the minimum that would be able to measure itself with it.   But such a fleet would make Germany fourth among the Sea-Powers of first rank, and place her incontestably in a position to play a great rôle on the sea, a rôle which would be worthy of her position in Europe.   For with her twenty battleships she would be able to throw an enormous weight into the scales, turn the balance by her adherence to an alliance, and consequently be as much sought after as an ally on account of her sea-power as on account of her land-power."

The Prince accordingly proposed that the German building programme should include 20 battleships with auxiliary screws, 10 frigates, 30 steam cruisers, 40 gunboats, and 80 gun-sloops ; and that the construction of these vessels should be spread over a period of ten years.   In this project we have that same principle of the gradual working up to a fixed standard of strength which has characterized all modern German naval legislation.   Nor can it be said that Prince Adalbert's plans were appreciably less ambitious than those of Admiral Tirpitz.

However, the Prince did not manage to persuade the Frankfort technical commission to adopt his scheme in its entirety, though the programme approved went a

long way towards meeting his views. Why this programme was never carried out has already been seen.
In the Memorandum just quoted from, Prince Adalbert
had written : " The entire nation unanimously demands
a German war fleet, for German, absolutely German, it
must be, a true representative of the new-born unity
of the Fatherland ;" and it must have been with a
heavy heart that he saw his vision melt away, and
went back to Berlin to employ his gifts in a more
restricted and less promising field.

The difficulties which opposed themselves to the
realization of the Prince's ideas will be appreciated,
when it is stated that the man who built the first
warship of any size which had been launched from
a German yard since the days of the Hanseatic League
is still alive. Wilhelm Schwarm, now ninety-four
years of age, was employed as a young man in
Klawitter's shipyard at Dantzic, and at the time when
the air was filled with talk of a future German Navy,
the firm very shrewdly sent him over to the works of
Robinson and Russell, on the Thames, to learn the art
of constructing vessels of larger size than were then
built on the Baltic. He brought back with him the
plans for a paddle corvette, which was built under his
supervision on the Klawitter slips, fitted with English
engines, and, under the name of *Dantzig*, was an important addition to the Prussian fleet.

At the time of the Crimean War this vessel showed
the Prussian flag at Constantinople for the first time in
history, and it was also with her that Prince Adalbert
experienced a rather grotesque adventure in the
Mediterranean in 1856. In the previous year a
German ship had been plundered by the Riff pirates,
and the Prince, happening to be in those parts with
the *Dantzig*, made a reconnaissance, in one of the ship's
boats, of the coast of Cape Tres Forcas, where the
outrage had occurred. The natives, as was their
custom, fired on the party from the shore. Annoyed
by this molestation, Prince Adalbert determined to

teach the Arabs a severe lesson. Having manned and armed all his boats, he stormed the steep and rocky shore and planted the Prussian flag on the summit of the cliffs. His triumph was, however, a very brief one, for the enemy immediately returned to the attack, and drove the landing party back to the boats with the loss of seven killed and twenty-three wounded. Official panegyrists extol this rash escapade as an "heroic deed," and declare that it did much to raise the confidence of the young Prussian Navy. As the Riff pirates were no doubt also exultant over their victory, the affair must have been one of those rare encounters with the issue of which both sides were equally satisfied. The *Dantzig* was sold a few years later in England, in the belief that her timbers were unsound, and was then passed on to Japan, where she was run ashore and burnt by her own crew during an engagement in the civil war.

The problem of obtaining properly qualified personnel for the corps of naval officers was not less difficult to solve than that of building efficient warships. England would have been the natural source on which to draw for instructors, but for political reasons it was decided not to seek assistance from that most competent of all quarters, and the services of three officers of the Swedish Navy were secured. For similar reasons a Swedish naval constructor was engaged. A few years later, however, permission was asked and obtained for a number of cadets to learn their profession on British men-of-war.

The year 1852 brought an event of the utmost importance for the development of the Prussian Navy —the acquisition of Wilhelmshaven as a North Sea base. At that time Prussia did not possess an inch of coast-line on the North Sea, and could obtain access to it only through the Belt and the Sound, then under the control of the superior naval power of Denmark. Among the innumerable projects with which the National Assembly had been deluged, was the scheme of three citizens of Rendsburg for the construction of a water-way pretty much along the line subsequently followed by the Kaiser Wilhelm Canal. This plan was, however, based on the false assumption that Schleswig-Holstein would at once become, and ever afterwards remain, German territory. It had also been proposed to the Frankfort Government by an Oldenburg official that the Jade Bay should be chosen as the North Sea base for the fleet, and this suggestion seems to have fixed the attention of Prince Adalbert on the inlet which is now the chief naval headquarters of the German Empire. The Grand Duke of Oldenburg was approached, and he consented to cede to Prussia the piece of marshy land which has since been covered by the harbours, docks, shipyards, workshops, barracks, and fortifications of Wilhelmshaven. Prussia paid a sum of 500,000 thalers for this invaluable possession, and at the same time took upon herself the protection of the coast and sea-trade of the duchy.

Herculean efforts and inexhaustible patience were required to adapt Prussia's acquisition on the Jade to its destined purposes. Years had to be spent in a careful survey of the bed of the harbour, in order to ascertain how far the channel was affected by the movements of sand and mud under the influence of the tide. Further years were consumed by the task of sinking piles in the treacherous peaty soil to obtain a solid foundation for dock and harbour walls. Frequently a storm or a spring tide destroyed in a few hours the fruits of months of strenuous labour. As Hanover refused to allow the construction of a railway across her territory, which lay between Prussia and Oldenburg, it was necessary to convey all the building materials to the spot by the long and tedious sea-route. At first not even drinking-water was to be had on the desolate site, and prolonged and costly exertions were needful before it could be procured in sufficient quantities. Sixteen years elapsed before the new harbour was formerly declared open by the Prussian King, afterwards the Emperor William I., in the presence of British ships, the officers of which probably regarded the works with indulgent curiosity, and little guessed the significance which Wilhelmshaven would one day possess for their own country.

When the second war with Denmark broke out in 1864, Prussia's fleet was still absurdly inadequate to deal with the naval force opposed to it. The ship establishment at the close of 1863 was composed as under :

Steamships with Fighting Value.

3 corvettes, mounting 27 or 28 guns each.
1 corvette, mounting 17 guns.

Steamships with little Fighting Value.

4 first-class gunboats, mounting 3 guns each.
17 second-class gunboats, mounting 2 guns each.
3 despatch-boats, mounting together 8 guns.

Steamship without Fighting Value.

1 corvette, mounting 9 guns.

Sailing Ships with little or no Fighting Value.

3 frigates, mounting a total of 112 guns.
3 brigs, mounting a total of 4 guns.
2 schooners, mounting a total of 4 guns.

Also without Fighting Value.

40 rowing-boats, mounting a total of 76 guns.

Denmark, on the other hand, had 31 steam war vessels, among which were 1 battleship, 5 frigates, 3 corvettes, and 4 armoured craft. Even with the assistance of a number of Austrian ships, which arrived in the North Sea from the Mediterranean, the Prussian fleet could contribute nothing decisive towards the issue of the war. At the most it prevented the Danish blockade of the German coast-line from being effective. The Prussian Government attempted to reduce its inferiority by hiring merchant vessels, and hurriedly purchased warships in France and

England. One of these latter, the monitor *Arminius*, which was of English build, was almost entirely paid for with the voluntary contributions which had continued to flow in. This fact shows how steady and keen the interest of a large section of the population in the development of the navy already was, and how erroneous it is to ascribe the naval enthusiasm in Germany of recent years entirely to the official agitation. Peace was concluded before the new ships could be made ready for sea.

The war of 1864 was one of the great cross-roads of British history. Difficult as it is to "overlook the cards of Providence," as Bismarck put it, there can be little doubt that we took the wrong turning. The great German Chancellor candidly admitted that the possession of Kiel and a strategic canal through Holstein were two of the principal objects which Prussia had in view when she drew the sword. The two leading members of the British Cabinet were in favour of backing up Denmark; and one of them, Palmerston, used language in Parliament which might well have led that country to count upon our support. A strong body of English public opinion also warmly espoused the Danish cause. But Queen Victoria, largely influenced by the sympathy for Germany which she had imbibed from the Prince Consort, threw all the weight of the Crown into the opposite scale.

There are few more agitated passages to be found in the records of diplomacy than those letters to Lord Granville in which she argued, threatened, entreated, and, finally falling back on the last strength of woman, her weakness, complained that she was "completely exhausted by anxiety and suspense," and "so tired and unwell she can hardly hold up her head or hold her pen." Her will prevailed in the end, and she was able to congratulate herself that, "owing to the determined stand she had made against her two principal ministers, she had saved the country from an

unnecessary war." When Prussia, completely reversing her attitude, made those very claims of the Danish
King which she had contested by force of arms her
pretext for annexing the two duchies under the " rights
of conquest," the Queen suffered a bitter disillusion-
ment, and, on her instructions General Grey wrote
to Lord Granville, that " Prussia should at least be
made aware of what she and her Government and
every honest man in Europe must think of the gross
and unblushing violation of every assurance and
pledge that she had given which Prussia had been
guilty of." It will hardly be contended now that a
war which should have left Schleswig-Holstein in the
hands of Denmark would have been anything but
exceedingly advantageous, economical, and opportune
for Great Britain.

Even before, in the formal division of the spoils,
Prussia had obtained Austrian recognition of her
right to Kiel, she had occupied that port and transferred her naval headquarters thither from Dantzic.
The construction of the North Sea Baltic Canal was
delayed many years, mainly by the opposition of
Count Moltke, who argued that its cost would be so
great that it would, on the whole, be cheaper to build
a second fleet with the money. He further urged that
the canal would be navigable only in the summer, and
that in the event of a war the army would be weakened
by the necessity of providing for its defence. But for
the doubts and jealousies of the sister service, the
German Navy might already be enjoying the benefits
of that prolongation of the Canal, contemplated by
Bismarck, which would have allowed its ironclads to
steam from Kiel to Wilhelmshaven without putting
out into the open sea.

In the hope that the lessons of the war would have
produced the desirable effect on the public mind, the
Prussian Government, in 1865, laid before its Parliament a bill that may be considered as the definite
inauguration of the naval policy which Germany has

ever since pursued. In the Memorandum submitted
to the House with the measure, it was contended
that the time had come for Prussia to join the ranks
of the Sea-Powers, in order that she might be in a
position to protect her own and the other German
coasts and maritime trade, and, for all future time, to
assert her European position as against such States
as were accessible only by water. " For the present,"
it was stated, " she is unable to enter into rivalry with
the first-class naval Powers, but she must occupy a
position commanding esteem among those of the
second-class."

Accordingly, the Government asked for authority
to build 10 armoured frigates of the highest efficiency,
an equal number of armoured vessels of the cupola
or turret type for coast defence, 16 corvettes for the
protection of sea-borne trade, 6 despatch-boats, and
at least 4 transports. It was calculated that ten years
would be necessary for the execution of this plan,
but rather for the training of the personnel and the
provision of the indispensable harbour works than
for the actual construction of the ships. The cost of
the proposed fleet was estimated at 34,500,000 thalers,
that of its annual maintenance at about 5,000,000 thalers.
In recommending the scheme to the Diet, Bismarck used
the following words, which contain very noteworthy
implications : " During the last twenty years no
question has so unanimously interested public opinion
in Germany as precisely the naval question. We
have seen associations, the press, and the Diets give
expression to their sympathy, and this sympathy
exercised itself in the collection of comparatively important sums. The Government and the Conservative
party have been reproached with the slowness and
parsimony with which action has been taken in this
direction. It was particularly the Liberal parties
which carried on this agitation. We believe, therefore, that we are doing you a great pleasure with this
Bill."

But the Liberal majority, then exclusively pre-occupied with the constitutional struggle against the masterful and autocratic Minister-President, threw out the Bill, and modified naval estimates were given the force of law by royal decree. The attitude of the Prussian Liberals of that epoch was very similar to that of the Socialists of to-day, and many of those who now support the latter would undoubtedly weaken in their hostility to army, navy, and colonial votes if concessions were made to them in other directions.

In the brief war of 1866, the Austrian fleet was tied down to the Mediterranean by the superior sea-power of Italy, and the operations of the Prussian ships were confined to a few cheap victories over the antiquated coast and river fortifications of Hanover. As the result of the war, Prussia was rounded off by the incorporation of the Kingdom of Hanover, Electoral Hesse, Nassau, and the old imperial town of Frankfort-on-Main. She thus secured for herself the entire German North Sea littoral, with the exception of the coast-line of Oldenburg, which by treaty was already hers in fact if not in law. Immediately after the conclusion of peace, all the States to the north of the Main were closely welded together in the North German Confederation, the first decisive step towards the creation of the Empire. An article in the Federal Constitution ran: "The Federal Navy is one and indivisible under the command of Prussia. Its organization and composition fall to His Majesty the King of Prussia, who nominates the officials and officers of the navy, and to whom they, as well as the crews, must take the oath of fealty. Kiel Harbour and the Jade Harbour are federal war harbours. The expenses necessary for the establishment and maintenance of the fleet and the institutions connected therewith will be borne by the Federal Treasury."

Two years later a fresh naval programme was submitted to, and approved by, the North German

Reichstag. It laid down that within ten years the
fleet should be brought up to the subjoined strength :

16 large and small armoured ships.	3 transports.
20 corvettes.	22 steam gunboats.
8 despatch-boats.	7 school-ships.

The new vessels actually needed for the attainment
of this establishment were 12 armoured ships, 12 corvettes, 6 despatch-boats, 2 transports, and 1 school-
ship. As native ship-builders had so far had no
experience in the construction of ironclads, only one
vessel of this type was placed in Germany, the State
yard at Dantzic being experimentally entrusted with
the work, while the rest were purchased or ordered in
England or France. No fact could illustrate more
vividly the tremendous progress which Germany has
since made in this respect.

Oddly enough, the great war with France was
succeeded by a marked cooling-off of the popular
enthusiasm for the navy in Germany. The reasons
for this appear to have been disappointment with
what the fleet actually accomplished and the complete
overthrow of the enemy without its assistance. Even
if all the federal ships had been in perfect trim and
manned by thoroughly trained crews, they were confronted by so overwhelming a superiority of force that
at best they could have achieved little or nothing. But
the outbreak of hostilities coincided with a series of
accidents which temporarily disabled several of
Germany's best war vessels, and at that time there
was not a single dock in the country in which they
could be repaired. Officers and crews were, too,
imperfectly trained and insufficiently familiar with
both engines and guns, the harbour equipments were
inadequate, and, in fact, everything was in a state of
unpreparedness.

That the French, with their great naval superiority,
effected so little, and did not even make a determined attempt to force the Jade and destroy the

works at Wilhelmshaven, can only be ascribed to their lack of initiative and the paralyzing operation of their crushing defeats on land. The only regular engagement fought at sea during the war was an encounter of uncertain issue between a small German gunboat and a French despatch-boat off the coast of Cuba. But in spite of the odds against the federal fleet, public opinion in Germany protested that it should have shown more dash and enterprise, and in some way have crowned itself with laurels. Even more prejudicial to the popularity of an ambitious naval policy was the patent fact that the hereditary and most formidable foe had been thoroughly and rapidly humbled by a purely land campaign, and that his superiority on the sea had availed him practically nothing. To such considerations must be attributed a large share of the indifference with which many Germans regarded their navy during the next thirty years.

The prevalent views were reflected in the Memorandum with which, in 1872, the Minister of Marine, Lieutenant-General von Stosch, ushered in the first naval programme of the new German Empire. This document stated that in a long war Germany must leave the offensive to her land force, and that the proper task of her navy was to assert the power of the Empire where smaller interests were at stake in places to which the army could not penetrate. An increase in the fleet was, however, stated to be necessary on the ground of the growth of German sea-borne trade, and it was proposed that the following vessels should be available by the year 1882:

8 armoured frigates.	6 despatch-boats.
6 armoured corvettes.	18 gun-boats.
7 armoured monitors.	28 torpedo-boats.
2 armoured batteries.	5 school-ships.
20 cruisers.	

The cost of these vessels was estimated at 73,000,000 thalers, that of their maintenance in the year 1882 at 1,300,000 thalers. The plan, which was much more modest in its pretensions than its predecessors, and in principle constituted a retirement from the position formerly taken up, was approved by the first Parliament of the new Germany.

The first royal review of the German Fleet took place in the Warnemünde roads in 1875. The ships present were four ironclads, a despatch-boat, and four schoolships; their total complements 2,862 officers and men.

When the year 1883 arrived, General von Stosch published a Memorandum on the execution of his plan. It is significant of the change that had come over public opinion that the Government had not dared to ask the Reichstag for a substitute for the armoured frigate *Grosser Kurfürst*, which was lost in collision off Folkestone, and that consequently one of the eight vessels of her type was lacking. The last of the six armoured corvettes had yet to be built, and instead of five monitors thirteen armoured gunboats had been constructed, because it was thought that the latter class of ship was better suited for the defence of the Jade, Weser, and Elbe. It had been decided not to build the floating batteries, which would have been an easy prey to the fish torpedo, introduced as a weapon of naval warfare since they were projected. One out of the twenty corvettes, and eight large and nine small torpedo craft were also still wanting. German national vanity had, however, scored a questionable triumph: the Empire was now entirely independent of foreigners so far as its warships were concerned. But if Germany had continued to purchase some of her warships in England while she was still but a tyro in the art of naval architecture, she would have saved much money, and have reached her present efficiency even more rapidly than has been the case.

General von Stosch simultaneously presented another Memorandum, dealing with the future development of the navy. In it he laid stress on the reasons which could be adduced against the principle hitherto followed, and since readopted, of fixing the building programme in advance for a longer period, and advised that it was inexpedient to look farther ahead than three or four years. While admitting that " the seas are ever more ceasing to separate the nations," and that " the course of history seems ever more to indicate that a State cannot withdraw from the sea if it is striving to maintain for itself a position in the world beyond the immediate future," he laid down the axiom that " naval battles alone seldom decide the destinies of States, and for immeasurable time the decision of every war will for Germany lie with her land army." Thus, though he admitted the desirability of "a concentrated high sea fleet always ready for action," he considered it best to defer the construction of battleships till further experience had shown whether their functions could not be equally well performed by vessels of a smaller type. The conclusion reached by the Memorandum was that it was necessary to add without delay to only one class of vessel—namely, that which served the purposes of coast defence. In this connection the following words were used :

" Here it is the torpedo-boat, which, especially when used in large numbers at night, will render the carrying through of a blockade almost impossible. Every night the blockading ships would be compelled to withdraw to a distance under steam. Their coal consumption would thereby be much increased, the tension of the crews, in consequence of the need for unremitting vigilance, would become intolerable, and at night the blockaded harbours would be accessible. Even when in motion, the blockading ships would not be safe at night. The torpedo-boats would follow them and recognize their aim by the lights which the enemy would not be able to do without when steaming in squadron formation. The torpedo-boat is a weapon which is of special advantage to the weaker on the sea. A few States already possess a considerable strength in torpedo craft. For the German Navy 150 torpedo-boats are considered necessary, and of these thirty-five will be ready for service shortly."

It was while the German Fleet was still impotent for all serious purposes that the Empire acquired the mass of its colonies: South-West Africa, Togo, the Cameroons, German New Guinea, the Bismarck Archipelago, and the Marshall Islands were all annexed in 1884. The decisive step towards the acquisition of German East Africa was taken in the following year. The political and commercial value of these possessions will be considered in a later chapter.

William I. lived just long enough to lay the foundation-stone of the Kiel Canal, which had been one of the dreams of the Frankfort patriots forty years earlier. His death was followed after an interval of three months by that of Frederick I., and with the accession of William II., in 1888, the latest era of German naval policy may be said to have commenced. Until, however, Admiral Tirpitz was put in charge of the Ministry of Marine, in 1897, practically nothing was done to add to the fighting strength of the fleet. Any progress which was made in connection with the navy was confined to developments of organization, and to the exchange of German rights in Zanzibar and Witu for the islet of Heligoland. This transaction was scoffed at by Bismarck, then in retirement, who, however, only contemplated the possibility of a naval war with France, and it was bitterly resented by German public opinion, and especially by that heated section of it which poses as the pioneer on the paths of militarism, navalism, and colonism. Only during the last three or four years has the conviction gradually begun to gain ground, that perhaps, after all, Germany did not make such a bad bargain, and Heligoland has simultaneously taken an ever more and more prominent place in the speculations of political prophets as to the probable outcome of an Anglo-German war.

The keen interest of the Emperor William, and his ambition to play the leading part on the stage of the world, would not, in themselves, have sufficed to bring about the change which has been wrought during the past fifteen years.　The decisive personal factors here have been the fixed purpose, the steady will, the unflagging energy, the inexhaustible patience, the profound political insight, and the rare diplomatic skill of Admiral Tirpitz, the nearest approach to a really great man that Germany has produced since Bismarck. He is the true creator of the German fleet that is and is to be.

CHAPTER IV

BRITISH INFLUENCE ON THE GERMAN NAVY

In a very special sense the German Navy is the child of the British Navy, which is the mother of all the great naval forces of the world to-day. From the very first it has been no secret that the German Fleet has been definitely planned on the model furnished by the many centuries' development of the British Navy, and the Emperor William has been one of the principal agencies through which this formative influence has been exerted in more recent years.* He came to the throne at a moment when naval sentiment in Germany was at its lowest point, and he assisted in the initial revival which occurred before Grand Admiral von Tirpitz came on the scene.

Old residents of Portsmouth still remember a boy whom they occasionally saw walking about the dock-yard looking at the ships with admiration and rapt attention. His greatest delight seemed to be to watch the great ironclads moving in and out of Spithead. Sometimes he would find his way on board vessels of the Royal Navy. This lad was none other than the present German Emperor. As a grandson of Queen Victoria, he was a frequent visitor in his boyhood and early manhood to his grandmother during the summer months when she was in residence at Osborne, and on one occasion his father and mother, then Crown Prince and Princess of Germany, rented Norris Castle, on the outskirts of Cowes, and lived there for several months with their children. Prince William, who was

* *Cf.* also p. 80

a great favourite of the late Queen, thus not only became an eager spectator of the naval pageants in
the Solent directly under the windows of Osborne
House and Norris Castle, but watched with interest
the gay assemblage in Cowes roadstead for the regatta
from year to year.

At this time the newly-created German Empire
had practically no fleet. During the Franco-Prussian
War the few ships which flew the flag of the North
German Confederation were so weak that they could
take no part in the conflict. The memory of these
recent events was still fresh in the mind of the future
Emperor when he visited England and watched the
activities of the British 'Navy, whose far - flung
squadrons performed the double task of protecting
the Motherland from fear of invasion, and safeguard-
ing all her oversea possessions. He determined that
he, too, would have a great fleet when he succeeded
to the throne of the German Empire.

This is no imaginary picture of the ideas which were
taking root in the mind of the ruler of the German
Empire to-day. Years afterwards—in fact, in 1904—
addressing King Edward, on the occasion of His
Majesty's visit to the Kiel Regatta, the Emperor paid
a tribute to the power and traditions of the British
Navy, with which, he added, he became acquainted as
a youth during visits which he paid to England. He
recalled that he had had many a sail in the *Dolphin*
and *Alberta*, old British yachts, and had seen mighty
ironclads constructed which had since served their time
and disappeared from the Navy List. " When I came
to the throne I attempted to reproduce on a scale
commensurate with the resources and interests of my
own country that which had made such a deep impression on my mind when I saw it as a young man
in England."

When he first advocated the construction of a big
navy, the German people viewed his dreams with
indifference and distrust. Shackled by a system of

conscription in order to provide the Empire with its huge army, they asked what it would profit them if to the burden of a great army they added the vast expense of a fleet capable not merely of defending their coasts, but of operating on the offensive in distant seas. At first the Emperor made little progress in educating public opinion; but he still nursed those dreams of sea-power—very moderate dreams at this date, before Admiral von Tirpitz came on the scene—which had first taken shape in his mind when he wandered about Portsmouth Dockyard, and viewed from the grounds of Osborne House the coming and going of mighty British warships. In the early days of the present century he referred with some pride to the persistency with which he had pursued his aims in spite of popular disfavour. At the launch of the *Kaiser Karl der Grosse* he said : "If the increase in the navy which I had demanded with urgent prayers had not been consistently refused me during the first eight years of my reign—I did not even escape derision and mocking at the time—in how different a manner should we now be able to promote our prosperous commerce and our interests overseas !" He had to wait for many years before he saw his dreams reaching fruition.

As the British Parliament is the mother of all popular representative institutions, so the British Navy is the mother of navies. If the records of most of the great fleets of the world are searched, it will be found that in greater or less degree they owe their birth to the more or less direct assistance of British naval officers, ofttimes acting with the direct authority of the British Admiralty ; while in almost every fleet in the world even to-day may be found ships designed by British brains and constructed of British material by the skilled craftsmen of these islands. It was to England that Peter the Great came to watch the shipbuilding on the Thames, and it was with a large body of British mechanics that he returned to Russia to create a fleet with which to defend his empire and ex-

tend its borders at the point of the gun. The prestige
of the Russian Navy in the seventeenth century was
due entirely to the skill and daring of Scotsmen. The
Greigs of four generations, Admiral Elphinstone,
Lord Duffus Gordon, and a number of other Scotsmen
entered the Navy of the Czar and did splendid service;
and some of the descendants of these pioneers of the
Russian Navy may still be traced in the fleet of to-day.
The American Navy was, of course, of distinctly
British origin; so were the fleets of many of the South
American Republics; while, as everybody knows, the
seeds of the sea-power of Japan were sown by British
naval officers, including first and foremost Admiral
Sir Archibald Douglas, and her ships were mainly built
in England. The excellence to which the Chinese Navy
once attained was also due to British instruction under
another Scotsman, Admiral Lang; and one of the principal shipyards of Italy, as well as her gun factory, is of
British origin, and is still linked with its British parent.

In the case of the modern German Fleet the British
Admiralty had little part in its upbuilding, but British
naval power fired the imagination of the Emperor,
and it was a kindly present made years before by King
William IV. to the then King of Prussia which first
directed his Majesty's thoughts towards the sea.
When the present Emperor was a boy, one of his
favourite recreations was to sail a beautiful model of
about 20 tons of a British frigate on the Havel lakes near
Potsdam. This little ship, of excellent workmanship,
was sent as a present to the then ruler of Prussia early
in the last century by our sailor King, and was a never-
failing source of pleasure to the present German
Emperor as a youth. From his earliest years at home
and in England the future ruler's aspirations were
always towards the sea, and we can now see that his
dreams of later years, which have taken such tangible
shape, were largely due to these vivid impressions
of sea-power which he obtained during his visits to
England, and which reached their climax in 1889, when

Queen Victoria, on the occasion of his visit to the Cowes Regatta, conferred on him the, then, unique rank of Admiral of the Fleet.

Though other foreign Princes and monarchs have since been made honorary officers of the British Navy, the German Emperor remained for some years the only person of foreign birth holding supreme rank. The commission conferred upon the Kaiser was of course purely honorary, but his Majesty has never concealed the pride with which he dons the British uniform with its deep gold cuffs and cocked hat, and he can claim that he is the only ruler of a foreign State who has ever commanded the British Navy in modern times.

Great Britain has boasted of her "splendid isolation," and the German Emperor's is the only alien hand which has controlled any of her fleets.   In times gone by a British squadron was placed under the orders of Peter the Great.   This incident occurred during the Czar's operations against Sweden, when he received the assistance of a squadron from these islands and hoisted his flag in command of the allied forces.   Between that date and the year when the German Emperor became an Admiral of the Fleet the British Navy maintained its absolute independence.   But soon after receiving the honorary rank from Queen Victoria, the Emperor seized the opportunity to emulate the example of Peter the Great, and he afterwards confessed in a speech he delivered on board the British battleship, *Royal Sovereign*, that the incident had left an indelible impression upon his mind.   "One of the best days of my life," he remarked, "which I shall never forget as long as I live, was the day when I inspected the Mediterranean Fleet when I was on board the *Dreadnought*,* and my flag was hoisted for the first time."

The Emperor at this time was making a cruise in the Mediterranean, and visited the Piræus to attend the

* This ship was, of course, the predecessor of the present *Dreadnought*.

wedding of his sister to the present King of Greece. Sir Anthony Hoskins, who was then only a Vice-Admiral, was in command of the British Fleet which had assembled in honour of the royal marriage. The German Emperor decided that in his new rôle as a British officer he would exercise command, and consequently the emblem of an Admiral of the Fleet, which consists of the Union flag, was broken at the main on board the old battleship *Dreadnought*, and Sir Anthony Hoskins, being a junior officer, was forthwith relieved of the control of the British men-of-war, and nominally, though not of course actually, the German Emperor, during the time that his flag was flown, was in command of the greatest of all the fighting squadrons of the British Empire.

On a subsequent occasion, at Malta, His Majesty again visited the British Fleet. Arriving at this great naval base he announced that on the following day he would inspect one of the men-of-war. Accordingly, he proceeded on board, and his flag was forthwith hoisted. It was thought that His Majesty would formally walk round the decks and then take some light refreshments and return to his yacht. This was not the case, however. No sooner did the Emperor reach the quarter-deck, where he was received with naval honours by all the officers, than he took off his coat and intimated that he was ready to go over the ship. His Majesty went everywhere, from the turrets to the engine and boiler-rooms, and kept the Captain fully occupied in answering a multitude of questions as to the design and equipment of the vessel. With all the impetuosity of his nature he dived into every hole and corner and saw everything, and the Captain was kept so busy that he forgot his duty as host and the wines he had laid in for the occasion. At last the inspection ended, the questions ceased, and His Majesty prepared, after complimenting the Captain on the smartness of his ship, to go down the companion ladder to his launch. As he did so, he turned to this commanding officer and said: " Yours must be the longest ship in the British Navy." "I think not, your Majesty," replied the Captain, "it's only 420 feet long." "Oh, you surely are mistaken," added the Emperor, and then the Captain remembered the naval slang as to "long-ships in the navy"—namely, those with long intervals between refreshments. He forthwith apologized profusely for the oversight, and implored the Emperor to return to the cabin. His Majesty would not, however, do so, but added: " January 27 is my birthday, and my orders are that on that day you entertain all your brother captains to dinner and drink my health." He then left, pleased at the result of the incident.

When the day arrived, the dinner was duly held, and the guests enjoyed themselves immensely. During the evening they despatched the following message to the Emperor : "The orders of our Admiral of the Fleet have been carried out, and we have drunk your Majesty's good health. But there is one point on which we cannot agree with your Majesty, and that is as to the length of H.M.S. ——." From this the Emperor, who is familiar with the language of the navy, was able subsequently to infer that on that evening there had been no lack of hospitality.

On many occasions the Emperor has visited British men-of-war in virtue of his commission as Admiral of the Fleet, and no visitor has been more welcome. His Majesty has always been very popular among British officers, and by many little incidents, characteristic of a ruler who has much of the sailor's roving nature and love of good fellowship, he has endeared himself to the men of the British Fleet. More than once, when yachting in Norwegian waters, he has fallen in with a cadets' training ship and entertained the future officers in the most delightful manner, throwing aside all that majesty which hedges round a King, and had made his young guests anticipate the meeting with some amount of dread. During his succession of summer visits to Cowes Regatta in the early years of his reign, he never lost an opportunity of further cementing his friendship with the British service.

After the lapse of many years during which the progress of the German Navy has become ever more and more the preoccupation of the British people, it is difficult to realize that when the movement for naval expansion on the other side of the North Sea first began to take shape it was regarded with sympathy by the British nation, and the German Emperor, wearing his uniform as an honorary British officer, was, of all monarchs, the most popular in this country. The two countries were on terms of growing cordiality when the Emperor succeeded his father in 1888. The absence of any reference by the new Emperor in his proclamation either to England or to France caused momentary anxiety, but that feeling quickly passed away, and in the following summer the new Emperor was the central figure in the great naval pageant at Spithead.

For the first time in the history of the British Fleet naval manœuvres had been held in 1885, and in the year after William II.'s accession the young ruler witnessed the greatest display of British sea-power which had ever been organized. The assembly of 1889 far exceeded in numbers and in the suggestion of power the Naval Review which had marked the celebration of Queen Victoria's Jubilee. It was the most powerful fleet ever brought together in time of peace. The Naval Defence Act, the culmination of a long and vigorous agitation, had been passed in the spring, and it was thought appropriate to mobilize the fleet as a demonstration in the eyes of the world. The German Emperor determined to visit this country for the special purpose of joining in this festival of British sea - power. In those days the act of mobilization occupied considerable time; though the ships in reserve were manned in the middle of July it was not until August 1 that the fleet assembled at Spithead. It included 20 battleships, 6 coast defence vessels, 29 cruisers, 3 gun vessels, 14 gunboats, and 38 torpedo boats. The great anchorage presented a brave appearance when, on the following day, the Emperor arrived, escorted by a squadron of his small navy. This force consisted of the battleships *Friedrich der Grosse, Preussen, Deutschland, Kaiser, Sachsen, Baden,* and *Oldenburg,* together with the despatch vessels *Zieten* and *Wacht;* while the training ship for German naval cadets, the *Niobe,* was also present, together with the corvette *Irene,* commanded by the Emperor's brother. The German Emperor and his ships received an enthusiastic welcome as he passed through the English Fleet on board his yacht, the *Hohenzollern.* The spectacle was one of the most brilliant and imposing ever witnessed in waters which had often been the scene of naval displays. On the following Monday, when the Prince of Wales, representing Queen Victoria, inspected the ships, His Royal Highness was accompanied by His Majesty, to whom, subsequently, all the principal officers were presented on board the *Victoria and Albert.* Early on the following day the fleet proceeded to sea, steaming past the German Emperor, who watched the evolution from the deck of the *Osborne,* moored in Sandown Bay.

Thus did the new ruler of Germany, on whom Queen Victoria had just conferred the honorary rank of Admiral of the Fleet in the British service, gain a unique knowledge of the size and efficiency of the British Navy normally maintained on a peace footing in home waters. The contrast in organization and in administration between the British Navy and the German Army can hardly have failed to impress the young Emperor, who had devoted himself with unremitting persistency to the study of the military machine of his own country. Looking back with the knowledge which we now possess of the rapidity with which a navy can be raised from a peace footing to a war footing as exemplified by the modern German Navy, we can imagine the impression which the

British mobilization made upon His Majesty. And then, when the time came for the ships to pass out of the anchorage into the channel, the delays and confusion which occurred must have suggested to the young ruler, familiar with the standard of efficiency attained by the German Army, that something was lacking.

A contemporary account of this evolution records that—"It was at half-past three in the morning that the fleet began to unmoor preparatory to proceeding to sea, but it was not until nearly eleven that Sir George Tryon—the Admiral in supreme command —was able to give the signal for his squadron to weigh anchor. Nearly all the delay was caused by trouble and mishaps connected with the anchoring gear of various ships. There is no part of the equipment of a man-of-war which requires more management and experience in handling than the ground tackle. Every vessel has peculiarities of her own in this respect, therefore it is due, probably, to the crews being in most cases quite strange to their ships, and to the officers not yet having got the hang of things, that so many shortcomings were made apparent. Soon after ten o'clock Admiral Baird, in command of the other section of the fleet, got impatient of further delay, for it was manifest that if he did not start speedily another review might have to be postponed. So he signalled the ships of his squadron to proceed to sea as soon as ready, and shortly afterwards they began filing out eastward in a long single line. But some ships could not obey the order; and amongst these were the *Anson, Collingwood*, and *Inflexible* still engaged in getting up their anchors."

This same writer concluded his account of the spectacle with the remark that "A grander, a more magnificent demonstration of England's Fleet it would indeed be difficult to imagine." But behind the seeming of things there stood revealed an organization which, though it had recently been greatly improved, still left much to be desired in rapid and efficient action. Moreover, at this time even in the Channel fleet, which then consisted of five ships, and was the only fully commissioned force in home waters, the main purpose of sea-power, to shoot straight, was certainly not kept in view. In his interesting book of reminiscences, "The Navy as I have Known It," Admiral the Hon. Sir Edmund Fremantle, describing the conditions which existed in the Jubilee year, records: "We had large crews and, as all the ships were masted, there was a fair amount of sail drill, while I fear gunnery was little attended to."

There is no record of the impressions which the German Emperor carried home with him from Spithead, but it is more than probable that, while his Majesty was impressed by the great display of ships and men, he was not less impressed by the failure to utilize these resources to the best possible advantage.

The British Navy was living on its past achievements. Though it possessed a mass of material and a large personnel, neither was well organized for war. The available resources exceeded anything belonging to any other nation, but the fleet still basked, content, in the glow of the triumphs achieved in the early years of the nineteenth century. The navy was unreformed. Steam had taken the place of sails, wood had been superseded, first by iron and then by steel, but the routine of the squadrons, the training of officers and men had undergone little change. The conditions of naval warfare had altered, but the British Fleet remained faithful to the old régime, holding fast to the belief that when war occurred there would be a sufficient interval to allow it to complete its arrangements, elaborate its plans and place all its resources on a war footing. As the British Navy in its influence on world policy inspired German ambitions, so German thoroughness in organization, when applied to the growing German Fleet, reacted upon the British Navy and gave it a new and vigorous life.*

* In the preparation of this chapter use has been made, with the permission of the editor of the *Nineteenth Century*, of an article entitled "The Kaiser's Dreams of Sea-Power."

CHAPTER V

THE GERMAN NAVY ACTS

AMONG the political developments of the last quarter of a century there is none more remarkable than the evolution of German naval ambitions as revealed in the legislation which has been passed since 1898.

One of the first acts after the Emperor ascended the throne was the reorganization of the central Navy administration, which had hitherto been presided over by a general officer of the army. This fact in itself indicates the subordinate position which the navy had hitherto occupied in the defensive machinery of the German Empire. The fleet itself was of extremely modest proportions. It consisted only of a few small battleships of heavy gun-power, but limited radius of action, whose rôle was the defence of the coasts of Germany, and more particularly the Baltic littoral, for at this period few men-of-war under any flag cruised in the North Sea. The spearhead of the British Navy was exposed in the Mediterranean, where the latest and most powerful ships were stationed, and the small Channel fleet spent most of its time not in the Channel, but ringing the changes on Vigo and other Spanish ports—Lisbon, Lagos, Gibraltar, Madeira, and Port Mahon. This squadron consisted of five obsolescent ships, and the only British vessels permanently in home waters — so complete was the domination of the situation in southern waters—were a number of port and coast-guard ships, half manned and distributed round the coast, and the unmanned vessels in reserve in the dockyards. The distribution of the French Fleet was on much the same lines, the majority of the modern ships being concentrated in the Mediterranean, while a small force was based upon Brest. Russia alone was represented in northern waters, and it was consequently in the Baltic that the German Fleet, such as it was, was trained and drilled. Except for a few gunboats, the German naval ensign was entirely unrepresented in distant seas, and public opinion showed no desire to increase the naval votes in order to enable German influence to be exercised beyond home waters.

After the Emperor's accession to the throne in June, 1888, and after the reorganization of naval administration, an effort was made to obtain an increased grant from the Reichstag, but only with partial success. From 1874 to 1889-90 the naval expenditure had increased gradually from £1,950,000 to about £2,750,000. In 1890-91 the Estimates had advanced to nearly £3,600,000, and in the following year they rose still further to £4,750,000, and then they began to fall once more under the pressure of the Reichstag, which viewed with no sympathy the new naval ambitions which were finding expression in the Press. During these years the Reichstag repeatedly reduced the votes put forward by Admiral von Hollmann, the Minister of Marine. Throughout his period of office, from 1890 to 1897, he failed signally to inoculate the Parliamentary majority with the new ideas and the new enthusiasm which dominated the Marineamt; and at last in 1897, after being repulsed, first by the Budget Committee and then by the Reichstag itself, the Marine Minister, whose ambitions were really extremely modest, retired from the scene compelled to admit defeat. He was a sailor and neither a statesman nor an administrator, and his blunt methods were not to the liking of the politicians. No surprise consequently was felt when three months after this final humiliation the Admiral resigned his office. One of the pioneers of German sea-power, Admiral von Holl-man began, under the inspiration of the Emperor, the naval movement which, a few years later, under the impulse that the Boer War imparted to public opinion, and with the help of an elaborate Press Bureau, was carried to such lengths by his successor.

On the resignation of Admiral von Hollman, the Emperor appointed as Naval Secretary a comparatively unknown naval officer named Tirpitz. Born on March 19, 1849, at Cüstrin, and the son of a judge, Alfred Tirpitz became a naval cadet in 1865, and was afterwards at the Naval Academy from 1874 to 1876. He subsequently devoted much attention to the torpedo branch of the service, and was mainly responsible for the torpedo organization and the tactical use of torpedoes in the German Navy—a work which British officers regard with admiration. Subsequently he became Inspector of Torpedo Service, and was the first Flotilla Chief of the Torpedo Flotillas. Later he was appointed Chief of the Staff of the naval station in the Baltic and of the Supreme Command of the German Fleet. During these earlier years of his sea career Admiral Tirpitz made several long voyages. He is regarded as an eminent tactician, and is the author of the rules for German naval tactics as now in use in the Navy. In 1895 he was promoted to the rank of Rear-Admiral, and became Vice-Admiral in 1899. During 1896 and 1897 he commanded the cruiser squadron in East Asia, and was appointed Secretary of State of the Imperial Navy Office in January, 1897. In the following year he was made a Minister of State, and in 1901 received the hereditary rank of nobility, entitling him to the use of the prefix "Von" before his name.

With the advent of this officer as Marine Minister, German Naval affairs at once underwent a change. His predecessor, who entertained very modest theories as to the size of the fleet which Germany should possess, had attempted to browbeat the politicians, thumping the table in irritation when he could not get his way. The new Minister from the first adopted other methods. He devoted himself to the education of the people by means of an elaborate Press Bureau, and was soon the undisputed master of German naval policy. He met opposition in the Reichstag with a smiling reasonableness, and set himself to win the support of opponents by good-tempered argument. In fact, Admiral von Tirpitz from the first revealed himself as a politician and diplomatist, and from the time that he took office, though now and again slight checks were experienced, naval policy in Germany made rapid—indeed, astonishing—progress.

In the year after Admiral von Tirpitz went to the Marine Office, a Navy Bill, far more ambitious in its terms than any proposal that had been put forward by Admiral von Hollman, was accepted by the Reichstag.

This measure was believed to embody at any rate the beginnings of a scheme which he had submitted to the Emperor some time prior to his appointment. At any rate, it enunciated a new and vital principle. As has been seen, the Government, whether Prussian or German, had on previous occasions drafted extensive naval programmes for the carrying out of which a period of ten or twelve years was required. Not once, however, had the establishment of ships and personnel been fixed by law ; and the Parliament in each case committed itself to the entire scheme only to the extent of passing the first annual instalment considered necessary by the Government as the initial step towards the desired goal. In this way neither Diet nor Reichstag bound itself or its successors for the future, but left both free to deal with the annual naval estimates as they thought fit. And in practice it had been found that very liberal use was made of the budgetary prerogatives, that standards once approved were not considered binding, and that the fate of the naval estimates depended to a considerable extent on the relations which happened for the moment to exist between the Government and the majority parties on questions totally unconnected with the naval requirements of the Empire.

Another disadvantage of the practice of leaving the Reichstag free to determine annually the number of vessels which should be laid down in a given year, was, that it gave the shipbuilding, armour-plate, and ordnance industries no sure basis for their plans for the future. The rule that Germany must build, engine, arm, and equip her own war vessels had been generally accepted, but the industries which should enable her to do this were still in their infancy, and were almost entirely dependent upon the orders of the home Government. If they were ever to be able to supply the demands of a powerful fleet, it was necessary that slips should be multiplied, plant increased, and workshops extended. But so long as the naval policy of the Empire was indefinite and subject to violent fluctuations, shipbuilders and manufacturers would not endanger their businesses by locking up large amounts of capital in appliances which could be used for the building and arming of warships and for no other purposes. If German industry was ever to be in a position to satisfy the demands of a large and efficient fleet, some guarantee of steady and remunerative orders must, it was urged, be afforded to the trades concerned. And apart altogether from its own needs, the Government also hoped that, some day, Germany would be able to claim a share in those large profits which Great Britain appropriated to herself as the world's shipbuilder.

It was by such arguments that Admiral von Tirpitz justified his demand that the strength of the fleet, the date at which it should attain that strength, and the age at which each ship should be automatically replaced by a new one, should be fixed by legal enactment. No portion of his Bill was more hotly contested than this. It was objected that, by accepting it, the

Reichstag would be depriving itself of a considerable portion of that power of the purse which constituted the only effective bulwark of its rights. But in the end the smiling and imperturbable patience of Admiral von Tirpitz gained the day, and the Reichstag satisfied itself with the formal right of drawing the absolutely unavoidable conclusions from its own enactment and passing every year the naval estimates, which could not be rejected without an infraction of the law. The repeated sections in the Act of 1898 which appear to reserve the Chamber's Budget rights, are, in reality, meaningless and valueless—except as a monument to the folly of those who believed they had a meaning and a value. Admiral von Tirpitz apparently drew from his first legislative experience the perfectly correct conclusion that the Reichstag can be made to do almost anything if one only treats it in the right way. The principle of fixed establishments and regular replacements has now become so recognized a feature of German naval legislation that opponents to it can be found only among the ranks of the Socialists.

In the explanatory Memorandum attached to the Bill, Admiral Tirpitz was able to adduce two convincing reasons why the fleet should at once be considerably augmented. One of these was the fact that Germany's naval strength had in recent years actually diminished. In case of mobilization, it was pointed out, she would have had only seven efficient battleships, whereas she had once had fourteen. Of the armoured cruisers which had been adopted in other navies for foreign service in times of peace, she did not possess a single example, and their work had to be done by three antiquated battleships. Moreover, to the tasks allotted to the fleet in the Memorandum of 1873, another of great importance had been added— namely, the defence of Germany's newly-acquired colonial empire. Further, it was contended that the growth of the Empire's population, trade, and industry, the development of her sea-fisheries, and the increasing investment of German capital abroad, had all added to the possibilities of her becoming involved in quarrels with other nations. The fleet which Admiral Tirpitz considered necessary to fulfil the old and the new sea rqeuirements of the Empire was as under :

THE BATTLE FLEET.

19 battleships (2 as material reserve).
8 armoured coast-defence vessels.
6 large cruisers.
16 small cruisers.

FOREIGN SERVICE FLEET.

Large Cruisers.

For East Asia	2
For Central and South America	1
Material reserve	3
Total	6

Small Cruisers.

For East Asia	3
For Central and South America	3
For East Africa	2
For the South Seas	2
Material reserve	4
Total	14

1 station ship.

The period proposed for the gradual attainment of this strength was seven years, but the Reichstag shortened it by a year, and thus it became known as the "Sexennat."* It was pronounced inexpedient to attempt to fix for some years in advance the

---

* The Clerical Party had suddenly come forward with a proposal to make a very important change in the Navy Bill, and their scheme was accepted by a large majority of the Budget Committee, and also by the Secretary of State for the Marine on behalf of the Government. The proposal was that the German Navy should be raised to the strength contemplated by the Government Bill at the end of six instead of seven years, as the Government had originally demanded.

Empire's requirements in torpedo craft, school-ships, and training ships.*

That this scheme was intended by its author to be merely a beginning has been shown by the sequel, but Admiral von Tirpitz himself little dreamed that he would so soon be able to take the next and decisive step, which should bring him to within measurable distance of his goal. Early in 1899 he said in the Budget Committee: "I declare expressly that in no quarter has the intention to submit a new navy plan in any way been manifested; that, on the contrary, in all quarters concerned, the firmest intention exists to carry out the Navy Law, and to observe the limits therein laid down." In other words, the law was to run its six years' course.

Nevertheless, before the year was at an end, the Bill which was to become the Navy Law of 1900 had already been announced by the Government.

In the light of the vast development of Germany's colonial and commercial interests the Navy Act of 1898 was of an unambitious character. The German Fleet was at this time still the weakest possessed by any of the Great Powers of Europe, except Austria-Hungary, which had no naval pretensions. If only as a matter of historical interest it is interesting to record that, at the moment when this effort towards expansion was made, Germany kept in commission only four ships which could be dignified with the description of battle-ships, together with four smaller armoured vessels. The only modern ships of the line under the German ensign consisted of these four battleships of the Worth class, vessels of 9,874 tons displacement in comparison with ships of 15,000 tons, which had already been incorporated in the British Fleet. The German ships, though nominally battleships, were really only coast-defence vessels, heavily gunned and thickly armoured, but with storage for only 680 tons of coal; whereas

---

* The Bill in the form in which it was passed into law will be found in Appendix I.

contemporary British ships of the Majestic class possessed a capacity of 1,850 tons.* The four vessels of this class, in addition to the *Worth*, were the *Weisenburg*, *Kurfürst Friedrich Wilhelm*, and *Brandenburg*. They marked a notable advance on the little armoured ships of three to four thousand tons of the Siegfried class, which had been built during the early nineties, but, owing to their limited fuel capacity, their radius of action was extremely restricted, and they were, in fact, only very powerful coast-defence ships, with a speed on trial of between sixteen and seventeen knots. The design of every armoured ship is a compromise between armament, armour, speed, and coal capacity, and in this German design a predomiance then unprecedented in any navy in the world was given to the two first-named characteristics. On paper these ships were vessels of great offensive power, as is revealed by the contrast given on p. 117, between them and the contemporary battleships of the Majestic class of the British Fleet, which displaced about 15,000 tons and attained a speed of eighteen knots, with 1,850 tons of coal on board.

These few details reveal the fundamental differences between the character of the British and German Navies at this time and the policy which they represented. The British Government, in accordance with precedent, was providing a fleet of the high-seas type, while the German Government was content with a small force built specifically for the purpose of coast-defence. These four large German coast-defence ships were at this time supported by the four vessels of the Sachsen type of 7,283 tons, already obsolescent; by six old ships—one dating back to 1868; by eight little armoured vessels of the Beowulf class, of about 3,500 tons, which had been constructed during the early nineties; and the tail of the list was brought up by eleven

* It is interesting to note, however, that even at this early date the German Admiralty made provision for the storage of oil in order to supplement the coal supply.

armoured gunboats each of 1,000 tons displacement. This enumeration of the naval forces of Germany indicates conclusively the modest ambitions which hitherto had animated her naval administration.

The German Fleet, except for the purposes of coastal defence, and specifically for the protection of

	Majestic Class.	Worth Class.
Length	Over all, 413 ft. (390 ft. at water-line).	380 ft. 6 in. (354 ft. 3 in. at water-line).
Beam	75 ft.	65 ft. 6 in.
Mean draught ...	27 ft. 6 in.	24 ft. 4 in.
Armour ...	Partial 9-in. Harveyed belt, 16 ft. broad, and 220 ft. long ; bulk-heads, 14 in. (max.) ; barbettes, 14 in. ; barbette-shields, 10 in. ; casemates (12), 6 in. ; protected deck, 2·5 to 4 in.; forward conning tower, 14 in. ; after conning tower, 3 in.	Complete belt, 11·8 to 15·7 in. (compound in earlier, steel in later, ships) ; barbettes and conning-tower, 11·8 in. ; ammunition-hoists, 11·8 in. ; gun-hoods, 5 in. ; cellulose cofferdam belt ; case-mate for 4·1-in. guns, 3 in. ; steel deck, 3 in., flat on top of belt.
Armament ...	4 12-in. 46-ton (wire-wound) breech-load-ing ; 12 6-in. quick-firers in casemates ; 16 12-pounder quick-firers ; 2 12-pounder boat-guns ; 12 3-pounder quick-fir-ing ; 2 Maxims ; 5 tor-pedo-tubes (18-in.), 4 submerged, 1 above water in stern.	6 11-in. Krupp breech-loading, 2 in each bar-bette ; 8 4·1-in. quick-firing of 30 calibres in a casemate forward of the centre barbettes ; 8 3·4-in. quick-firers of 30 calibres ; 2 2·3-in. breech-loading boat or field guns ; 12 1-pounder quick-firers ; 8 machine ; 3 torpedo tubes, 2 sub-merged.

her Baltic shores, was a negligible quantity, having no influence either upon European or world policy. The truth of this statement is conclusively proved by the following table showing the relative strength of the only five navies in the world which were, at that time, of appreciable importance, the fleets of Japan

and of the United States being then still in their
infancy:

	Britain.	France.	Russia.	Italy.	Germany.
Battleships :					
First-class ...	29	14	6	8	4
Second-class ...	7	8	4	2	4
Third-class ...	18	7	5	3	6
Total battleships	54	29	15	13	14
Coast-defence ships	14	16	13	—	18
Cruisers :					
First-class ...	23	8	6	—	1
Second-class ...	47	13	3	5	3
Third-class ...	34	9	1	9	9
Total cruisers ...	104	30	10	14	13
Torpedo gunboats	34	19	8	15	4

It must be confessed that at this time the German
Fleet bore no reasonable relation to Germany's growing trade and oversea interests. But the people of
the German Empire were still unconscious of any
deficiency, and, blinded by the success of their armies
during the war with France and the small influence
which naval power exerted in that struggle, they had
refused for many years to take upon themselves the
burden which the new naval ambitions represented.

But with the passage of the Navy Act of 1898, and
the widespread agitation carried on by the Navy
League, under the highest patronage, and—even more
important—by the Press Bureau under Admiral von
Tirpitz, a change immediately occurred; and the
success with which the British forces were enabled to
conduct their military operations in South Africa, while
Europe was forced to stand by inactive, owing to the
supreme control which the British Fleet possessed of
sea communications, produced a revulsion of feeling.
The current of European events, and the reception

with which the Emperor's speeches met, convinced the Government, within a comparatively few months of the passage of the Act of 1898, that they might safely abandon this modest measure and replace it by a new Bill.

What had happened in the meantime? This: the the outbreak of the Boer War had generated in Germany an absolutely unprecedented hostility to Great Britain, which was afterwards roused to white heat by the seizure of the mail steamer *Bundesrat* and other German vessels on the African coast. Admiral von Tirpitz had a unique opportunity such as was never likely to present itself to him again. He made prompt and full use of it, and while Great Britain was in the thick of the embarrassments of the early stages of the South African War, the great Navy Bill of 1900 was passed into law.

The seizure of the German vessels was admitted by the British Government to have been a blunder. An apology was tendered to Germany on account of it, and promises made that similar incidents should not recur. The action of the British warships did nothing but harm, and would certainly never have been taken if the Foreign Office in London had been properly informed on the situation in Germany by its representatives in Berlin, and had itself kept the Admiralty fully posted as to the possible political consequences of a molestation of neutral shipping.

Consequently, in the spring of 1900, the Act of 1898 was replaced by a new one, in face of all Admiral von Tirpitz's protestations of two years before. This measure set up an establishment of almost twice the size of the former one, and embraced ships intended for battle purposes on the high seas. During the discussion of the measure in the Reichstag the Centre Party compelled the Government to modify their original scheme, and to drop five large and five small cruisers for service on foreign stations, while the reserve of cruisers was reduced by one large and two small vessels. In the course of the debate the Naval Secretary announced that, while the Government were compelled to agree to the amendment of their proposals, they still insisted upon the necessity of providing the original number of ships for duty in foreign seas, but would agree to postpone the final settlement of the question until a subsequent date.

In its final form, as it received the approval of the Reichstag and of the Emperor, and as it was published in the *Imperial German Gazette* of June 20, 1900,[*] the Bill set up the following establishment for the Fleet:

THE BATTLE FLEET.

2 fleet flagships.
4 squadrons, each of 8 battleships.
8 large cruisers for scouting purposes.
24 small cruisers for scouting purposes.

FOREIGN FLEET.

3 large cruisers.
10 small cruisers.

RESERVE.

4 battleships.
3 large cruisers.
4 small cruisers.

The new Act was based upon the same calculation of the effective life of ships as the one of 1898, and provided that, except in the case of total loss, battleships were to be replaced after twenty-five years and cruisers after twenty years. It was provided that the age of ships was to be reckoned from the grant of the first instalment in payment for the ship to be replaced to the passing of the first instalment in payment for the ship to be built as "substitute" (Ersatzschiff). It was proposed to keep half the battle squadrons— the First and Second—fully manned on a war footing, together with one-half of the torpedo craft and all the school-ships and auxiliary vessels. The Third and Fourth battle squadrons were to form the Reserve

* See Appendix I.

Fleet, half the ships of which were to be kept in permanent commission. The Act also made provision for nucleus crews for the second half of the torpedo-boats, for the requirements of ships serving abroad, and for the needs of the shore establishments.

More remarkable, perhaps, than the actual terms of the Navy Act was the character of the explanatory Memorandum put forward by the Navy Department.* In this notable document occurs the following statement of the new naval policy of the German Empire:

"To protect Germany's sea trade and colonies, in the existing circumstances, there is only one means: Germany must have a battle fleet so strong that, even for the adversary with the greatest sea-power, a war against it would involve such dangers as to imperil his position in the world.

"For this purpose it is not absolutely necessary that the German battle fleet should be as strong as that of the greatest naval Power, because a great naval Power will not, as a rule, be in a position to concentrate all its striking forces against us. But even if it should succeed in meeting us with considerable superiority of strength, the defeat of a strong German fleet would so substantially weaken the enemy that, in spite of a victory he might have obtained, his own position in the world would no longer be secured by an adequate fleet."

The whole Memorandum well repays study in the light of subsequent events. Almost at the moment of its publication Admiral von der Goltz, a former Chief of the Admiralstab, gave a less reserved exposition of German policy, thus reflecting the opinions held by the naval officers responsible for the character of the proposed expansion of the German Fleet.

"Let us consider," he said, "the case of a war against England. In spite of what many people think, there is nothing improbable in such a war, owing to

* Cf. Appendix II.

the animosity which exists in our country towards England, and, on the other side, to the sentiments of the British nation towards all Continental Powers, and in particular against Germany. These are not Chauvinistic exaggerations, but the opinion of the whole of the people of Great Britain, who are jealous of our commercial development. If England should ever lose her mercantile supremacy on the seas, the decline of her naval dominion would only be a question of time, and she realizes the fact instinctively. Of course the British Government will make every effort to prevent the violent explosion of these sentiments, preferring peaceful competition to war. But how long can that last? Violence becomes a right to a people which fears for its existence.

"The opinion is generally held in this country that any resistance against England at sea would be impossible, and that all our naval preparations are but wasted efforts. It is time that this childish fear, which would put a stop to all our progress, should be pulled up by the roots and destroyed.

"At this moment (1900) we are almost defenceless against England at sea, but already we possess the beginnings of a weapon which statesmanship can put to a good use, and our chances of success in a war against England grow more favourable day by day.

"The maritime superiority of Great Britain, overwhelming now, will certainly remain considerable in the future; but she is compelled to scatter her forces all over the world. In the event of war in home waters, the greater part of the foreign squadrons would no doubt be recalled; but that would be a matter of time, and then all the stations oversea could not be abandoned. On the other hand, the German Fleet, though much smaller, can remain concentrated in European waters.

"With the increases about to be made it will be in a position to measure its strength with the ordinary British naval forces in home waters (then consisting only of the small and inefficiently manned Channel squadron); but it should not be forgotten that the question of numbers is far less important at sea than on land. Numerical inferiority can be compensated by efficiency, by excellence of material, by the capacity and discipline of the men.   Careful preparation permitting rapid mobilization can ensure a momentary superiority."

With the passage of the Navy Act of 1900, Germany proceeded to develop a High-Sea Fleet—a naval force capable of going anywhere and doing anything. Hitherto her ships had represented in their design the domination of a coast-defence policy.   She now entered upon the construction of ships of the first class.   Naval construction was regularized, and forthwith proceeded with great rapidity.   During the five years—1886 to 1890—no ship even nominally of the battleship class was launched.   During 1891 to 1895 only four vessels, and between 1890 and 1900 only six vessels, and these all of relatively modest fighting power, were put in the water, but in 1901 no fewer than five first-class battleships were sent afloat.

At the time when the Navy Act of 1900 was passed Germany had just completed the five ships of the old Kaiser class, with a displacement of about 11,150 tons, and mounting four 9·4-inch guns of 40 calibre as battle weapons in association with a large number of secondary guns—eighteen pieces of 5·9 inches.   The technical advisers of the German Admiralty at this date pinned their faith to a storm of projectiles from quick-firing guns, and in order that weights might be kept down and the ships might be restricted to dimensions to enable them to navigate the Kiel Canal, reliance was placed upon the 9·4-inch gun at a moment when in practically all the navies of the world a 12-inch weapon was being mounted.

The type of battleship design which was introduced with the passage of the Act of 1898, and which was yet in hand when the measure of 1900 was prepared, still combined a weak main armament of four 9·4-inch guns with an exceedingly heavy secondary armament and a complete armoured belt.   Whereas British ships at this time, such as those of the Duncan class, were being given only partial belts, and these only 7 inches thick amidships, tapering off fore and aft, the German vessels received thicker belts extending over their whole length. Of this new design —known as the Wittelsbach class—five units were building when the 1900 Act was passed. They had a maximum coal capacity of 1,770 tons of coal, with 200 tons of oil, and were capable of steaming at a speed of about eighteen knots, thus reflecting the rise of German ambition for something more than a coast-defence fleet. The belts of these ships were 7·5 inches wide, with a thickness amidships of 8·9 inches, while the four 9·4-inch guns were protected with armour 9·8 inches thick, and the secondary turrets and casemates carrying the eighteen 5·9-inch guns were protected with armour 5·9 inches thick.

After the passage of the Navy Act of 1900 the 9·4-inch gun, as the battle weapon, was abandoned in favour of an 11-inch of 40 calibre, and the displacement of the new ships of the Deutschland class, as they are generically termed, although there are minor differences in the ten vessels, was nearly 13,000 tons. These ships really represented the entrance of Germany upon the high seas as a first-class naval Power, possessing vessels fit to lie in the line and to fight the men-of-war under any foreign flag. The new design may be contrasted with advantage with that of the Worth class which has already been described :

DEUTSCHLAND CLASS.

Armour.

Krupp, complete belt, about 7 feet wide,* 8·9 inches amidships, tapering to 3·9 inches at ends ; lower edge amidships, 6·7 inches ; lower deck side amidships, 5·5 inches ; main turrets and barbettes, 11 inches to 9·8 inches ; secondary turrets, 6·7 inches ; battery, 5·9 inches ; conning-tower, 11·8 inches ; s.t.—aft, 5·5 inches ; deck, 2·9 inches on slopes, 1·6 inches on flat.

---

* The five later ships were given a belt with a thickness of 9·4 inches amidships, but otherwise their protection and armament closely resembled those laid down at an earlier date.

Armament.

Four 11 inches (40 calibre) in pairs in turrets, fore and aft ; 14 6·7 inches (40 calibre), 10 in battery on main deck, 4 singly in turrets on upper deck ; 12 3·4 inches (24 pounder) ; 4 machine ; torpedo tubes, 6 (18 inches), 4 submerged, 1 bow, and 1 stern.

Simultaneously with the construction of these ten battleships, six armoured cruisers, ranging in displacement from 8,800 to about 11,000 tons, were laid down, and in 1906 a single clause amending the Act was passed increasing the foreign fleet by five armoured cruisers and the fleet reserve by one armoured cruiser, thus fulfilling in part the original programme of the Navy Department with which the Reichstag had interfered.

At about the same date German naval opinion made a complete *volte face* in regard to the fighting value of the submarine. About the time when the Act of 1900 was passed the British Admiralty, after a careful study of the progress of submarine navigation in France and America, decided that it could no longer ignore this type of man-of-war. It was forthwith decided to buy an experimental ship from the Holland Company of the United States, which had already demonstrated the practical value of this particular type of submersible torpedo-boat. The original craft which was purchased under these circumstances was a little ship with a submerged displacement of only 120 tons, and a water-line displacement of 104 tons. She was propelled on the surface by a four-cylinder gasoline engine giving a speed of eight to eight and a half knots, while below the surface she was driven by an electric motor, and was capable of only six or seven knots.

The entrance of this little ship into the British service was hailed in Germany with something approaching derision, and in the technical papers the futility of the submarine was urged with a wealth of argument. The little Holland boat, however, was merely the foundation from which the British authorities proceeded to develop a type of craft in keeping with the offensive rôle of the British Navy, and in 1906 submarines were being built for the British Fleet mounting two torpedo tubes on a displacement of about 300 tons, and possessing a surface speed of fourteen knots in combination with a submerged speed of ten knots. When it is added that these craft possessed a full speed radius of about 3,000 miles on the surface and were estimated to be able to travel 150 miles under water, it is not surprising that German naval opinion as to the advantages of the submarine underwent a sudden and dramatic change, Henceforth the submarine was to be treated by German naval officers with respect. Without the formality of any public announcement, either in the Reichstag or in the Press, an under-water boat was laid down at the Germania Yard at Kiel in 1906, and thenceforward an energetic policy of construction was pursued, although it was not until two years later that legislative provision was made for the building of this type of warship.

A very remarkable feature of German policy has been the persistency with which cruisers have been built even at a time when other naval Powers, including Great Britain, were inactive. As a matter of course, during the period when the German Government was content to provide a fleet mainly for the purposes of coast defence, great importance was attached to the efficiency and adequacy of the cruiser squadrons. At the time of the passage of the Navy Act of 1900, for instance, there were eighteen cruisers completed and nearly a dozen others in hand. Under the Act of that year provision was made to continue this policy while attaining a higher standard of battle strength.* Even when, in 1908, legislative effect was given to the ambition of the Marine Office further to expedite battleship construction, in spite of the heavy cost involved by the transition from mixed armament ships to the all-big-gun ships of the Dreadnought era,

* See Appendix I.

the Reichstag was asked to stereotype the cruiser programme. The Act made provision for two light cruisers to be laid down annually, and in the measure passed in 1912 an addition of two "small cruisers" was made for the period 1912-1917. A notable contrast is provided by a study of Germany's action and the policy of the British Admiralty charged with the protection of a vast oversea trade and half the shipping of the world. During the later years of the last century and the first four years of the present century a persistent policy of construction was pursued both in armoured and protected cruisers, and then for several years there was a complete cessation of this form of shipbuilding activity. Other countries, Germany only excepted, either acting on their own initiative or accepting the lead of the British authorities, also desisted from cruiser construction. The advance in the size and cost of large armoured ships threw heavy burdens upon the respective Exchequers and no doubt the saving effected was a welcome relief at a moment when under every flag naval expenditure was advancing at an unparalleled rate. The result of the persistent policy adopted by Germany became apparent in 1911, when in modern swift cruisers suitable for scouting the two fleets were practically upon an equality. It was in these circumstances, faced by evidence of German progress in cruiser construction, that the British authorities again decided to embark upon the building of new squadrons of cruisers of small size and high speed — in fact, of considerably smaller size than the ships then in hand in Germany.

But in battleship construction German policy has necessarily been less continuous and consistent. The war between Russia and Japan in the Far East, and the lessons which it taught to the naval world were destined to upset completely the theories upon which battleship and larger cruiser design in Germany had been based in the early years of the present century

The German naval authorities had persisted in attaching primary importance to the secondary gun, still believing in the moral and material effect of a storm of projectiles from numerous quick-firing guns. They were still proceeding with the construction of ships—battleships and large cruisers—embodying these ideas when a new Board of Admiralty in London, with Admiral Sir John—now Lord—Fisher as First Sea Lord, appointed a Committee to reconsider the design of British ships in the light of the information which the gunnery tests of the fleet and the struggle in the Far East had supplied.

Thanks to the British alliance with the Japanese, British officers, and British officers only, had been permitted to be present with the Japanese Fleet during the decisive battles of the war. With the advantage of the information thus obtained the designs of British ships were reconsidered. The report of this Committee was treated as confidential. In presenting the Navy Estimates for 1905 to the House of Commons, the Earl of Selborne, the First Lord, contented himself with making the following statement as to the work of this body, and of the new programme of construction:

"I may claim that the work of the Committee will enable the Board to ensure to the navy the immediate benefit of the experience which is to be derived from the naval warfare between Russia and Japan, and of the resultant studies of the Naval Intelligence Department. I can, however, hold out no hope that it will be consistent with the interests of the public service to publish either the reference to the Committee or its report.

"It is proposed to begin during the financial year 1905-06: 1 battleship, 4 armoured cruisers, 5 ocean-going destroyers, 1 ocean-going destroyer of the experimental type, 12 coastal destroyers, 11 submarines.*

"His Majesty has approved that the battleship should be called the *Dreadnought*, and the first of the armoured cruisers the *Invincible*."

* One of these "armoured cruisers" was not built.

It was not until many months later that it gradually became known that the British Admiralty were embarking upon the construction of an entirely new type of battleship, and it was even later that information was available as to the character of the "armoured cruisers" mentioned in the First Lord's statement. In the following spring a partial revelation of the change in British design was made in the *Naval Annual*:

"The *Dreadnought*, officially laid down at Portsmouth on October 2, 1905, though some material had already been built into her, was launched by His Majesty on February 10, 1906. The Admiralty announce that the period of building for armoured vessels is to be reduced to two years, but the *Dreadnought* is to be completed in February, 1907. The rapidity of her construction will therefore out-rival that of the *Majestic* and *Magnificent*, which were completed within two years from the date of the laying of their first keel plates.

"The *Dreadnought* represents a remarkable development in naval construction, which has been for some time foreshadowed, notably by Captain Cuniberti, the famous Italian naval constructor. The Russo-Japanese War, more particularly the Battle of Tsushima, established the fact that naval engagements can, and will, be fought at greater distances than were formerly considered possible. Hence the medium armament is held by many authorities to lose much of its value."

In the *Naval Annual* of that year, it was reported that the Japanese contemplated laying down a battleship with an armament of four 12-inch and ten 10-inch guns. It was then announced that the *Dreadnought* was to carry a main armament of ten 12-inch 45 calibre guns, of 50 per cent. greater power than those carried by the *Majestic*, while the medium armament was to disappear entirely.

The question of protection entered also very largely into the consideration, and the *Times*, in describing the new ship, said that it was understood that " she was to be made as nearly unsinkable as possible from the explosion of a torpedo or mine." It was even stated that there would be no openings in the water-tight bulkheads, and this proved to be the fact. Moreover, this ship was the first large vessel in the world to be fitted with turbines.

Particulars of the *Dreadnought* were never made public officially, but the following is condensed from *Engineering*, February 9, 1906:

" On the forecastle there will be mounted two 12-inch guns in a barbette on the centre line, being considerably above the water-level. On each side, a short distance to the rear, there will be two other pairs of 12-inch guns on the upper-deck level, and in order to enable these guns to be fired ahead an embrasure is formed at each side of the forecastle, so that all six 12-inch guns may take part in a running fight. At the same time four of them can be used on each broadside. Aft there are two pair of guns, both in the centre line of the ship, one pair to the rear of the other ; but with this difference, as compared with the American design, that both pairs of guns are on the same level and a considerable distance apart. These four guns, therefore, firing on either beam, cannot be fired astern, although they have a very considerable arc of training abaft and forward of the beam. The arrangement reduces the astern fire to two guns, which is less than in any preceding ship where there are either 9·2-inch guns or 6-inch quick-firers on each quarter. But the pair of 12-inch guns should be adequate, in view of the other qualities of the *Dreadnought*, in connection with probable combatants. Her speed of twenty-one knots would probably enable her to outclass any more powerfully armed vessel, as in most foreign Powers the question of cost must militate against high speed with such gun-power. None of the guns are at a less height than the upper-deck level, and the two forward barbette guns are on the forecastle. Another important point in reference to the armament is the protection against attack by torpedo and submarine boats. In the *Dreadnought* the intention is to adopt an entirely new weapon, using an 18-pound shot.

"The placing of the guns on the upper deck has materially simplified the arrangement of the armour, and the adoption of the turbines has assisted towards the higher gun-platform, because the weights with turbine machinery are lower in the ship, and thus the centre of gravity is considerably lower; at the same time the top hamper in the ship has been reduced. The main belt in the way of the machinery has been increased in thickness to 10 inches, and the upper deck is armoured. The gun mechanism is protected by thick heavy hoods, as in the case of the earlier barbette guns; and the gun-mountings, while largely protected by the main broadside armour, are further shielded by armour barbettes or cylindrical casings.

"The adoption of the steam turbine has not only increased the speed, but has resulted in the improvement of the manœuvring quality of the ship. Four shafts are adopted, and this has greatly facilitated the fitting of a double stern with two rudders—a form of stern advocated for some time for heavy battleships. The cutting away of the deadwood in combination with a balanced rudder has improved the turning moment of later single-stern battleships by 30 per cent.; and as the double rudder enables a larger area to be utilized effectively, without increasing the torsion on the threaded shaft of the steering gear, there will be still better facility in manœuvring. While there is no change so far as the upper works are concerned, the stern of the ship is doubled under water, with two rudders quite 20 feet apart. The contract for the turbine machinery was placed with Messrs. Vickers, Sons and Maxim, Limited, and it is anticipated that with the four propellers running at over 300 revolutions, the power developed will be equal to 23,000 I.H.P. There will be two high-pressure turbines and two low-pressure turbines, each on separate shafts, and each shaft will also carry an astern turbine, two of which will take high-pressure and two low-pressure steam. The high-pressure main and astern turbines are to be on the wing shaft, and the two inside shafts, in addition to carrying the low-pressure ahead and astern machines, will also have turbines of small diameter for cruising purposes. Steam for the low powers will pass from the boiler into the cruising turbines, thence to the high-pressure wing turbines, and back to the low-pressure turbine before entering the condenser. This will enable a full range of expansion to be economically attained, even with a small volume of steam. The steam pressure is to be higher than in any previous turbine ship, as the eighteen Babcock and Wilson boilers are to be worked at 250-pound pressure, which will be slightly reduced at the high-pressure turbines.

"The boilers, consistent with the latest practice, will be fitted for working not only with coal, but with oil fuel. In order to reduce the power necessary to attain a speed of twenty-one knots, and to reduce the draught for a given displacement—the *Dreadnought* when ready for sea will be about 18,000 tons on 26 feet draught—it was decided to increase the length of the ship from the 410 feet of the *Lord Nelson* to close upon 500 feet, with a beam of 82 feet. This increase in length has the further advantage that it will afford greater room forward and abaft for magazines under the 12-inch guns without interfering with the under water torpedo-tube gear in connection with the five submerged tubes."

It was stated unofficially that this new ship of the all-big-gun type rendered obsolescent practically all the battleships of the world with mixed armaments— that is with guns of varying size. The British naval authorities continued to maintain a discreet silence as to the character of the new vessels, and the design, as its main characteristics became known, was assailed with a good deal of criticism. The controversy was at its height when President Roosevelt called upon Commander Sims, the Inspector of Target Practice in the United States Navy, to make a report upon the advantages possessed by the all-big-gun ship of high speed and complete armour protection in view of the criticism of Admiral Mahan of the British design.* Commander Sims, who had made a life-study of gunnery questions, prepared a long report describing

* It has since become known that the Americans had designed an all-big-gun ship before the British *Dreadnought* was laid down.

the character of the revolution in design, and its influence upon the navies of the world. It is interesting to recall some passages from this report, which in its essential portions appeared in the proceedings of the United States Naval Institute, particularly as the British Admiralty have never considered it wise to enter upon a detailed defence of their policy. Commander Sims stated :

" Concerning the advisability of building all-big-gun ships, that is, discarding all smaller guns (except torpedo-defence guns) and designing the ships to carry the maximum number of heavy turret guns, these alone to be used in battle against other ships, I think it could be clearly shown that Captain Mahan is in error in concluding that it would add more to our naval strength to expend the same amount of money that the big ships would cost, for smaller and slower ships, carrying the usual intermediate guns (6-inch, etc.) ; and that, as in the question of speed, this error is due to the fact that much important information concerning the new methods of gun-fire was not considered by the author in preparing his article. (Note.—Unfortunately these methods of gun-fire cannot at present be specifically explained in a published article, as this would involve a discussion of our methods of controlling our ships' batteries, and bringing our ships into action with an enemy.)

" I may, however, assure the reader that, from the point of view of the efficiency of gun-fire alone, it would be unwise ever to build a man-of-war of any type whatever, having more than one calibre of gun in her main battery. In other words, it may be stated that the abandonment of mixed-battery ships in favour of the all-big-gun, one calibre ship was directly caused by the recognition of certain fundamental principles of naval markmanship developed by gunnery officers.

" Therefore we have but to decide what the calibre for each class of ships should be, a decision which should present no special difficulty, provided it be first determined how we are to defeat the enemy—whether by the destruction of his ships (by sinking them or disabling their guns) or by the destruction or demoralization of their personnel.

" In this connection the following facts should first be clearly understood—namely :

" 1. Turrets are now, for the first time, being designed that are practically invulnerable to all except heavy projectiles. Instead of having sighting-hoods on the turret roof, where sights, pointers, and officers are exposed to disablement (as frequently happened in the Russian ships) there will be prismatic sights, projecting laterally from the gun trunnions, through small holes in the side of the turret, and the gun-ports will be protected by 8-inch armour plates, so arranged that no fragments of shells can enter the turrets.

" 2. On the proposed all-big-gun ships the heavy armour belt will be about 8 feet above the water-line, and extending from end to end. The conning-tower, barbettes, etc., will be of heavy armour ; and there being no intermediate battery (which could not be protected by heavy armour, on account of its extent), it follows that in battle all the gunnery personnel, except the small, single fire-control party aloft, will be behind heavy armour, and that, therefore, neither the ship or her personnel can be materially injured by small calibre guns.

" Considering, therefore, that our object in designing a battleship is that she may be able to meet those of our possible enemies upon at least equal terms, it seems evident that it would be extremely unwise to equip our new ships with a large number of small guns that are incapable of inflicting material damage upon the all-big-gun one-calibre ships of our enemies, or upon the personnel manning their guns."

In the same paper Commander Sims explained the principal tactical qualities that are desirable in a fleet —namely, compactness of the battle formation and the flexibility of the fleet as a unit—that is, its ability to change its formation in the least possible time and space with safety to its units. Proceeding to elaborate his views, Commander Sims stated :

" For example, suppose two fleets of eight vessels each, composed of ships that are alike in all respects, and suppose their personnel to be equally skilful, with the exception of the Commanders-in-Chief, whose difference in energy and ability is such that one fleet has been so drilled as to be able to manœuvre with precision and safety while maintaining one-half the distance between its units that the other fleet requires.

"This is putting an extreme case, but it shows:

"1. That the short fleet, being about half the length of the other one, can complete certain important manœuvres in about one-half the time and one-half the space required for similar manœuvres of the long fleet.

"2. That, when ranged alongside each other, the defeat of the long fleet is inevitable, since the rapidity of hitting of the individual units is assumed to be equal, and each of the four leading ships of the long fleet receives about twice as many hits as she can return, though the eighth ship of the short fleet would suffer a preponderance of gun-fire from the fifth or sixth vessel of the long fleet, the seventh and eighth being too far astern to do much damage, as would also be the case if the long fleet had several vessels astern of these.

"It is because of the principle here illustrated that the constant effort of competent flag-officers is to reduce the distance between the units of their fleets to the minimum that can be maintained with safety under battle conditions—that is, while steaming at full speed, without the aid of stadimeters, sextants, and other appliances that should be used only for preliminary drills.

"Doubtless some flag-officers, by constant competitive exercises in manœuvring, may succeed in attaining an interval between ships that is less by 15 or 20 per cent. than that attained by others; but manifestly there is hardly any possibility of much greater improvement in this respect, because the minimum practical interval between ships depends upon their lengths and manœuvring qualities. For example, the German interval is 300 metres from centre to centre, while larger ships, say 400 feet long, require about 400 yards, and those between 450 and 500 feet in length require about 450 yards.

"If we accept Captain Mahan's advice and build comparatively small, low-speed battleships, while our possible enemies build large, swift, all-big-gun ships, it seems clear that we will sacrifice the enormous advantages of fleet compactness and flexibility, the superior effect of heavy-gun fire and the ability to concentrate our fire—the loss of these advantages to be fully realized twenty-five years hence, when our enemies have fleets of big ships while we still have those of our present size."

Finally, this officer added :

" If it be claimed that it would be better to reduce the speed of the large vessel to sixteen knots and put the weight saved into guns, it may be replied that the heavy turret guns cannot be mounted to advantage (so as to increase the hitting capacity of the vessel) without very considerably increasing the size of the ship, because the number of heavy turrets that can be placed to advantage is governed largely by the length of the ship—which increases slowly with the displacement. This point is fully discussed in a recent article in a German publication. I do not remember the displacement used by the author to illustrate the principle, but, supposing the ones quoted below to be correct, he shows that if it requires a displacement of 20,000 tons to obtain a broadside fire of, say, eight 12-inch turret guns, you could not advantageously mount any additional turrets on 21,000 or 22,000 tons, but would have to go to 25,000 or 26,000 tons to obtain the necessary space. And, conversely, if you design a 20,000-ton battleship for sixteen instead of twenty knots, you cannot utilize the weight saved to increase the gunpower by adding 12-inch turrets, as you could by adding a number of intermediate guns.

" It is now hardly necessary to state that adding superimposed turrets (by which the number of guns could be doubled, if the weights permitted) does not materially increase the hitting capacity of the ship as a whole, because of the ' interference ' caused by having four guns in one two-story turret, while it decreases her defensive power by adding to the vertical height of her vital targets.

" Captain Mahan characterizes the sudden inclination in all navies to increase the size of the new battleships (from about 15,000 to about 20,000 tons) as a ' wilful premature antiquating of good vessels ' . . . ' a

growing and wanton evil.' If these words are intended
in their true meaning, the statement is to me incomprehensible. I can understand an individual being
wilful and wanton, but I cannot believe that the naval
officers of the world could, without good cause, be
suddenly and uniformly inspired in this manner. On
the contrary, it seems to me that the mere fact of there
being a common demand for such large vessels is conclusive evidence that there must be a common cause
that is believed to justify the demand.

"This common cause is undoubtedly a common
belief that the same amount of money expended for
large war vessels will add more to a nation's naval
power than the same amount expended for small
vessels, for it cannot reasonably be assumed that the
tax-ridden nations of Europe expend their great naval
budgets wilfully and wantonly. Undoubtedly each
nation earnestly strives so to expend these sums as
to derive the greatest increase of naval power. The
same is true in reference to their armies. As the
mechanical arts improve each nation endeavours to
improve its war material. When a nation adopts new
rifles, it is not a wilful premature antiquating of several
million excellent ones, it is a case of *force majeure*—it
must adopt them or suffer a relative loss of military
efficiency, and it must make no mistake as to the relative
efficiency of its weapons. In 1870 the French suffered
a humiliating defeat as a direct result of the colossal
conceit which rendered them incapable of accepting
conclusive evidence that the German field artillery was
greatly superior to theirs.

"The same law—that of necessity—governs the
evolution of battleships. As might have been expected,
this evolution has, as a rule, been gradual as regards
increased displacement. The exception is the sudden
recent increase (4,000 to 5,000 tons) in displacement.
This exception therefore needs explanation. . . . It
was due to a complete change of opinion as to the
hitting capacity of guns of various calibres. This is
now well understood by all officers who have recently
been intimately associated with the new methods of
gunnery training. These methods have demonstrated
this point in such a manner as to leave no doubt in
our minds as to the correctness of our conclusions.

The rapidity of hitting of the heaviest guns has been increased several thousand per cent., and that of smaller guns about in proportion to their calibre.

" . . . The inception of the epoch-making principles of the new methods of training belongs exclusively to Captain (now Rear-Admiral) Percy Scott, Director of Naval Practice of the British Navy, who has, I believe, done more in this respect to improve naval marksman-ship than all of the naval officers who have given their attention to this matter since the first introduction of the rifled cannon on men-of-war; nor should we forget that this degree of improvement was rendered possible by the introduction of telescope sights, the successful application of which to naval guns was made by Com-mander B. A. Fiske, U.S. Navy, as early as 1892.

"As soon as the above facts gained general accept-ance in Great Britain and the United States, the evolution of the all-big-gun, one-calibre battleship became a foregone conclusion; and the reason for the great increase in displacement, as I understand it, is simply that you cannot build an efficient ship of this class on less than about 20,000 tons, because you can-not mount more than two 12-inch turrets to advantage upon a battleship of much less displacement, because the length and breadth are not sufficient."

The Dreadnought design and all that it meant threw the German Admiralty into confusion. At the moment they were still engaged in the construction of the vessels of the Deutschland class, of about 13,000 tons, in which primary importance was given to the secondary gun—fourteen 6·7-inch weapons—to the sacri-fice of the big gun—four 11-inch pieces—and speed; whereas the new British design ignored the secondary gun in order to mount no fewer than ten big guns, and develop the speed to the extent of three or four knots above battleships then building. Before the *Dreadnought* of the British programme of 1905 had been laid down at Portsmouth, two German battle-ships of the familiar design with mixed armament had been begun—the *Schleswig-Holstein* in the Germania Yard and the *Schlesien* at Dantzic. So completely were the German authorities unprepared for the revolution initiated by the British Admiralty, that from the summer of 1905 until July, 1907, the keel of not a single further battleship was laid in Germany.   In the meantime, while British yards were busy with vessels of the new type, the design of the German ships was reconsidered.   After an interval of two years the keels of two vessels of the Dreadnought type were laid down, and two more keels were placed in position a month later—that is, in August, 1907.   These four ships—the Nassau class—inaugurated the Dreadnought policy in Germany.   Two were completed in May, 1910, and two in September following.

These ships embody the all-big-gun principle in association with a powerful secondary armament, consisting of a dozen 5·9-inch guns and sixteen 24-pounders. Moreover, whereas the British *Dreadnought* had been provided with only ten big guns, which was held by the British gunnery experts to be the maximum number which could be carried with advantage on the displacement then considered advisable, the German vessels were given twelve guns, not of the 12-inch but of the 11-inch type.   Each of these ships displaces 18,600 tons, and has a nominal speed of twenty knots.   Their normal coal capacity is 885 tons, with a maximum storage of 2,655 tons.   On the other hand, the early British *Dreadnought*, with about the same displacement and coal-carrying capacity, attained a speed of one or two knots more, owing to the use of turbines in place of reciprocating engines.   The contrast between the armour and armament of the British and German ships, comparing the four Nassaus of the German Fleet* with the Superb class of the British Navy, is given in the table on p. 140.

By energetic action the British Admiralty had

---

* British naval opinion held from the first that these ships of the Nassau type vitiated the Dreadnought principle of simplicity of armament, and were so over-gunned as to be ineffective units. Sea-service has tended to confirm this view.

obtained a lead in the new type of battleship.* Moreover, even after the character of the Dreadnought
became known, the German authorities remained
ignorant of the fact that the " armoured cruisers " of
the Invincible class were really swift battleships carrying the same type of battle gun as the *Dreadnought*,
in association with a speed exceeding twenty-five
knots, and an armour belt not inferior to that placed

	Superb Class.	Nassau Class.
Armour ...	Krupp : Complete belt, about 16 ft. wide (narrower aft), 11 in. amidships, tapering to 6 in. forward and 4 in. aft ; turrets, 8 in. ; barbettes, 12 in. ; forward conning-tower, 12 in. ; after conning-tower, 8 in. ; deck, sloping, 2·7 in.	Krupp : Complete belt, 12 in. amidships, tapering to 3·9 in. forward, and 3·9 in. aft ; lower deck side, 7·9 in. amidships, 3·9 in. narrow belt at ends ; turrets and barbettes, 11 in. ; battery, 6·1 in. ; conning-tower, 11·8 in. ; deck, sloping, 2·9 in.
Armament...	10 12-in. (45 calibres) in pairs in turrets, 1 forward, 1 on each beam, 2 aft on centre line ; 16 4-in. (50 calibres), 2 on each turret (except No. 4), 8 in superstructure ; 5 machine ; torpedo tubes, 5 18-in., submerged, broadside, and stern.	12 11-in. (45 calibres) in pairs in turrets, 1 forward, 1 aft, and 2 on each beam ; 12 5·9 in. (45 calibres) in battery ; 16 3·4 in. (24-pounder) ; torpedo tubes, 6 18-in., submerged, bow, stern, and broadside.

on the latest pre-Dreadnought German battleships.
By this decisive move, the British authorities had
depressed the value of all mixed armament battleships,
in which the British Fleet was becoming weak in face
of foreign—and particularly German—rivalry, and had
started the competition in armaments on an entirely

* In the three succeeding years, in accordance with the British
Government's policy of a limitation of naval armaments, and as an
example to other Powers, this advantage was partially lost, and hence
the large programme of 1909-10.

new basis upon terms of advantage. No sooner was the true inwardness of the Dreadnought policy realized than the German authorities began the preparation of a new German Navy Act. It was eventually decided that the best means of accomplishing the end in view—namely, the construction of a larger number of ships of the armoured classes in the next few years than was provided in the Act of 1900, was to reduce the nominal effective age, and legislate for the replacement of all battleships and large cruisers within twenty years. Accordingly, attached to the new Act passed early in 1908, which was over two years after the laying down of the Dreadnought, was a schedule setting forth that four large armoured ships should be laid down annually between 1908 and 1911, both inclusive, and that in 1911 onwards to 1917, two keels annually should be placed in position. By means of this single clause measure, which became law on April 6, 1908, the construction of ships of the Dreadnought type was accelerated, and, whereas the British Admiralty had definitely abandoned the construction of large cruisers of the armoured class—as the German authorities knew by this time—the Marine Office decided that each of the "large cruisers" specified in the Act of 1900 should be swift Dreadnoughts.

This point is an important one. Between 1897 and 1904, Great Britain laid down 27 battleships and 35 armoured cruisers—a total of 62 armoured ships in eight years, or an average of 7·75 ships a year. In this period Germany built 16 battleships and 5 armoured cruisers, or 21 armoured ships—equal to an average of 2·62 ships a year. In 1905 the Admiralty determined to cease building armoured cruisers. In that year they laid down 4 "capital ships"—all of them Dreadnoughts; in the next two years 3 annually, and in 1908, 2 ships only. While the British authorities abandoned the building of armoured cruisers, Germany decided to accelerate her battleship construction, and she also decided that all the "large cruisers" specified in her Law should be swift Dreadnoughts, and thus from 38 battleships and 20 armoured cruisers, she rose to an establishment of 58 battleships.

At the end of 1911, when it was imagined that the German programme would fall from 4 large ships annually to 2 ships, a new Navy Bill was produced.* Incidentally this measure added to the establishment 3 battleships and 2 unarmoured cruisers, and made provision for the construction of a maximum of 72 submarines.

The significance of the successive changes in shipbuilding policy in Germany, reflecting in an ascending scale the naval ambitions of the Marineamt, may be realized from the following summary, showing the establishment of large armoured ships fixed under successive measures:

Act.				Establishment of Ships Adopted.	
				Battleships.	Large Cruisers.
1898	...	...	...	...	17	8
1900	...	...	...	...	38	14
1906	...	...	...	...	38	20
				Dreadnoughts.	
1908	...	...	...	...	58	
1912	...	...	...	...	61	

Under the operation of German naval legislation, it is now intended to provide sixty-one large armoured ships of maximum power, all of them less than twenty years old. The Act does not specify the character of the vessels of the various classes which are to be laid down. It is elastic in this respect. It leaves to the Marine Office complete freedom in the matter of design; but, on the other hand, it ties effectually the hands of

* *Cf.* Appendix I.

the Reichstag, and it cannot, except it repeal the Navy
Law, reduce in any year the number of keels to be laid
down. There can be no reduction in the output of
naval material until a new Navy Law has been passed.
This is a point which is frequently forgotten in
England.

But the notable feature of the Navy Act passed by
the Reichstag in 1912 was not the additions to the
shipbuilding programme, though these were notable,
but the steps taken to increase the instant readiness of
the fleet for war. Prior to the passage of this measure
it had been the practice in the British Navy to maintain
only about half the men-of-war of various classes on a
war footing, relegating the remainder to reserves
representing various stages of preparedness for action.
The German Navy Act of 1912 set up an entirely new
standard with a view to obtaining the maximum
advantage from a conscript service, where the pay is
low, in competition with a voluntary service, such as
obtains in the British Fleet, with very much higher
rates of pay. In the speech which he delivered in
Committee in the House of Commons on July 22, 1912,
Mr. Winston Churchill, the First Lord of the Admiralty,
gave a lucid explanation of the essential features of this
German Navy Act. He said :

" The main feature of that Law is not the increase in
the new construction of capital ships, though that is an
important feature. The main feature is the increase in
the striking force of ships of all classes which will be
available, immediately available, at all seasons of the
year. A third squadron of 8 battleships will be
created and maintained in full commission as part of the
active battle-fleet. Whereas, according to the un-
amended Law, the active battle-fleet consisted of 17
battleships, 4 battle or large armoured cruisers,
and 12 small cruisers ; in the near future that active
fleet will consist of 25 battleships, 8 battle or large
armoured cruisers, and 18 small cruisers ; and, whereas
at present, owing to the system of recruitment which
prevails in Germany, the German Fleet is less fully

mobile during the winter than during the summer months, it will, through the operation of this Law, not only be increased in strength, but rendered much more readily available.

" Ninety-nine torpedo-boat destroyers—or torpedo-boats, as they are called in Germany—instead of 66, will be maintained in full commission out of a total of 144. Three-quarters of a million pounds had already been taken in the general estimate for the year for the building of submarines. The new Law adds a quarter of a million to this, and that is a provision which, so far as we can judge from a study of the finances would appear to be repeated in subsequent years. Seventy-two new submarines will be built within the currency of the Law, and of those it is apparently proposed to maintain fifty-four with full permanent crews.

" Taking a general view, the effect of this Law will be that nearly four-fifths of the entire German Navy will be maintained in full permanent commission—that is to say, instantly and constantly ready for war. Such a proportion is remarkable, and so far as I am aware, finds no example in the previous practice of modern naval Powers. So great a change and development in the German Fleet involves, of course, important additions to their personnel. In 1898 the officers and men of the German Navy amounted to 25,000. To-day that figure has reached 66,000.

" Under the previous Laws and various amendments which have preceded this one, the Germans have been working up to a total in 1920, according to our calculations, of 86,500 officers and men, and they have been approaching that total by increments of, approximately, an addition of 3,500 a year. The new law adds a total of 15,000 officers and men, and makes the total in 1920 of 101,500.* The new average annual addition is calculated to be 1,680 of all ranks, but for the next three years by special provision 500 extra are to be added. From 1912 to 1914, 500 are to be added, and in the last three years of the currency of the Law 500 less will be taken. This makes a total rate of increase

---

* In his speech in the House of Commons on March 26, 1913, the First Lord corrected this figure. He stated that the maximum to be attained under the new Fleet Law in 1920 was 107,000 apart from reserves.

of the German Navy personnel of about 5,700 men a year.

"The new construction under the Law prescribes for the building of three additional battleships—one to be begun next year (1913), one in 1916, and two small cruisers of which the date has not yet been fixed. The date of the third battleship has not been fixed. It has been presumed to be later than the six years which we have in view.

"The cost of these increases in men and in material during the next six years is estimated as £10,500,000 above the previous estimates spread over that period. I should like to point out to the Committee that this is a cumulative increase which follows upon other increases of a very important character. The Law of 1898 was practically doubled by the Law of 1900, and if the expenditure contemplated by the Law of 1900 had been followed the German estimates of to-day would be about £11,000,000. But owing to the amendments of 1906 and 1908, and now of 1912, that expenditure is very nearly £23,000,000. But the fact that the personnel plays such a large part in this new amendment, and that personnel is more cheaply obtained in Germany than in this country, makes the money go farther there than it would do over here.

"The ultimate scale of the new German Fleet, as contemplated by the latest Navy Law, will be 41 battleships, 20 battle or large armoured cruisers, and 40 small cruisers, besides a proper proportion—an ample proportion—of flotillas of torpedo-boat destroyers and submarines, by 1920. This is not on paper a great advance on the figures prescribed by the previous Law, which gave 38 battleships, 20 battle or large armoured cruisers, and 38 small cruisers. That is not a great advance on the total scale. In fact, however, there is a remarkable expansion of strength and efficiency, and particularly of strength and efficiency as they contribute to striking power. The number of battleships and large armoured cruisers alone which will be kept constantly ready and in full commission will be raised by the Law from twenty-one, the present figure, to thirty-three—that is to say, an addition of twelve, or an increase of about 57 per cent. The new fleet will in the beginning include about twenty battleships and large cruisers of the older types, but gradually, as new vessels are built, the fighting power of the fleet will rise until in the end it will consist completely o modern vessels.

" This new scale of the German Fleet—organized in five battle squadrons, each attended by a battle or armoured cruiser squadron, complete with small cruisers and auxiliaries of all kinds, and accompanied by numerous flotillas of destroyers and submarines, more than three-fourths—nearly four-fifths, maintained in full permanent commission—the aspect and scale of this fleet is, I say, extremely formidable. Such a fleet will be about as numerous to look at as the fleet which was gathered at Spithead for the recent Parliamentary visit, but, of course, when completed it will be far superior in actual strength. This full development will only be realized step by step. But already in 1914 two squadrons will, so far as we can ascertain, be entirely composed of Dreadnoughts, or what are called Dreadnoughts, and the third will be made up of good ships like the Deutschlands and the Braun-schweigs,* together with five Dreadnought battle-cruisers. It remains to be noted that this new Law is the fifth in fourteen years of the large successive increases made in German naval strength, that it encountered no effective opposition in its passage through the Reichstag, and that, though it has been severely criticized in Germany since its passage, the criticisms have been directed towards its inadequacy."

In these words the First Lord of the Admiralty described in full detail the exact character of the latest German Navy Act, and then he proceeded to make some general observations, which, in view of the organization of the British Navy, prior to the expansion of the German Navy, are of particular interest :

" There are two points with regard to navies and naval war which differentiate them from armies and land war. The first is the awful suddenness with which naval warfare can reach its decisive phase. We see on the continent of Europe immense military establishments possessed by nations dwelling on

* These two groups of ships are of practically the same design.

opposite sides of political frontier lines; yet they
dwell and have dwelt for a whole generation in
peace and tranquillity. But between those armies
and any decisive collision there intervenes an inevitable period of delay that acts as a great buffer,
a cushion of security. I mean the vast process of
mobilization, the very first signs of which must be
noticed, and which, once it begins, lays idle the
industry of both countries, and dominates the whole
course of national life. So it is that through all these
years nations are able to dwell side by side with their
tremendous military establishments without being a
prey to undue anxiety as to immediate attack. But
none of these considerations apply to fleets. The fleet
which was assembled for the manœuvres the other
day was fully capable of going into action as soon as
the ammunition could be brought up and put by the
side of the guns. And that is true of all the great
highly efficient navies of the world.

"I am bound to say, looking far ahead, and farther
than the purposes of this Vote, at the aspect which
Europe and the world will present when the power of
States, which has been hitherto estimated in terms of
armies, will be estimated very largely in naval strength,
and when we have a number of great Powers all
possessed of very powerful navies, the state of Europe
and of the world would seem to contain many more
germs of danger than the period through which we
have been passing in our lifetime.

"The second general point to which I would
direct attention is the extreme slowness with which
naval preparations can be made. Small ships take
eighteen to twenty months to build; large ships four
years. Docks take more than four years to build.
Seamen take from two to three years to train; arti-
ficers take much longer; officers take between six and
seven years. The efficiency which comes from the
harmonious combination of these elements is a plant
of very slow growth indeed. Cool, steady, methodical
preparation, prolonged over a succession of years, can
alone raise the margin of naval power. It is no use
flinging millions of money about on the impulse of the
moment by a gesture of impatience, or in a mood of
panic."

Such is the evolution which German naval ambitions have undergone since the Reichstag in the early years of the Emperor's reign refused to believe that four relatively small battleships in full commission, with the same number of ineffective coast-defence ships of small size, did not represent the maximum naval power which Germany need provide, and that an expenditure of two and three-quarter millions sterling was not sufficient burden to impose annually upon the Teutonic peoples over and above the cost in money and service of the predominant army.

Nothing reveals the statesmanship of Admiral Tirpitz so strikingly as the character of the naval legislation for which he has been responsible, and the manner in which he has bent every influence in Germany and every occurrence abroad to promote his ends. Prior to the introduction of the Navy Act of 1898, the only example of a continuous naval policy was the Naval Defence Act of 1889, under which seventy ships of various types were added to the British Navy during a period of four years. Of these vessels only ten were of the armoured classes. This measure was confined to shipbuilding, and it made no provision for increasing the personnel or for setting up a fixed standard of commissioning. It merely provided a certain number of ships and left it to Parliament to provide or not to provide crews with which to man them, and, as a matter of fact, Parliament did not provide the necessary officers and men until long after the ships were at sea. Admiral von Tirpitz was not satisfied with so unmethodical and unstatesman-like a measure of procedure when he went to the Marineamt in 1897. He presented to the Reichstag, as may be seen from the terms of the Fleet Law of 1898, given in an appendix, a complete scheme of naval expansion, making provision not only for the construction of ships in specified numbers over a period of six years, but providing also for the due expansion of the personnel and for the attainment of a fixed establishment of ships first in full commission, secondly with nucleus crews, and thirdly in reserve. In obtaining the assent of the Reichstag to this measure, which to a great extent removed the naval expansion movement from the annual control which it had hitherto exercised annually on the presentation of the Estimates, the Minister of Marine achieved his first great triumph.

This Act was to have remained in operation for a period of six years, and was represented as an embodiment of German needs, quite independent of the naval preparations then being made by other Powers. During the next two years no development occurred in the naval programmes either of Great Britain or other foreign countries, but an Anglophobe wave passed over the Continent as a result of the South African War. German sympathies in particular were aroused, and Admiral Tirpitz at once seized the opportunity to repeal the fixed and immutable Fleet Law of 1898, and to replace it by a new enactment providing a Battle Fleet of roughly twice the strength of that legalized in the establishment of the former measure. This measure was to have remained in force until 1917. Six years later, however, an amendment representing another expansion was passed ; two years after that the fourth Fleet Law became operative, and in 1912 another measure was adopted by the Reichstag under the influence of a renewed Anglophobe movement in Germany. Experience has shown that German Fleet Laws are regarded as immutable and fixed when proposals in the direction of a limitation of armaments are made, but as flexible as though no Fleet Law existed when political circumstances are favourable for making a further effort towards a higher standard of naval power.

Nor does this study exhaust the remarkable features of this naval legislation. An ordinary statesman, ignorant of naval matters, might have so framed the successive Naval Laws as seriously to tie the hands of the naval authorities in the development of the fleet, whereas Admiral von Tirpitz, with great skill, restricted the powers of interference on the part of the Reichstag, while leaving the Marine Office with almost complete freedom in shaping the naval machine in the process of expansion.   This double end was achieved by the use of generic naval terms in the loose manner adopted by those unfamiliar with their significance. Admiral von Tirpitz made up his "paper" establishment in the Fleet Laws by styling every ship of slow speed but carrying an armoured belt "a battleship," and then, under the terms of the Law, he made provision for these dummy vessels to be replaced by veritable battleships of maximum power.   Thus ships of 4,000 tons displacement have been replaced by Dreadnoughts of 25,000 tons, carrying the heaviest guns, and protected by thick armour.   The establishment fixed by the Reichstag has not been exceeded, but by a simple process of conjuring, small coast-defence ships have been quietly converted into first-class sea-going battleships, ranking in strategical and tactical qualities with the most formidable ships in the British Fleet.   The naval authorities have by this means been able to prove to the uninitiated when challenged that they have kept within the four corners of the Law, that the number of battleships has remained fixed according to the establishment between the periods of each enactment, and at the same time they have been in a position to follow an active shipbuilding policy, at the same time raising from year to year the necessary personnel for manning the new vessels.   This is another notable feature of Admiral von Tirpitz's policy.   The legislation has been so elastic as to enable him to raise the necessary number of officers and men to suit the requirements of the Fleet.   When a Dreadnought, requiring 1,106 officers and men, has been completed for sea to take the place of a ship of the Hagen class, with a crew of only 306, the additional personnel has been instantly ready.

The same process has been adopted in increasing
the cruiser squadrons of the German Navy.   The Law
has specified that a certain number of "large cruisers"
shall be built, and it has been left to the discretion of
the naval authorities to interpret this elastic term in
tons, guns, armour, knots of speed, and personnel.   In
accordance with the Law, Admiral von Tirpitz has
thus been able to replace cruisers of negligible fighting
value and of small size by Dreadnought battle cruisers
mounting guns of immense power and attaining speeds
hitherto without precedent.   Similarly, small torpedo-
boats have given way in the establishment of the Navy
to torpedo-boat destroyers of large size, and step by
step the naval strength of Germany has been increased
by a process, the cleverness and ingenuity of which
even the German people themselves have not realized.

Germany has immensely increased her resources of
ships and men, but she has done more than that: she
has forced other Powers to organize and train their
squadrons on a standard of efficiency never attempted
in the past.   She has increased the strain and stress
of peace until it resembles closely the actual conditions
of war, and having determined year in and year out
to keep four-fifths of her fleet always on a war footing,
always instantly ready for action, she has compelled
other countries, in accordance with the dictates of
ordinary foresight, to take similar action, however
onerous the financial burden.   It is on Great Britain
and the United States that the weight of this burden
bears most heavily, for in those States alone is reliance
placed on a voluntary system of manning.

CHAPTER VI

GERMAN SHIPS, OFFICERS, AND MEN

In material, in the art of constructing and equipping ships of war, Germany now ranks far above most of the Great Powers, and she is little, if anything, behind even Great Britain in workmanship, rapidity and cheapness. Her personnel also stands high, for she has succeeded in translating into naval terms the professional and disciplinary codes which have raised the German Army to a position of pre-eminence. Above all she has succeeded, in a degree never before attempted by any country, in keeping ships and men in constant association. The German naval authorities have recognized that, while a conscriptive system of manning a fleet brings into the organization certain grave and ineradicable disadvantages, it does at least enable large numbers of officers and men to be borne for service at a relatively small annual cost. Realizing this economic benefit of conscription, the Marineamt has had no hesitation in increasing the personnel rapidly from year to year. The expansion of this element of naval power has kept pace with the activity of the shipyards. This policy of simultaneous increase of ships and of men, accompanied as it has been by the expansion of her shipbuilding and allied industries and of her dockyards, has been the secret of the rapid rise of Germany as a maritime Power wielding world-wide influence.

Within the memory of the present generation German ships of war, if not built in England, were constructed

in Germany with materials obtained entirely or in part from England. Her earliest armoured ships of any account—the *Deutschland*, the *Kaiser* and the *König Wilhelm*—were all constructed on the banks of the Thames at the old Samuda Yard. The great industry which Germany and other foreign nations helped to support is now dead, and on the other side of the North Sea is to be seen an activity more intense and on a far larger scale than the Thames establishments could boast even in the day of their greatest prosperity.

Though there are many shipbuilding yards and engine-making establishments in Germany, the naval authorities depend exclusively upon the vast establishment of Krupp for armour and guns, and the repute of the firm in both respects stands very high. The vast establishment which supplies the German and many other Governments was founded in 1810 by Friedrich Krupp, who bought a small forge and devoted himself, with little commercial success, to the manufacture of cast steel. In this he was ahead of Germany's requirements, but on the basis thus laid by the father, the son built; and in 1851 a solid steel ingot which he exhibited at the Great Exhibition in London completely took the metallurgic world by surprise, and his fortune was made. He turned his energy and knowledge to the making of guns, armour, weldless steel rails, and other manufactures; and the modest works at Essen continued to expand until to-day they and the associated establishments give employment to about 70,000 men, not all of whom, of course, are engaged on the manipulation of armaments.

For many years the Krupp process of armour manufacture was adopted in every country in the world, but lately the British Admiralty have, it is common knowledge, adopted a superior process which produces a plate of greater resisting power, and the German cemented type of armour no longer holds the premier position which it occupied when its advantages over the Harvey plate were demonstrated. On the other hand, the Krupp firm still claim that their ordnance is not equalled by any in the world, and on the strength of this claim they have obtained most valuable orders, extending over a long series of years, from foreign Governments. British guns are made on the wire-wound system—that is, steel ribbon is wound under great pressure round the gun, and over this is placed an outer hoop; Krupp's, on the other hand, still remain faithful to the solid steel tube to resist the gas pressures exerted, arguing that their method of steel manufacture enables them to submit it to strains which other steel might not stand. There has been endless controversy as to the merits of the two systems; and the subject was again discussed as recently as the end of 1912, when the Italian Minister of Marine laid a report before the Italian Parliament with reference to the armaments of the principal fleets. According to this statement the British, Italian, and Japanese are the only Navies to mount wire-wound guns; the probable life of the Italian and Japanese 12-inch guns was given at 80 rounds, whereas the English gun was good for only 60 rounds. On the other hand, the Austrian and German guns were given from 200 to 220 rounds, and the American 14-inch gun was estimated to have a probable life of 150 rounds. Particulars with reference to British and German guns were given as follows:

	British.		German.		
Calibre in inches	12	13·5	12	14	15
Length in calibres	50	45	45	50	50
Weight in tons	69	80	53	83	102
Weight of projectile in pounds	850	1,240	850	1,360	1,650
Initial velocity	2,950	2,800	3,000	3,000	3,000
Energy at muzzle in metric tons	16,540	22,150	17,520	27,650	33,910
Energy per kilogramme in kilo-metres	240	277	330	330	330
Probable life in rounds ...	60	60	200	200	200

The attention of the First Lord of the Admiralty was directed to these statements in the House of Commons, and he reiterated the assurance of former Ministers that the expert advisers were satisfied as to the wisdom of retaining the wire-wound system. He gave no data as to the foundation of this confidence, and in the German technical press—no doubt with an eye to foreign orders—the superiority of the German gun over the British was repeated with at least equal assurance.

The great advantage of the wire-wound system, it has always been claimed, is that after much use, when the rifling is worn, the gun can be given a new inner tube, a comparatively simple and cheap operation which results in practically a new gun being made available for sea service in a short time. All that can be said as to the two systems from practical experience is that the Japanese found the British-made weapons give eminently satisfactory results during the war with Russia, while the Krupp artillery guns used by the Turkish Army in the Balkan War of 1912 did not realize expectations.

Probably in naval material—in ships, their armour, armament, and engineering equipment—there is little difference as between the leading navies. One may be thought to have an advantage in some particular respect, but this may possibly be counterbalanced by the rival's superiority in another. No final judgment on the relative merits of material, certainly as between the British and German Navies, can be passed in the absence of war experience. Generally the British ships mount fewer guns but of larger calibre, and to the experienced eye they look very workmanlike; while the German ships carry smaller guns in greater number and have a crowded appearance which does not appeal to British naval opinion in its desire for simplicity of design and plenty of working room. Which school represents the nearest approximation to ideal war conditions only war itself can show. Virtually, all the instruments for exerting naval power as they exist to-day are experimental, based upon empirical knowledge. When the war between the United States and Spain occurred, it was anticipated that it would throw light upon these problems, but these anticipations were not realized, and even the struggle between Russia and Japan failed to satisfy fully the natural curiosity of the naval constructor and the naval officer owing to the inefficiency with which the Russian ships were handled, and the deplorable slackness of the administration.

It is the fashion to calculate the relative strength of fleets in tons and guns,* but the probability is that on the day of trial these nice paper computations will be entirely upset by the course of events. Morale, as Napoleon observed, dominates war. This dictum is no less true to-day than it was in the past. Man is still greater than the instruments of his creation, and the experience of war will certainly confirm the teaching of history—that the important element in naval power is men rather than ships. On the eve of the Battle of St. Vincent, when Jervis, in command of fifteen ships, was pacing the quarter-deck of his flagship and the Spanish Fleet was entering the field of vision, the numbers of the enemy were reported by the Captain of the Fleet to the Commander-in-Chief as they were counted. "There are eight sail of the line, Sir John," "Very well, sir," answered the Admiral. "There are twenty sail of the line, Sir John." "Very well, sir," Jervis responded. "There are twenty-five sail of the line, Sir John." "Very well, sir," the Admiral again replied imperturbably. "There are twenty-seven sail of the line, Sir John," the Captain of the Fleet at length reported, and when he had the temerity to remark on the great disparity between the British and Spanish Fleets, the Admiral, confident in the efficiency of his small fleet, replied: "The die is cast, and if there be

* A comparison of the gun-power of the British and German Fleets, drawn from official sources, is given in Appendix VII.

fifty sail, I will go through them." We may be sure that the victor of the Battle of St. Vincent, who by stern but wisely directed measures created the fleet which Nelson used with such dramatic effect at Trafalgar, would have scorned and ridiculed an entire reliance on mere paper calculations of guns and tons, realizing that victory or defeat depends mainly upon the personal element and morale.

It is in respect of officers and men that there is the greatest contrast between the British Fleet and the Navies of the continent of Europe. The British service is organized on a voluntary system, while the Continental fleets are manned mainly by conscripts; the former serve for many years, while the latter for the most part submit to only the short period of duty required by law and then pass into the reserve. In the matter of officers, however, the German Fleet is certainly not worse served than the British Navy; though the cadets begin their training at a somewhat later age, a thoroughly good sea officer is produced. The marked distinction between the two services is that, whereas under the White Ensign special duties are assigned to special classes of officers—gunnery, torpedo, navigation, signalling and physical training— in the German Navy no hard-and-fast lines are drawn. It is held that the British system would entail a larger number of officers than are available on the other side of the North Sea. However this may be, the German authorities can certainly pride themselves upon a corps of executive officers which in many respects is not excelled in any country. As in the British service, special lines of officers are trained for engineering, medical, and accountant duties and these have no executive standing.

The method of training executive officers for the German Fleet differs in some important respects from that which obtains in England. In the British service the cadets, who enter when they are, on the average, thirteen and a half years of age, have not completed their general education, and consequently spend four years at the Naval Colleges at Osborne and Dartmouth respectively before they go afloat in a training ship. The German naval officer receives much the same general education as any other boy before he enters the navy, whereas the British cadet, after entering, is submitted to an educational course specially devised with a view to his future naval career; his studies embrace physical science and practical engineering, and emphasis is laid upon athletics and as much sea experience as can be obtained in small craft. When the four years ashore are completed he goes afloat at about the same age as the average German cadet and makes a six months' cruise. Which is the better system? Who shall say? This is certain, however, that British naval officers have always held that lads for the sea service cannot be caught, broken in, and inoculated, so to speak, too early.

The training and the position subsequently occupied by the naval officer in the German organization is peculiar to the country in some respects. His relation to the navy, to the technical side of naval power, and to the Emperor, as the supreme head of the fleet, was admirably presented by two foreign officers who, after studying the German naval system, compiled the following notes :*

Private workshops will construct the ships, will mount the guns, will provide the technical personnel, will instal all the machinery and all the arms for immediate and perfect action ; only skill in directing and rapidity of action will be required of the officers. It is on this principle that the organization of the German Fleet is founded, and to this principle is subordinated every detail of the education of the officers. It is not claimed that the officers possess a profound scientific knowledge of the mechanism nor even sufficient practical acquaintance with the details for handling it. The

* Translated from the *Rivista Generale di Marina* of November, 1911, and published in the *Journal of the Royal United Service Institution.*

first is the province of the naval architects; and for
the second there exists the class called " deck officers "
(warrant officers), to whose function the Saxon nature
readily adapts itself; a class between petty officers
and officers, composed of individuals whose practical
knowledge of one single subject is being constantly
improved by frequent alternations of practical experience and teaching in the schools. From this class
are drawn and placed respectively under the officers
concerned, experts in gunnery, torpedo and engineering, highly trained by constant and exclusive employment of the one machine, and perfected in the schools
by theoretical instruction limited, in extent, but of
great efficiency.

Relying on these assistants, the German naval officer
does not require a profound knowledge of the scientific
part of his machinery, nor familiarity with details,
but concerns himself solely with the direction of the
whole.

There are, besides, other peculiarities of race and of
political organization which influence details, and are
at first sight incomprehensible to us. In war and
executive matters the control of the Emperor is absolute and personal. He issues his orders directly to
the chiefs of the different departments, without the
intervention of the Minister, which is only exercised
in the administrative part. Contracts, construction,
etc., are under the Minister's control, but the Commanders-in-Chief of the fleets and of the naval stations,
the heads of the departments of artillery and of torpedoes, and those of the centres of instruction receive
orders directly from the Emperor. Their personal
responsibility to him is therefore unavoidable and
effective.

The Emperor, for his part, issues concise orders without entering into details, and this compels the subordinate to exercise his own initiative. The result of this
system is, first, a perfect knowledge on the part of the
Emperor of the fitness of the personnel; and, secondly,

that each individual is accustomed to act on his own responsibility and on his own initiative unhampered by any other consideration than that of carrying out the design of the Emperor.

It is evident that this tends to produce admirable results in the spirit of the war organization, but on the condition that the personal fitness of the Emperor is fully equal to the great requirements of such an important rôle. Everything depends on this.

There are other important factors which must not be overlooked, if we would understand and judge the organization of this navy. The democratic spirit, claiming equal chances for all, which influences all the acts of Governments of the Latin nations, has not yet impressed itself upon the Teutonic race. It is therefore not surprising to find strict rules excluding the lower grades of society, such, for example, as the rules determining the entrance to the Academy in the first instance, and later on to executive rank, or those which forbid the lower grades of engineers to marry if they aspire to the rank of officers.

This same spirit of differentiation which pervades the whole fabric of society, and is accepted by the lower classes themselves, facilitates the exercise of military authority without requiring great scientific or intellectual knowledge.

The combination of these circumstances creates an atmosphere absolutely different, not only from our own, but from that of all maritime nations. It is not thought necessary to give officers an extensive knowledge which might be useless, and would probably quench in them an activity which should be applied rather to stimulating qualities of another order. Neither is there any intention of adopting the system of evolution, which other nations have initiated in the organization of engineers; there will continue to be, above all, practical men with a career limited to the post of Commander; because, it is said, they have not the wherewithal to fill the higher posts.

The course of instruction of the personnel of the different branches is founded upon these ideas.

As to the executive branch of officers the maximum age for admittance as a cadet is eighteen, and a certificate of the standard of education of "bachelor" is sufficient to qualify him for entrance. A Commission of the Inspectorate of Schools examines the antecedents of the candidate's family more closely than his diploma, and his admission is then determined. It is possible also to enter before the age of sixteen, without having attained the standard of "bachelor," but in this case, and with the consent of the Board, the candidate must pass a qualifying examination in arithmetic, algebra (including quadratic equations), geometry, plane and solid (elementary), plane trigonometry, the rudiments of physics (mechanics, light, heat, and electricity), French, and English (to read and translate).

During the first six months the cadets receive military training on land, and then at once embark in the cruisers exclusively reserved for this purpose. These vessels, of 5,000 tons, are the *Hertha, Freya, Hansa,* and *Victoria Luise.*

The instruction given in these cruisers, which are at the same time schools for seamen apprentices, is of a practical character; they are taught the principles of seamanship, including practical navigation and pilotage, and sufficient astronomy for the determination of latitude by the meridian. In gunnery they learn the handling of the guns and firing at the target. In the engine-room they perform the mechanical duties of each department in all their details. Every midshipman must have kept at least twelve watches of two hours each as stoker mechanic, and twenty-four as artificer in the engine-room. The study of gunnery and of engineering is purely descriptive. They learn, besides, French and English.

During the first year the progress made in their studies is carefully watched, and at the close of the course the students pronounced competent undergo an examination on board the same ship before they can pass into the Kiel School as midshipmen; whilst those classed as competent, but who fail in the examination, may repeat the course.

The school at Kiel occupies at present a building which, although sumptuously furnished and decorated, does not fulfil the modern requirements for space in establishments of this character. The German Government, alive to this defect, is constructing an edifice adapted for the purpose at Sonderburg.

The midshipmen remain a year in this school. The table on p. 163 gives the list of lectures delivered, and the time devoted to each subject in the year's course, which is the only one of a theoretical character in the career of the German officer.

In addition, the afternoons are employed as follows :

(*a*) In summer, weekly : Two double hours seamanship ; one hour gymnastics ; one hour fencing ; one hour signalling. Monthly : One double hour in engineering, and, during the term, seven double hours of navigation.

(*b*) In winter : Six double hours gunnery ; five hours construction ; one hour gymnastics ; one hour fencing ; one hour signalling ; one hour riding ; one hour dancing.

The textbooks for the course of instruction contained in these lectures could scarcely be more elementary. The one for mathematics includes arithmetic, algebra, geometry, and trigonometry. It consists of 450 pages, and the previous knowledge of the four rules of arithmetic with whole numbers is all that is required for its study. The theories of arithmetic and algebra are confined to the first 88 pages. Plane geometry, with numerous applications to pilotage, occupies the next 100 pages. Trigonometry is studied in all its branches ; this science, with the principles of solid geometry, which are indispensable for the comprehension of all that relates to the sphere, and with application to cosmography and nautical astronomy (triangulation) occupies the rest of the book.

The German officer does not study calculus. Analytical geometry is epitomized in 80 pages, which treat principally of the parabola, and touch lightly

TABLE OF STUDIES IN THE SCHOOL.

Subjects.	Hours Weekly in Classes.	Observations.
Navigation, seamanship, and knowledge of the ship	6	One and a half hours a week in navigation work, and a practical course in a sailing vessel during one week.
Gunnery and hydraulics	2	—
Engineering	3	—
Organization of the departments	2	—
Construction	2	—
Mathematics	2	—
Natural sciences	2	—
Electro-technics	2	—
English	2	—
French	2	—
Mines (in summer) ...	1	—
Land tactics (fortifications in winter)	1	During the summer twelve double hours approximately for land tactics. During the winter six double hours given to the same subject in such form as the Director of Studies may decide.
Drawing and languages optional	—	—

on the other curves of the second degree. This book contains all that is required for the mathematical course.

All that refers to natural sciences is contained in a little book of 94 pages, devoted to all the most elementary principles of mechanics, heat, light, magnetism, electricity, and chemistry.

The class-books on the applied sciences do not go much farther. Cosmography, navigation, meteorology, oceanography, and surveying are contained in a volume of 280 pages.

Engines occupy 300 pages in a book, which, after some elementary explanation of thermo-dynamics, gives a description of the engines actually in use in the German Navy, not only for propulsion, but for every kind of use on board. It describes, therefore, reciprocating engines, turbines, internal combustion, all kinds of auxiliary engines, dynamos, electro-motors, refrigerators, ventilators, pumps, etc. It is all in a very condensed form, and the scientific is subordinated to the popular character.

Gunnery is the subject of a much larger work, and is divided under three heads. The first is the description of the material in use in the German Navy; the second part, of 50 pages, is a fairly complete and very practical study of external ballistics and fire control; and the third portion is a very elementary treatise on internal ballistics, powder, and ammunition.

When the course of study has been completed in the school, the students pass into the gunnery school of Sonderburg, where, for three months, they devote themselves exclusively to the theory and practice of this arm; after which, having satisfied their instructors in this course, they pass into the torpedo school on board a special ship, where they remain two months. Another examination follows, and they are then attached for one month's purely military service to one of the colonial battalions. After this stage of apprenticeship the midshipmen have the privilege of wearing swords, and then enter for a year's service afloat.

The examination at the end of this last year closes the period of instruction, and the place which the student takes in the examination, together with his previous record in the schools, determines his seniority in the list. But whatever may be the result of this examination, the student does not enter the Executive Branch of Officers until all the officers at the station to which he belongs, whether Kiel or Wilhelmshaven, have given their votes in his favour. Should even one officer alone raise objection to the entrance of the candidate on the ground of the dignity and reputation of the corps, it is sufficient to delay his admission pending the decision of the Emperor.

The commanders of the ships have the power to delay the final examination for six months, and even to propose retirement on professional or social grounds. This is granted by the Inspectorate of Schools, of which Board a Vice - Admiral is head.

Promotion to the higher grades of the corps goes practically by seniority, because, although the regulations direct promotions by selection, this method is little employed, at present at all events.

The officers of the Executive Branch of Officers performing the duties of naval lieutenants are selected, not on their initiative, but by the direction of their superiors, to go through a course of gunnery which comprises two standards : the lower, which requires two months, is for the guns of cruisers ; the higher, lasting three months, for the heavy guns of battle-ships. Should three years elapse without these officers being employed in the capacity for which they have specialized they forfeit their title of specialist.

In the same way the " Oberleutnants " (lieutenants of less than eight years' seniority) have to go through a further torpedo course, which lasts three months. As in the previous case, the title of specialist is forfeited by three years' unemployment. In reality neither the torpedo nor the gunnery course gives any personal advantage or differentiation in the service.

Promotion in the ranks of Engineer Officers is practically limited to the comparative rank of "Kapitän-leutnant" (naval lieutenant of over eight years' service), because, although there are posts ranking with major and lieutenant-colonel in the Army, their number is so small relatively to that of the officers that it is by only an exception that these posts can be obtained. On the other hand, the pay is always higher than that of other officers of equal rank. Their position on board is that of combatant officers, although inferior to that of the officers of the Executive Branch, who hold certain privileges, such as Presidency of the Mess, etc.

The candidates for entry as engineer sub-lieutenant must, as students, be under twenty-two years of age; they must have attained the standard of education of "bachelor," or followed part of the course for this certificate like the students of the Executive Branch of Officers; they must pass a theoretical examination in elementary mathematics, the rudiments of mechanics, and mechanical drawing, as well as a practical examination in what concerns their profession; they must, besides, show that they have served in private works for at least twenty-four months, of which four must have been passed in boiler works, two in copper, and three in iron foundries, and fifteen in machinery workshops. Having satisfied their examiners on these points, they then receive an exclusively military training for three months, and the other nine months of the first year are spent in naval vessels. At the end of the year they are examined on board ship by a commission composed of one captain, one commander, and three engineer-officers. They pass two years more on board an armoured vessel; or one year in an armoured ship and one in a torpedo-boat as petty officer, keeping their watches, and pass on to Wilhelmshaven for a theoretical course.

The programme for this first year is as follows :

Subjects.	Hours per Week.
Engines	5
Electro-technics	3
Mechanics	4
Physics	2
Chemistry	2
Higher mathematics	6
Languages	4
Drawing	3

At the end of this year, the fourth of their career, they are promoted, and return as " deck officers " (warrant officers) to the ship. There they do duty as assistant chiefs of the watches in the engine-room and stoke-hold, subordinate to the engineer officers, who are the chiefs of the watches. After four years' duty they return again to Wilhelmshaven, where they go through a year's course, comprising both theoretical and practical work. The following subjects are studied :

Subjects.	Hours per Week.
Engines	6
Electro-technics	4
Mechanics	3
Physics	2
Chemistry	2
Mathematics	5
Languages (French and English)	4
Torpedoes	4

This ninth year of their career closes the period of training and the result of the examination, combined with that of the previous examinations, and with the reports of their commanding officers, determines their seniority in the list of officers ; but in order to take their place among the officers a favourable vote must be obtained, as in the case of the officers of the Executive Branch, only in this case the officers of the Engineer and the Executive Branch vote. Those who aspire to become officers cannot marry until after they have attained their position.

After the first six months of study, a certain number of the engineer students are selected from the others, and trained in torpedo-boats exclusively. Later they spend a year at Wilhelmshaven, and when they have been advanced to torpedo "deck officers" they spend six months in the floating torpedo school, on board the *Württemberg*. After this course they pass on to the school for torpedo practice on board the armoured cruiser *Friedrich Karl*, where they remain three months. Another year is spent in practical work in the torpedo workshops. After four years, reckoned from their advancement to "deck officers," they return to Wilhelmshaven and go through the second course with the engineers, and are finally promoted to officers under the same conditions as the other engineer officers. The most distinguished among those of both branches are afterwards sent for a two years' finishing course in civilian schools and institutes.

The electricity department is confined in Germany to engineer officers, excepting the machinery required for the guns, which is under the control of the officers of the Executive Branch, assisted by "gunnery engineers," so-called. These latter are recruits, who can prove that they have served three years in private workshops. They are at once sent to the artillery division, where they are put through a three months' practical course on board; then they spend two months in the *Kronprinz* (course of electricity); five months in gun factories, and in workshops for the construction of dockyard machinery; one-and-a-half months in the school for gunnery; one-and-a-half in arsenal workshops. Having completed this course of training they are appointed to ships, and having given evidence of their aptitude and skill, they are then recommended and promoted to petty officers.

The most proficient among them, after a fixed time of duty in the workshops and four years on board ship, return to the gunnery school, where they qualify for advancement to "deck officers."

These are the various methods by which officers are trained, and it only remains to add that owing to the drastic action of the Emperor the average age of German officers, which was formerly very high, has been reduced. As an illustration of His Majesty's methods it may be recalled that one year after naval manœuvres two admirals, a captain, and four younger officers were placed on the retired list; and on other occasions energetic steps have been taken in order to secure to the service only those officers whose intellectual and seaman-like characteristics fit them for the arduous duties of the sea service.

Throughout the years of naval expansion the German authorities have been struggling to eliminate as far as possible the disadvantages of conscription in its application to naval conditions. The War Department is responsible for putting in force the conscription law, and periodically the navy sends in its requisition, stating the number of recruits who will be needed, and where and when they are to join. The men selected are passed direct into the fleet without preliminary training each October. Under the British system boys are entered at about sixteen years of age, and receive a short training first in one of the shore or stationary sea establishments, and are subsequently drafted into one of the ships of the Training Squadron, thence joining the sea-going fleet. A certain number of youths are also entered at an average age of about seventeen and a half years, and these recruits dispense with the preliminary course, but are also drafted to the Training Squadron before joining the fleet. Nearly all the men of the fleet sign on for twelve years' active service, and the best of these are permitted to re-engage for another ten years in order to earn pensions. A relatively small number of men, not boys, join the British Navy for a term of only five years, with the obligation to remain in the Reserve for seven years. Five years, consequently, is the minimum in the British Navy, and applies to only a relatively small number of men; but three years is the maximum period of German conscripts, and during this time the officers and warrant officers have to do their best to transform the raw material provided by the State into skilled seamen.

It is easy to imagine the difficulties which assail the administration in Germany in these circumstances. Every year one-third of the naval conscripts complete their period of active service and are passed into the Reserve, and their places are taken by an equivalent batch of raw recruits. The result is that in the winter months the officers and petty officers of the fleet are occupied in licking into shape these embryo sailors, and from October until May the fighting ships of the Empire become practically training vessels.

If this were a complete representation of the conditions in the German Fleet its efficiency would be of a low order. The Navy is, however, stiffened by a proportion of conscripts who re-engage voluntarily, and by a certain number of volunteers who enter as boys. These lads engage at ages ranging from fifteen to eighteen years. They agree to undergo an apprenticeship of two years followed by seven years of active fleet service. Volunteers are not trained ashore or in fixed naval establishments as in the United Kingdom, but are drafted to sea-going training ships, which cruise in home waters during the summer months and pass into the Mediterranean during the winter. By these two expedients the German naval authorities have been able to secure about 25 per cent. of the German personnel on what passes in Germany for a long-service system. The boy volunteers and the conscripts who re-engage constitute the class from which petty officers are drawn, and these men are the backbone of the naval organization ashore and afloat, and it is to their efforts that the high standard of efficiency which Germany's Navy has attained may in a large measure be traced.

Year by year, in order to provide crews for the larger number of ships passed into the fleet, the

Marine Office has been compelled to increase the number of conscripts required for sea service, and thus the task of training the Navy has been increased in advance of the expansion of the material, because men must begin training before their ships are ready for sea. The officers and petty officers have had not only to train raw recruits embarked to take the place of conscripts at the end of their three years' term, but to find means also of training the additional recruits entered as net additions to the naval strength. When it is added that in 1894 the number of officers and men in the Navy was less than 21,000, whereas it is now 66,000, and under the Navy Act of 1912 is to be raised to 107,000, some conception may be formed of the character of the problem which presents itself, not only to the central administration ashore, but to the officers afloat, intent upon attaining the highest standard of efficiency at sea. Admission of these difficulties was made by Admiral von Tirpitz in the explanatory Memorandum which accompanied the last Navy Bill presented to the Reichstag and which directed attention to "two serious defects" in the organization of the fleet:

"The one defect consists in the fact that in the autumn of every year the time-expired men—*i.e.*, almost one-third of the crew in all ships of the battle fleet, are discharged and replaced mainly by recruits from the *inland population.* Owing to this, the readiness of the battle fleet for war is considerably impaired for a prolonged period."

When it is recalled that the maritime population of Germany amounts only to 80,000, and that compulsory service in the active fleet lasts for only three years, it will be realized that most of the recruits taken for the German Navy must necessarily be landsmen. The personnel in 1912 numbered roughly over 50,000, after deducting from the total the executive officers, engineers, cadets, and volunteers. If approximately 13,000 of these are regarded as long-service men there remain roughly 37,500 conscripts, one-third of whom pass annually into the Reserve, and are replaced by raw hands. Under the new Navy Law it is intended to strengthen the personnel in the next few years by 6,400 annually, and, consequently, if allowance is made for a certain number of the net additions being volunteers, it follows that the raw recruits to be embarked will number between 18,000 and 19,000 men, or about one-third of the total personnel, excluding officers and long service ratings. It is proposed to utilize the third squadron of the High Sea Fleet largely for training purposes, and thus to raise the standard of efficiency in the First and Second Squadrons by the elimination, as far as possible, of the raw recruit. This apparently is the best expedient which has occurred to the naval authorities in the difficulty in which they are placed by the conscriptive law which is essential to the Army, but is a serious handicap to the Navy—not only in Germany, but in every country on the continent of Europe. While the average period of service in the British Navy, including the relatively small number of five years' men entered for short service, is about ten years, the average in the German Fleet does not amount to as much as half this period.

It is possible to attach too much importance to the fact that the German Navy is recruited " mainly by recruits from the inland population." The inherited sea habit counts for less to-day than at any time since men attempted to navigate the seas. Ships of war have become vast complicated boxes of machinery, and naval life requires the exercise of qualities different from those it demanded in the sail era. Then brute courage, endurance, and familiarity with the moods of the sea were the main attributes of sailors, but to-day a large proportion of the crews must be experts in the handling of complicated mechanical appliances. In these changed conditions the compulsory system of education in Germany has proved of the greatest advantage in providing recruits of a high standard of intelligence, who probably acquire in six months as complete a familiarity with their work as it would have taken a seaman of the old school as many years to attain. At the same time, while resisting the temptation to place too great importance upon the inherited sea habit, it would be no less a mistake to ignore entirely its influence upon naval efficiency. Familiarity breeds contempt for the terrors of the sea and for the horrors of a naval action, and it is reasonable to expect that in the hour of trial the long-service men of the British Navy will exhibit a moral standard when projectiles are falling fast and thick far higher than that of the conscript. A modern Dreadnought is intended to fire its guns in broadsides and not in succession, and when it is borne in mind that at one discharge these guns will deliver on an enemy's ship, if they are fired accurately, between five and six tons of metal, it will be realized that at such a moment the calibre of men will count more than the calibre of guns.

Let there be no mistake, the German naval authorities realize the disadvantages under which they are working owing to the restrictions of the conscriptive law. When the Act of 1900 was introduced the Reichstag was informed by Admiral von Tirpitz in a Memorandum that "as, even after the projected increase has been carried out, the number of vessels in the German Navy will still be more or less inferior to that of other individual Great Powers, our endeavours must be directed towards compensating this superiority by the individual training of the crews and by tactical training by practice in large bodies. . . . Economy as regards commissioning of vessels in peace time means jeopardizing the efficiency of the fleet in case of war." Never since navies existed have a body of officers and men been worked at higher pressure than those of Germany: drill never ceases; no effort is spared to obtain the last ounce of value out of every one on board the ships. The promotion of officers rests with the Emperor, and he is unsparing in his punishment of anything like slackness; an officer who is not enthusiastic, alert, and competent, stands no chance of rising in rank. The German Navy has no use for anything but the best which the Empire can provide, and in order that the highest expression of the *esprit de corps* which has contributed to German influence on shore may be instilled into the Navy, no officer, however influential or brilliant, can enter either the executive or engineering branch unless, as we have seen, his claims are endorsed by all his contemporaries; one black ball—if the term may be used—is sufficient to disqualify an aspirant, though he may have passed all the prescribed examinations brilliantly.

The German Navy is recognized as a vast complicated machine which has to be worked at the highest pressure, and therefore no sand must impede the engine nor salt water get into the boiler; everything must be made to go smoothly and quickly; so far as it can be eliminated, there must be no distraction. It may be that the officers and men are being submitted to a régime which is inimical to their staying power, that their endurance is being unduly tested, and their nerves kept too continuously on the strain. This may be so, but the German naval authorities have in view a kind of war different from any which has hitherto been known. It is not to be a long-drawn-out contest in which patient courage, sturdy tenacity of purpose, and incapacity to recognize defeat can triumph after months or years of hostilities. The German Fleet is intended to be used—if used at all— like a thunderbolt. The whole record of its evolution and training confirms this conclusion, and we have notable confirmation of this view in the series of "notes" by two Spanish officers already quoted. They have written as follows:

"The German Navy has a definite and immediate objective; everything must be prepared for a rapid, energetic and decisive action. Her ships, equipped by her national industry, rich in resource of every kind, provided with war material of the highest efficiency, must be ready to dart at a given moment against an enemy whose fleet awaits them almost at the mouth of the German ports. The first encounter, fierce and terrible, will decide the campaign, and will influence the future of both nations. The partial actions, the long blockades, the prolonged manœuvres of fleets, which require such seamanship, such skill in the personnel, will necessarily be eliminated in the future war. All that is required is men of action, with the determination to win in one day of supreme and fierce struggle."

The ideal of the German naval authorities somewhat resembles that of the American manufacturer. The latter does not attempt to produce an article which will last a lifetime, because he foresees that in a few years inventive genius will have produced something better. He provides a motor-car, locomotive, or stationary engine which will run well and do good work for a reasonable time, and he sells it at a price which justifies the owner in scrapping it directly a better article is available representing a gain in power or speed. So the German naval authorities are intent on creating an instrument which will look well on paper when tons and guns are compared, and thus achieve a diplomatic objective, and which will be trained to the highest pitch of efficiency for a sudden coup, representing a triumph over the disadvantageous conditions traceable to the law of conscription; but it will never be the kind of fleet which St. Vincent fashioned and which maintained the blockade for month on month off the French coast and still preserved undiminished its ability to go in and win whenever battle offered. Also it will not be the kind of fleet which British officers, faithful to their inherited traditions, still desire to preserve—a body of well-manned ships which can go anywhere and do anything, whether the service be short and sharp, or whether it be a long and wearisome task.

Germany is creating a navy as a powerful political instrument which at a favourable moment and in an instant can exert its maximum power. The German Fleet has its limitations, but within those limitations it probably has no superior in the world : the ships are well built, the officers are capable sailors, and the men are raised to the highest pitch of efficiency possible under a short-service system.

CHAPTER VII

WILLIAM II. AND HIS NAVAL MINISTER

THE German Fleet as it is to-day, and as it will be when its statutory establishment has been reached, may be regarded as the work of two men—the Emperor William II. and Admiral von Tirpitz ; and in the present chapter an attempt will be made to allot to each his due share of credit for their joint achievement. The task is by no means an easy one, and in the present generation it cannot be performed with more than an approximation to accuracy. It must be left to the historian of a distant future, with access to State archives and the epistolary confidences of German statesmen now living, to tell the full and authentic story of this, as of all other episodes, of the reign of William II.

Even for those who have lived long in Germany, it is difficult to form a judgment as to the aims and motives of the Emperor William's naval policy, and of the part which he has played in its carrying out. With regard to their sovereign, Germans are inclined to fly to one of two extremes ; according to the class to which they belong, they represent him either as a heaven-born genius of universal gifts, or as a busybody whose meddlesomeness is rendered specially mischievous by medieval delusions as to the functions of monarchs and their relations to the Deity. Everything that he does or says is set down as quite right by the one party and as quite wrong by the other. Moreover, the opinions of those brought into closest contact with

him are vitiated by the prevalence of a type of syco-
phancy which is fortunately becoming extinct in other
countries. As all offices, high and low, in the Empire
and in Prussia are dependent, directly or indirectly,
on the Emperor's will, and as he intervenes in all the
details of the public administration, it is inevitable
that the desire to deserve his favour should be the
predominant motive in the minds of the servants of
the State. And, rightly or wrongly, the idea obtains
that an attitude of unqualified and unquestioning
adulation is the surest means of finding the way into
his good graces. Over the unofficial sections of his
subjects he exercises a similar influence as the foun-
tain of all honour. The German is vain, and delights
even more than other men in decorations, ranks, and
titles. And by the infinite multiplication of these
petty prizes of life which has taken place during his
reign, the Emperor has been ministering to a popular
appetite. Members of all professions and occupations,
artists, authors, and musicians, ministers of religion,
doctors, lawyers, and engineers, captains of industry,
commerce, and finance, compete with one another
eagerly for a share in the annual largesse of titles,
decorations, and patents of nobility, and their judgment with regard to the giver of the feast is perverted
by either the anticipation or the enjoyment of its
pleasures. It is true that this evil also exists in other
countries, but nowhere else has it assumed such dimensions as in Germany, for it is there alone that a single
individual endeavours to direct every force of the
national life along the channels of his own convictions
and tastes. On the other hand, disgust at the fulsome
flattery of the people who flock round the throne and
prostrate themselves before it has excited a reaction
in the minds of those to whom even the Emperor is
but a man to be measured by human standards, and
has prevented them, in their turn, from forming a just
opinion of his actions. Little wonder if it is well-nigh
impossible, in the confused picture resulting from

these discordant colours, to discern the true lineaments of its subject.

For the foreigner, the task is further complicated by an apparent incongruity between the Emperor's own opinions and actions, which it has been urged can be accounted for only by the theory of deliberate duplicity. Throughout his reign he has repeatedly protested his friendship for Great Britain, and his wish to live on terms of peace and amity with her, but at the same time he has, just as consistently, followed a line of policy which is admittedly a challenge to her position in the world, and can legitimately be construed as a direct menace to her very existence.   The apparent contradiction can, perhaps, best be explained by taking his words, or at any rate some of them, at their face value, and considering them in relation to his responsibilities as the head of the German Empire, and to certain marked traits in his character.   It is his obvious duty as German Emperor to do what lies in his power to fortify his country against attack, and to claim for it in the world the place to which he believes it to have entitled itself by its great military record and by its wonderful achievements in science, art, and industry. Though he has been more communicative than any monarch of modern, and perhaps of any other, times, his position has naturally prevented him from explaining his point of view as to his country's deserts and aspirations, but we shall be able to form some idea of it if we examine the opinions of those of his people who are animated by the sentiments which we call "national pride" in ourselves, but are apt to call "national vanity" in others.

The patriotic German, who is familiar with his country's history, knows that, five or six hundred years ago, his forefathers monopolized the markets and policed the seas of Northern and Western Europe. He realizes keenly that Germany's maritime and industrial progress was first checked, and then retarded for centuries, by political division and internecine and foreign wars. Possibly he still remembers that great crescendo of victory in which Prussia smothered Denmark, then overthrew Austria in a single battle, and finally, at the head of the kindred Teutonic States, humbled France in the dust, and welded Germany together in one indivisible whole. Even if he does not remember it as part of his own personal experience, all its vivid and stimulating episodes have been a thousand times impressed upon his mind by school-master, politician, historian, and journalist. That after this tremendous martial achievement he should regard his country as the mistress of the continent of Europe is no matter for surprise. But he sees, too, that the Germany of Luther and Goethe, of Ranke, Liebig, Helmholz, and Mommsen, of Bismarck and Moltke, has become also the Germany of Krupp, Siemens, Rathenau, Ballin, and Gwinner; that the products of German industry, the fruits of an unexampled applica-tion of the discoveries of science to the processes of manufacture, have been carried by German ships to the remotest ends of the earth; that the material prosperity of his country is advancing in every direc-tion by leaps and bounds. And he thus believes Germany to be strong, wise, and wealthy, and in every way fitted to stand at the head of mankind. But in one respect he feels, to his bitter mortification, that she is powerless. Wherever he goes on the world's oceans, he is confronted by those iron walls of Great Britain, which mean that he is there only by the sufferance of one who is immeasurably stronger than himself. With one nation he recognizes with chagrin that he cannot afford to quarrel, for by doing so he would expose his floating merchandise and his colonies to certain loss, and his home industry to the paralysis that would inevitably follow upon the closing of the routes along which it exchanges its finished products for the exotic raw materials indispensable to its existence. And these facts are all the more galling to him because he regards them as resulting from the accidents, and not from the intrinsic nature of things. For he is convinced that his country has the men and the money, and could soon be in a position to build and arm the ships as easily, as quickly, and as well as any other State. That any substantial improvement of Germany's position in this respect would endanger, not merely the prosperity, or the development, or the prestige, but also the very existence of Great Britain, is a consideration which we cannot ask him to take into his calculations. He cannot be expected to regard even the existence of another State as a legitimate bar to the gratification of his ambitions, especially if he is convinced that that other State occupies the place which, by moral right, belongs to his own country.

No doubt he could not, and would not, cherish such ambitions if it had been made clear to him that they could never be realized, that no efforts on the part of Germany could materially alter the balance of sea-power to her advantage as against Great Britain, and that she would be compelled to fight for her pretensions long before she was in a position to give battle on anything like equal terms. Unfortunately this has not been made clear to him. On the contrary, he knows that a very great change to his country's advantage has already taken place in the relationship of the Fleet of Germany to that of Great Britain, and he sees no reason why the process should not be indefinitely continued. He is persuaded that Germany will soon be rich enough to spend as much on her fleet as Great Britain does, and in manning it will have an enormous advantage in the inexhaustible resources of conscription among a population of eighty or ninety millions. He further believes that the British nation is unnerved and effete, that it is losing both its martial and industrial vigour, that its energies have been sapped by too much wealth and prosperity, and that it is rapidly following the downward path. Finally, he is convinced that the British Parliament, under the influence of an aggressive democracy, exclusively concerned with its own immediate material needs, is losing the capacity to realize and grapple with the larger problems of international politics, and that the Cabinets proceeding from it will, in timorous anxiety, procrastinate and vacillate till it is too late to strike. In this idea he has been only confirmed by the pacifist movement in Great Britain, by the British agitation for disarmament by international agreement, and by the well-meant but unfortunate attempt of Sir Henry Campbell-Bannerman to effect by example what much amiable precept had done nothing to accomplish. These phenomena he looks upon not as evidence of good-will and peaceableness, but as symptoms of physical, moral, and financial exhaustion.

Such is the view of many in Germany to whom we cannot fairly deny the name of "patriot" if we are to claim it for an analogous disposition among ourselves. It is the view that is almost universally held by the officers of the German Army and Navy, and, with certain qualifications and reservations, it may be said to be the view of the Emperor William. This will be evident if, with the help of his many spoken and written utterances, we attempt to follow the main lines which, with many sudden and violent deviations, his thought has taken on this subject. He has, for example, in his speeches repeatedly dwelt on the power and renown of the Hanse League—"one of the mightiest undertakings that the world has ever seen," which "was able to raise fleets such as the broad back of the sea had probably never borne up to that time," which "won such high prestige for the German name abroad," which "created markets for the German industrial regions," and which "only failed because it lacked the support of a strong united Empire obedient to a single will." At Hamburg, in June, 1911, he used these words: "I have only acted historically, for I said to myself on my accession, that the tasks which the Hansa attempted to solve by itself, and which it could not solve because the strong Empire was not at its

back, and the defensive and executive power of the
Empire did not exist, must unquestionably at once fall
on the shoulders of the newly-arisen German Empire;
and it was simply the obligations of old traditions
that had to be resumed." It was in one former Hanse
town that the Emperor spoke the familiar words, "Our
future lies on the water;" in another that he declared
"The trident should be in our hand;" in a third that
he uttered the appeal, "We have bitter need of a strong
German Fleet."

Again, he has repeatedly extolled the Great Elector
—"the one among my ancestors for whom I have the
most enthusiasm, who has from my earliest youth
shone before me as a bright example," who, "looking
far ahead, carried on politics on a large scale, as they
are carried on to-day." In his great speech at Bremen
in 1905, the Emperor said: "When as a youth I stood
before the model of Brommy's ship, I felt with burning
indignation the outrage that was then done to our fleet
and our flag;" and these words undoubtedly referred
to the injudiciously-phrased note in which Palmerston
threatened that vessels which undertook belligerent
operations under the colours of that greater German
Empire, which then was not and was never to be,
would render themselves liable to be treated as
"pirates." The present realities of sea-power had
been early revealed to him when, as he told the
officers on board a British flag-ship in the Mediterranean, he "was running about Portsmouth Dockyard as a boy;" and, as he said in a speech made
during the visit of King Edward to Kiel in 1904, "the
stupendous activity on the sea at the headquarters
of the greatest navy of the world impressed itself
indelibly on his youthful mind," and made him, "as
Regent, endeavour to realize on a scale corresponding
to the conditions of his country what he had seen as a
young man in England."

From such reflections, and from the imposing facts
of Germany's recent development, arose the dream of

world-empire which William II. sketched out in the Bremen speech already referred to. But perhaps this very speech furnishes the key to the riddle which his policy presents, for in it he declared with emphasis that his vision was one of pacific and not of warlike conquests. After using the significant words, "We are the salt of the earth," he said :

"As the result of my reading of history, I have pledged myself never to strive after an empty world-rule. For what has become of the so-called world-empires? Alexander the Great, Napoleon, all the great heroes of war swam in blood, and left behind them subjugated nations which rose on the first opportunity and brought their empires to ruin. The world-empire that I have dreamed of would consist in this, that, above all, the newly-created German Empire should on every side enjoy the most absolute confidence as a tranquil, honourable, peaceable neighbour, and that if history should one day tell of a German world-empire, or of a Hohenzollern world-rule, it should not have been based on conquests with the sword, but on the mutual trust of nations striving towards the same goal."

Of all the innumerable speeches of the Emperor William, there is perhaps none that throws more light than this upon the motives of his policy. If it is regarded as a sincere expression of the speaker's feelings, it disposes entirely of the idea that his fleet is being built with the deliberate intention of attacking Great Britain and opening the way to her shores for the hordes of the German Army. And those who have studied with care the Emperor's words and deeds will hardly doubt its sincerity. It is quite true that among his utterances are to be found many explosions of a bellicose and minatory type, but if all their circumstances are examined, it will be seen that they can easily be explained by a histrionic sensitiveness to the incidents and environment of the moment and an impulsive reaction to passing impressions, which are among the traits as to the existence of which in the character of William II. both his panegyrists and his critics are agreed. To those who have looked beneath the surface of German national life, it is, too, no secret that the Emperor's most inveterate and dangerous opponents are the rampant Chauvinists who, intoxicated by the exuberance of their own patriotism, are for ever calling on him to pick up an imaginary gauntlet, and who criticize him with great asperity on the ground that he carries his love of peace to excess and sacrifices Germany's interests and honour rather than draw the sword in their defence.

The theory so frequently advanced that the character of William II. is of a Machiavellian quality, that he is inspired by hostility to Great Britain and a determination to destroy her, and that his assurances to the contrary are merely designed to lull her into a false sense of security till he is ready to strike a fatal blow at her heart, is, in fact, absolutely untenable. The Emperor is essentially a man of warm impulse and frank utterance, and his professions of liking for England and the English are undoubtedly perfectly sincere. He is exceedingly impressionable, especially to appreciation of his own merits, and it is quite certain that he has been deeply touched by the enthusiasm with which he has been welcomed in the streets of London, and not a little puzzled how to reconcile it with the supposed political antipathy of Great Britain towards Germany. The free and unconstrained atmosphere of English social life also appeals strongly to a side of his nature which he may not so easily indulge in his own country, where he can never quite forget that he is the Sovereign, to whom none can speak on equal terms and with an open mind. In England, on the contrary, he can feel that he is a man among men, and consequently enjoy in all its fulness that spontaneous and unfettered social intercourse for which he often craves.

In his admission of the debt which the German Navy owes to its elder British sister, the Emperor has been frank and generous. "Not only," he said at a luncheon given to the Duke of Edinburgh at Berlin, "is the English Navy a model for the German from the technical and scientific standpoints, but the heroes of the British Fleet, Nelson and the rest of them, have always been, and will always be, the guiding stars for the officers and crews of the German Navy." And again, on board the *Royal Sovereign*, he said : "Ever since our fleet has existed we have always striven to form our ideas on yours, and to learn from you in every way." This is assuredly not the language of envy, hatred, and malice, and if such sentiments have played a part in German naval policy—as they undoubtedly have—they are at any rate not to be sought in the mind of the Emperor William.

No doubt the words quoted above seem out of harmony with the Emperor's expressed hope some day to control a fleet "which will be as powerful an instrument for the German Empire as my ancestors on the Prussian throne possessed in the Army," and thus to be able to "dictate peace on the seas also." But it is evidently the deep sense of the pacific nature of his own plans which prevents him from realizing that Germany can dictate peace upon the seas only when the British Empire has ceased to exist, and in all probability his mind is so completely devoid of all aggressive or violent designs that he is unable to understand the suspicions with which his naval policy is regarded. This hypothesis will be received with incredulity only by those who have not recognized the defects as well as the qualities of the Emperor's intellectual apparatus. His mind is one which leaps boldly at its final goal over all intervening stages and obstacles. It sees ends and ignores means ; it revels in grand spectacular effects, and does not trouble itself with the detailed work by which alone they can be attained ; it loses itself in dazzling ideals, and is oblivious of the difficulties that stand in the way of their realization ; it chafes under restraint, and is

heedless of that rule of consistency which, in defiance
of the law of human nature, public opinion attempts
to impose on statesmen and politicians. Above all,
it reacts instantly and irresistibly to the impressions
of the moment. It is these qualities which make
William II. at once the most charming of conversa-
tionalists and the most incalculable of monarchs.

The record of the Emperor is full of sayings of which
it is impossible to believe he realized the full bearing
when he spoke them. When he called the nations of
Europe to "defend their most sacred possessions"
against the power of heathendom that was arising in
the Far East, and when he promised "the three hundred
million Mohammedans living on the earth" that he
would "always be their friend," he cannot have fully
realized that he was threatening one set of peoples
and encouraging another to extravagant and unfulfill-
able hopes. Similarly, it is hardly conceivable that
he had thoroughly considered the significance of his
words when he spoke of dictating peace upon the seas.
What the Emperor expresses by such utterances are
ideals, not fixed aims of policy; visions, not the calculated expectations of statesmanship; speculations,
not positive predictions. Other monarchs and statesmen cherish such ideals, see such visions, and indulge
in such speculations, but they differ from the German
Emperor in this—that they say nothing about them in
public. William II. is exceptional in allowing us to
see so much of the workings of his mind, and if we
employed in his case the standard usually applied to
the words of monarchs, we should be doing him an
injustice. That he permanently and steadily desires
Germany to have a powerful fleet and to be immune
to attack from the sea, that he dreams of a day when
she shall be supreme in the council of the nations, is
indubitable and not unnatural; but just as certain is it
that he, personally, has no aggressive designs against
any of his neighbours, that he regards his fleet as an
instrument of peace, and that the destiny he wishes

Germany to fulfil is that of leading the world in art and science, industry and commerce, not that of overrunning it with the violence of armed hosts.

How far the Emperor has helped to realize his own naval ambitions, and how far his efforts have actually told against them, it is also very difficult to determine with anything like exactitude. His agitation for a bigger fleet has been open and unwearying, and outside Germany the idea is very prevalent that he not only contrived the naval policy of the Empire, but also, almost single-handed, generated the degree of popular support without which it could not have been carried out. This idea will be seen to be erroneous. The Emperor's influence upon his own people is very greatly overrated in other countries, and even the crisis of 1908, in which the storm of discontent which had long been gathering burst with full force upon his head, does not seem to have been properly understood outside Germany. On that occasion, the Imperial Parliament listened without a protest, without a murmur, as a Liberal deputy, slowly, deliberately, and with dramatic emphasis, spoke the following words : "In the German Reichstag not a single member has come forward to defend the actions of the German Emperor." The incident was without a parallel in the history of parliaments. Even the Conservative party, which has always gloried in being the chief prop of the throne, passed and published a resolution expressing the wish that the Emperor should "in future exercise a greater reserve in his utterances," and declaring that "arrangements must be made to prevent with certainty a recurrence of such improper proceedings." It may be remarked, in passing, that this blow fell upon William II. because he had confessed to having had Anglophile sentiments, and to having performed friendly services to Great Britain, at a time when the general feeling of the German people was one of hostility to this country. Nor was it without significance that when, after holding aloof from public affairs for several weeks, he at last emerged from the solitude of his palace at Potsdam, it was in England that he sought the recuperation and rest of which he stood in need.

As the debate in the Reichstag on the *Daily Telegraph* interview unmistakably showed, the Emperor at that time had the whole of his subjects against him in a solid body. But that would have been impossible if the interview had been merely a single isolated incident. It was, in fact, the culmination of a long period of accumulating resentment and opposition. William I., then Crown Prince of Prussia, fled to England in 1848 to escape the wrath of the populace : but he lived to concentrate on his person a hoard of personal popularity such as had, perhaps, never before fortified a monarch's throne. Only a few months after his grandson's accession, this inestimable treasure was already being rapidly dissipated. The causes of the change are not far to seek. All Germany realized that under the first Emperor it was Bismarck who really governed, and whatever there was of opposition or political discontent in the country was directed against the Minister alone. From the outset, William II. made it clear that he intended to be his own Chancellor, to take the initiative in all branches of government, and to extend his influence to many departments of the national life which had hitherto been regarded as lying outside the competence of the monarch. As he claimed for himself the credit, so he became the target for the criticism, of everything done in his name, and his intrusion into the realms of theology, art, music, literature, and the drama conjured up for him many opponents who would never have troubled themselves one way or the other about his specifically political theories and actions. If he had adopted an impartial attitude of general patronage towards all the various endeavours of his people, his intervention might have had a purely beneficial and stimulating effect. But the contrary was the case ; everywhere he appeared on the scene as a convinced and almost fanatical partisan, and nothing could be more indicative of the antagonism he aroused and of the limitations of his personal influence than the fact that every tendency which he has denounced and opposed, whether in politics, religion, or the arts, has at no other time flourished and prospered in Germany as it has precisely during his reign.

That his unconcealed determination to rule personally and in all things, and his openly-avowed belief in the divine origin and inspired character of his office, also aroused antagonism, will have surprised few who have so much as a superficial acquaintance with the German nation. The average cultured German is Liberal in conviction and sceptical in habit. He is well aware that many of the episodes which led to the Hohenzollern ascendancy in Germany had little enough of the divine character in them, and, above all, that the one really great Prince in the genealogy of his ruling house was an ardent disciple of the most iconoclastic of unbelievers. How indeed should he reconcile the idea that the family of Hohenzollern has prospered under the direct and special protection of a conventional Providence, with the fact that it was the Voltairian, Frederick the Great, who first gave the dynasty œcumenical importance ? Impatience of the Emperor's conception of his functions in the State and his position in the universe allied itself with many other types of dissent and discontent to form the great German Socialist party. In no direction has the Emperor's activity been more strenuous and persistent than in his efforts to eradicate Socialism, but in no other country, and at no other epoch, has this form of political error made such prodigious strides forward as in Germany during his rule.

But the political opposition which he has aroused has not been confined to the democratic elements in the German population. Even the Prussian nobles, the strong pillars on which the structure of the Hohenzollern monarchy rests, have more than once faltered in their allegiance. They perhaps understood his cosmopolitanism and universality less than any other class of his people. Strongly tinged with anti-semitism, as they are almost without exception, they were at a loss to comprehend his intimacy with Herr Ballin, the managing director of the Hamburg-America Shipping Company, and other prominent Jews whose work is of national import, or whose wealth has assisted him in carrying out his schemes. It is they, too, who furnish the Officers Corps of the Army, which, ever jealous of favours shown to the sister service, was especially apprehensive that it might be starved to provide money for the ambitious naval projects which the Emperor had made quite evident were the principal preoccupations of his mind. With their material interests resting on an almost purely agrarian basis, the Junkers were also filled with anxiety when they saw their Sovereign associating familiarly with the directors of banks and industrial companies, and heard him dilate on the importance of oversea trade in manufactured products. Their misgivings were transformed into overt opposition when, under the chancellorship of Caprivi, the corn duties were reduced, and commercial treaties concluded which admitted agricultural products into Germany on terms more favourable than those that had hitherto prevailed. It was then that some, at any rate, of the Conservatives openly threatened to "join the Socialists in the opposition." Some years later, a great project to link up the Rhine and the Elbe by a system of canals was submitted to the Prussian Diet, but the Conservatives feared that the proposed waterway would provide an easy channel for the introduction of foreign wheat into the heart of the Empire, and, though the Emperor let it be known that he had the scheme much at heart, the Bill was rejected. He is understood to have said: "None the less it will be built," but that was fifteen years ago, and the first sod of the canal has yet to be cut. Because the Emperor staked his personal influence in favour of the scheme, a certain amount of the opposition which it engendered among the most loyal section of his people was inevitably directed against himself.

The dismissal of Bismarck and the subsequent attempts of the Emperor to depreciate the life-work of the man to whom he owed the Imperial crown, were, of course, the principal causes of the spirit of opposition which flared up with such startling suddenness in 1908. The popularity of William I. was in no small measure due to his absolute trust and confidence in his Chancellor, and the abrupt ejection of this incomparable statesman from his office will never be forgotten or forgiven till the generation of his contemporaries has passed away.

These things go far to explain why it was that, in spite of the vigorous naval agitation of the Emperor, the German Fleet, as was pointed out in the Memorandum attached to the Bill of 1898, became weaker instead of stronger during the first ten years of his reign. From the day of his accession he had lost no opportunity of manifesting his interest in the fleet and his desire that it should be largely increased. Among his earliest acts as monarch was his unheralded appearance in admiral's uniform at a parliamentary luncheon given by Bismarck, to decorate one of the guests who had displayed sympathies and wishes with regard to the Navy similar to his own. Year after year, tables of diagrams, showing the disparity between the fleet of Germany and those of the leading naval Powers, and prepared, it is said, by the Emperor's own hand, were sent out over his signature to the Reichstag, the Government departments, and all public institutions where it was thought they might meet the gaze of appreciative eyes. At a soirée given at the New Palace at Potsdam in 1895, he assembled round him a group of members of the majority parties of the Reichstag, and lectured them for two-and-a-half hours on Germany's

need of sea-power. Bismarck's eightieth birthday was
then approaching, and the Emperor concluded his
remarks by urging upon his hearers that they should
seize the opportunity of "doing the founder of our
colonial policy the pleasure of passing the sum
absolutely required for the Navy."   A couple of
years later, he delivered a similar address after a
dinner given to members of the Reichstag by the
Finance Minister, von Miquel, illustrating his arguments with the diagrams of warships mentioned
above. About the same time, an English illustrated paper published a picture of the foreign war
vessels on the East Asian station. Among them,
as the sole representative of Germany, was a
small gun-boat, which, as was pointed out in the
accompanying text, was "under sail only."   Against
these words the Emperor wrote, "What mockery
lies therein," and the picture, with this comment, was
laid before the Budget Commission of the Reichstag,
then engaged in the discussion of the naval estimates.
Moreover, the monarch had himself recourse to the
paint-brush, and exhibited in the Berlin Academy of
Arts a picture of an attack by a flotilla of torpedo
craft on a squadron of ironclads. No doubt he
hoped in this way to arouse sympathy for his ideas in
some who were not accessible to the ordinary methods
of political persuasion. The "Song to Aegir," the
Scandinavian Neptune, of which he composed the
music, was probably also intended to have a similar
operation.

But all these pleas and cajoleries had little or no
positive result. Indeed, taken in conjunction with
other phases of the Imperial activity, they seem rather
to have excited opposition in the breasts of the
members of the Reichstag, who possibly considered
themselves just as well qualified as the monarch to
estimate the degree and appreciate the needs of
Germany's maritime interests, and at any rate half-
suspected that his efforts directly to influence their

deliberations involved an encroachment on their constitutional privileges. The first naval estimates submitted in the new reign, which provided for the laying down of the unusually large number of four battleships, were got through the Reichstag without much difficulty, but when Admiral von Hollmann became Minister of Marine in the following year, he found that quite a different temper had taken possession of the Parliament. It was not only that the Emperor's general governmental acts had begun to stir up opposition; his oratorical flights in praise of sea-power and world-empire had also generated strong suspicions that he was urging Germany along a path which would lead her to ruin at home and disaster abroad. Hollmann's by no means exorbitant demands were branded both in the Reichstag and the press as "unconscionable," his programme as "boundless," and on every side were heard contemptuous and impatient references to "the awful fleet." For a decade the naval estimates were ruthlessly and recklessly cut down to, on an average, not far short of half their original figure, and finally, in 1897, the ministerial career of Hollmann was terminated by the unceremonious rejection of three out of the four cruisers which, in a special Memorandum, he had sought to prove were indispensable for the protection of the Empire's stake on the seas. And all this time the Emperor had never ceased to agitate, by word and deed, for the ideas which he had so much at heart and to which the Reichstag nevertheless showed itself so completely indifferent, if not actually hostile.

The change that came with the appointment of Admiral von Tirpitz to the Ministry of Marine was as complete as it was sudden, and it is to this very able man that we must look if we wish to find not only the intellectual author of German naval legislation, but the statesman who devised and directed the means by which it was popularized and passed through the Reichstag. The transformation which he effected was one both of policy and of method. The three rejected vessels which brought about Hollmann's fall represented a principle—that of "cruiser warfare." At that time the imperfectly-thought-out strategy of the German Naval Ministry was based on the two ideas of coastal defence and commerce destruction. Pitched battles between ships of the line on the high seas played a very secondary part in its calculations. In the programme which he submitted to the Reichstag, Hollmann laid it down that fifteen battleships would be sufficient for Germany's purposes, and those who are best qualified to form a judgment of the Empire's naval policy at that epoch are of opinion that this number was intended to be not merely a provisional, but a final estimate of the country's requirements in this type of vessel.

There are good reasons for supposing that in the Hollmann era no clear idea existed as to the problems with which Germany might be confronted in a naval war, and that his programmes were the product rather of vague general principles than of calculated odds and chances. In fact, one of his main difficulties with the Reichstag was his inability to justify his estimates by numerical demonstrations.

On the other hand, Admiral von Tirpitz's strength always lay chiefly in this, that he knew exactly what he wanted and why he wanted it. When he came into office, it was generally stated that he had years previously already laid before the Emperor a Memorandum embodying his conception of Germany's maritime needs, and how they could be satisfied, and it is certain that the main outlines of his policy were at any rate clearly sketched out in his head long before he was given an opportunity of carrying it out. He was recalled from the command of the East Asian Squadron to take charge of the Naval Ministry, and he seems to have employed his leisure on the homeward voyage in drafting a programme, which he had worked out in all its details before he took over his portfolio. In its very fundamental principles it was a reversal of that of his predecessor, for it was based on the idea, probably adopted from Mahan, that battleships alone are the decisive factors in naval warfare. As he himself put it to the Reichstag: "If we have a strong battle fleet, the enemy will have to defeat it before he can blockade our coasts. But in such circumstances he will, before he declares war on Germany, consider very carefully whether the business will cover its expenses and justify the risk." It was this principle of risk which he took as his standard of the Empire's naval requirements. From the literature which he has inspired it is evident that he is one of those who believe that Germany is destined some day, in the not very distant future, to occupy the position on the seas which now belongs to Great Britain. It was, however, impossible for a Minister of State to argue this belief in public, for the open confession of it would have at once produced incalculable complications in international affairs which would certainly not have contributed to its realization. Besides, the consummation which he wished for could in any case only be reached by gradual stages over a long period of years. The defensive formula which he invented was quite as effective for his immediate domestic purposes, and, as the sequel showed, was not appreciated abroad in its true and full significance. It was that "the German Fleet must be so strong that not even the greatest naval Power will be able to enter upon a war with it without imperilling its position in the world."

It was only after a good deal of hesitation, and some resistance, in high quarters that Admiral von Tirpitz was able to make his view prevail. Even courtly panegyrists admit that at the commencement of his term of office deep-seated differences of opinion existed between him and the Emperor on cardinal points of naval policy. The monarch was then a firm adherent of the cruiser-war theory, and no doubt had been responsible for its adoption by his Ministry of Marine.

It may be regarded as his most substantial contribution to the present strength of the German Fleet that he finally yielded to Admiral von Tirpitz's arguments.

In one other very essential respect the new Minister revolutionized the policy of his predecessor. In the Memorandum already referred to, Hollmann defined the needs of the navy only for the three succeeding years, and in the course of the debate on the estimates, he used these words : " Neither the Federated Governments nor the Reichstag will ever agree to be bound to a formal programme for years in advance. That is quite impossible, and even if both factors desired it, impossible. for the very simple reason that the art of war is changeable on sea just as it is on land, and that to-day no Naval Ministry can prophesy what we shall need ten years hence. It can only tell you what are our immediate requirements, and if the circumstances change, then our demands will change too. As to that there is no doubt whatever." Here again, Admiral von Tirpitz not merely modified, but diametrically reversed the policy of his predecessor, and, it may be added, of the Emperor. Starting from the conclusion that the main types of war vessel and their respective functions remain unaltered in principle throughout the ages, he induced the Reichstag to commit itself statutorily to a fixed warship establishment, a building programme of nearly twenty years' duration, and an automatic renewal of the units of the fleet when they had reached a prescribed age. This is the one absolutely new feature of German naval legislation, and it was undoubtedly the idea of the new Minister. That it has its merits appears from the facts that it has been imitated by France and found warm advocates in England.

Admiral von Tirpitz has, in fact, been the Bismarck of German naval policy, and just as the Iron Chancellor fulfilled the hopes of the men of the Frankfort National Assembly, so the smiling and urbane Minister of Marine has gone far towards realizing the dreams

of Friedrich List and Prince Adalbert of Prussia. It
may be questioned whether he would not have done
this work quite as effectually without the Emperor's
loud and tempestuous advocacy of his schemes on the
open stage of the world. The trumpet tones in which
William II. proclaimed his dreams of world-wide rule
and maritime dictatorship, not only exercised a disquieting effect in foreign countries, but conjured up in
the minds of many Germans unpleasant visions of
provocative and perilous adventure. Other nations
were anything but delighted at the prospects of being
swallowed up in a universal Teutonic Empire, however peaceful its conquests and however beneficent its
rule, and they took steps by which the successive
moves of German naval policy were successively
counteracted. But for the blunders of British and
French diplomacy over the annexation of Bosnia and
the Morocco affair, Germany would at this moment
have been much weakened both internally and externally by precisely the measures which were intended to make her strong. If, on the other hand,
there had been less hurry and less noise, and the
inevitable ebullitions of German Anglophobia had been
quietly and unostentatiously exploited as they occurred,
the Imperial Fleet might have been steadily built up
without causing a condition of chronic alarm throughout Europe, and without giving rise to such effective
counter-measures. It would not, perhaps, so soon
have reached its actual dimensions, but its comparative value would probably have been even greater
than it is. Germany would, too, have avoided that
rapid accumulation of taxes and debts, which, in spite
of her prosperity, has made those of her people who
must live on small incomes the most discontented
class in Europe. And here, possibly, we have one of
Admiral von Tirpitz's few mistakes, for if he had little
to do with the noise he was at any rate responsible for
the hurry. Whether it will prove to be a mistake in
the long run, the future must be left to show.

If we may judge from the discretion which he has shown by keeping as far as possible in the background, Admiral von Tirpitz would, if left to himself, have built up the German Fleet with the same silent and systematic persistency with which Bismarck, Roon, and Moltke prepared to crush France, and to some extent he combines in his character the qualities of these three. He is at any rate the adroitest politician, the ablest organizer, and the most far-sighted strategist in the Imperial service. Long before he was thought of as Naval Minister, he had won for himself among his colleagues, by the skill and thoroughness with which he grappled with every problem allotted to him, the title of "The Master." It was he who, against the ignorant protests of the older school of naval officers, chiefly concerned for the smartness of their paint, the cleanness of their decks, and the brightness of their brasswork, forced the torpedo upon them, and brought the service of this weapon up to the high pitch of efficiency which it has to-day attained in the German Fleet. As Chief of the Staff to the General Command of the Navy, he evolved fresh rules of strategy and new tactical formations, and insisted upon manœuvres being carried out in such a way as to test the value of both. He has been no less successful as statesman, politician, and diplomatist. Here, too, he deserves the name of "Master" among his contemporaries, for what he has done has been the greatest ministerial achievement of our day. It is true that he was favoured by an extraordinary run of luck that was vouchsafed to none of his forerunners, and that he would never have been able to drive his machine but for the energy generated by a series of international dissensions, but at the same time it must be conceded that he took advantage of his opportunities with rare promptitude and address.

He at once took the measure of the Reichstag, and saw how he could make it obedient to his will. It is

traditional in the higher ranks of the German official
hierarchy to despise popular assemblies, and to treat
them with an air of pedagogic superciliousness.
Hollmann had become so impatient at the continual
mutilation of his estimates that at last he thumped his
fist menacingly on the table. That precipitate action
sealed his fate. Admiral von Tirpitz recognized that it
would be better for him if he disguised his contempt,
and smothered his anger in his beard. In one of
Rostand's plays, a lady is asked how she passed the
sentries who were posted round a jealously guarded
camp, and she replies: "I smiled at them." If the Naval
Minister were to be asked how he induced the parties
who had been so obdurate to his predecessor's demands to pass his own so much more expensive
projects, he, too, might have replied: "I smiled at
them." Completely breaking with the tradition of
schoolmasterly superiority, he was all complacency
and urbanity to the ignorant mediocrities who had it
in their power to frustrate his designs. His beaming
rubicund countenance was ever the brightest and
most ingratiating feature in the debates on his bills
and estimates. His good humour was inexhaustible,
his courtesy unflagging, his patience undisconcert-
able. He knew exactly what he wanted, and thought
only of that. His mind was not clouded, like those
of so many of his ministerial colleagues, by religious or political prejudices. He was ready to accept
ships from the hands of Catholics or Socialists.
Whether they ranked the Pope above the Emperor,
or preferred a republic to a monarchy, was quite indifferent to him, if only they would grant him the
ships and the men he asked for.

In one of his many veiled conflicts with the Foreign
Office, Admiral von Tirpitz is understood to have exclaimed: "Politics are your affair—I build ships!"
and it was precisely because he attended strictly and
conscientiously to his own business that he was able
to do it so well. It was incumbent upon him as

administrator of the Navy to make it as strong and efficient as possible, and it lay with the Chancellors to decide whether the line he was following was consistent with the general policy of the Empire. That, against their own convictions and what they conceived to be Germany's foreign interests, they allowed him to have his own way, only proved their weakness and his strength.

While he was amiable and polite to all parties and persons who could assist him in the carrying out of his ideas, flattered their vanity by pretended confidences from the region of high politics, took them for cruises in war vessels, and had them deferentially escorted round Imperial shipyards, the Admiral was quick to appreciate the importance of winning the good graces of the Catholics, without whose favour, as party relationships stood and were likely to stand, he could hope to effect little. Young and active members of the Centre party, who showed a particular interest in the details of naval policy, were singled out for special attention, and soon were numbered among his most devoted champions. He likewise realized the value of popular support, and this was secured through the instrumentality of the Press Bureau of the Ministry of Marine. This institution was, and is, administered in the same spirit which gained the Admiral his parliamentary triumphs. The naval officers by whom it is manned receive all journalists, domestic and foreign, with open arms, and, according to the objects and nationality of their visitors, furnish them with ideas, information, and directions. No German writer on naval affairs could afford to dispense with official assistance so profusely and willingly supplied. The Press Bureau placed at his disposal all the historical and statistical data which could be used to demonstrate Germany's need of a big fleet, all the articles from the foreign press which were likely to have a stimulating effect upon his readers, all the details of ship and gun types which could safely be made public, all the rules of naval strategy and tactics which might be of service to him in the formulation of his themes. If diffidence or a spirit of independence prevented him from coming to the Press Bureau, the Press Bureau went to him, as will be seen from the following document which found its way into print :

"IMPERIAL MINISTRY OF MARINE,
 "NEWS OFFICE.

" BERLIN,
" ...., 1907.

"It has become known here that, some time ago, you published in —— articles of a maritime nature. For this reason the News Office gladly takes the opportunity of enquiring whether you would care to receive occasional batches of service material and press comments for possible use in further articles. In view of the impending Navy Bill, your support in the Press might be particularly valuable in the immediate future.

" Your most obedient servant,
" BOY-ED."

By such means the Admiral succeeded in obtaining a control, gentle, persuasive, and veiled, but none the less effective, over practically the entire body of writers on naval topics in the German Press. He would have been a less able and a less successful statesman if he had openly egged on his army of scribes to a violent campaign against Great Britain. He was much too shrewd to do that. While he flooded Germany with information of a provocative character, the Press Bureau was careful to impress upon its callers that nothing was farther from his thoughts than the wish to inspire articles calculated to inflame international animosities.

The unanimity of view on naval subjects which the Bureau imported into the German Press was naturally most effective. When the simple citizen found that all the papers to which he had access spoke with one voice, simultaneously adopting an identical attitude to a fresh situation or propounding a novel theory, he could only assume that they must be in the right.   The proposal that Great Britain should abandon her Two-Power standard and accept in its stead a ratio of three to two, which appeared almost at the same moment in a score of different papers while the 1912 Navy Bill was under process of dilution, is an instance in point.   Up till then all naval writers in Germany had been unanimous in protesting that agreements to fix a naval ratio between two countries were in their very nature impossible, and the suddenness and simultaneity of their conversion must have been due to the intervention either of Providence or the Marine Minister.   Indeed, the Minister's statement a year later in the Reichstag Budget Commission definitively set at rest any doubt that might have existed as to the original source of the proposal.   Since Bismarck, no one has shown such adroitness as Admiral von Tirpitz in the management of the Press.

In addition to controlling the naval views of independent publications, the Press Bureau also makes important direct contributions of its own to periodical literature with the annual *Nauticus* and the monthly magazine *Die Marine Rundschau*.   Both these publications are further testimonies to the ability with which the Admiral performs the duties of his office.

But with all his cleverness, perseverance, and patience, Admiral Tirpitz would never have reached his goal had not Germany been swept by successive waves of Anglophobia.   Both speeches in the Reichstag and articles in the Press make it quite evident that the motive uppermost in the minds of most deputies when they voted for the Navy Bills was the desire to impress, annoy, or terrify Great Britain.   The truth is that, but for the Boer War, the Bill of 1900 could never have been so much as introduced ; but for the perpetual international friction over Morocco and the fantastic legend of King Edward's designs against Germany, the Bills of 1906 and 1908 would have had but small chance of acceptance ; and but for Mr. Lloyd George's speech and Captain Faber's indiscretions—and, it should be added, the misrepresentations of both of them by Admiral von Tirpitz's Press—the Ministry of Marine would never have been able to win its last victory against the opposition of the Treasury and the misgivings of the Chancellor. The lesson of 1848 cannot be too thoroughly learnt. The naval movement of that year was almost entirely popular in its character. It arose out of a sense of wounded dignity, and fits of national temper, blind to all the prudential considerations of domestic and international politics, have given Germany to-day the second largest fleet and the largest Socialist party in the world. It may seem almost like a contradiction in terms to suggest that a national sentiment has contributed to swell German Socialism to its present dimensions. But, as will be be seen later, this is—for Germany, at any rate—no paradox, for in no other country does so small a proportion of the population constitute what is in practice and in effect the " will of the people."

It should have become clear that the part which the Emperor William has played in the formulation and carrying out of Germany's naval policy has been quite insignificant in comparison with that played by his Minister. The really effective work which the monarch has done for his fleet has been that of which the wider public has heard least. The Emperor's brain is not an originating or creative one, but it is keenly apprehensive, appreciative, and assimilative, and its owner was quick to perceive the value of many of the forces and institutions which have made the British Fleet supreme, not only in numerical strength but also in *esprit de corps* and organization. From his visits to England he took back much useful information as to the construction and handling of ships, and in many other respects he found British models which he considered worthy of imitation in his own country. Thus the Institute of Naval Architects was provided with a German counterpart in the Schiffbau-technische Gesellschaft, the ideals of self-discipline of sport were fostered in the Imperial Navy, and when the temperance movement in the British Fleet had developed sufficient strength to attract attention, the Emperor inaugurated a similar propaganda among his crews. As has already been seen, William II. has generously admitted the debt of the German Fleet to its British sister, and beyond all doubt he has done more than anyone else to incur it.

The Emperor has also been able to do a good deal towards the propagation of his naval ideas through his autocratic control over the official machinery of Prussia, which constitutes more than three-fifths of the area, and nearly that proportion of the population of Germany. In a country where the tentacles of the central authority reach to the remotest village this control means a great deal. In particular, through the Ministry of Education, the rising generation is being initiated into the mysteries of "world-policy" and sea-power. The teaching of history and geography is utilized to impress upon susceptible minds the importance of colonies and fleets, and to suggest with more or less precision and emphasis that Great Britain is the jealous rival who chiefly obstructs Germany's path to that "place in the sun" which is her due. The process which is commenced in the schools is continued at the universities. Indeed, here as elsewhere, Germany's professors have been the pioneers of her progress, and were putting forward her claim to sea-power long before the Emperor was born. Friedrich List, the father of German economics, urged, in 1840, that Denmark and Holland should be taken into the Germanic Confederation, which "would then obtain what it at present lacks—namely, fisheries and sea-power, ocean-borne trade, and colonies." In another passage he said:

"What intelligent citizens of those sea-ports (Hamburg and Bremen) can rejoice over the continual increase of their tonnage, when he reflects that a couple of frigates, putting out from Heligoland, could destroy inside twenty-four hours the work of a quarter of a century."

List also maintained that Germany was "called by nature to place herself at the head of the colonizing and civilizing nations," and "that the time had come for the formation of a Continental alliance against the naval supremacy of England." Treitschke, writing ot the European situation in the later thirties, said:

"Against so absolutely ruthless a commercial policy, inciting and making mischief all over the world, all other civilized nations seemed natural allies. England was the stronghold of barbarism in international law. To England alone was it due that, to the shame of humanity, naval warfare still remained organized piracy. It was the common duty of all nations to restore on the seas that balance of power, long existing on the Continent, that healthy equipoise which permitted no State to do exactly as it liked, and consequently assured to all a humane international law. The civilization of the human race demanded that the manifold magnificence of the world's history, which had once commenced with the rule of monosyllabic Chinese, should not end in a vicious circle with the empire of the monosyllabic Britons. As soon as the Eastern Question was reopened a far-sighted statesmanship was bound to attempt at least to restrict the oppressive foreign rule which the English Fleet maintained from Gibraltar, Malta, and Corfu, and to restore the Mediterranean to the Mediterranean peoples."

At the same time the Professor was teaching his students at the Berlin University that "the settlement with England will be the most difficult of all," and that "the result of our next war must be, if possible, the acquisition of some colony."

The modern schoolmasters and professors of Germany are working to produce a race inspired with the ambitions of List and the rancours of Treitschke, and imbued with the idea that an unexampled destiny awaits their nation. That the Emperor William early recognized what schools and universities might be made to do in this direction is clear from the speech with which he opened the Educational Conference convened by him in 1890, and in which he complained that the traditional curriculum " lacked a patriotic basis." "We should," he exclaimed, " rear patriotic Germans and not young Greeks and Romans." It was also with a political purpose that he recommended a reversal of the usual order in which history was taught —that is to say, that the most recent periods should be taken first, and the student led back step by step to the events of antiquity.

While the Emperor is not omnipotent in legislation, he is, in Prussia, at any rate, practically unfettered in administration—that more extensive and equally important branch of Government—and so the impulsions of his will can be forced down through the reticulations of the bureaucratic system till they are felt by the humblest official. He thus has at his disposal a large body of zealous co-operators anxious to comply with his desires even if they should have no direct relation to their official duties.

To appreciate the operation of this force, it is only necessary to turn over the pages of the German Navy League Handbook and notice how prominent a part the provincial agents of the central authority and subordinate members of the official body play in the propaganda of that organization. It is impossible to avoid the conclusion that, wherever difficulty has been experienced in forming a local branch of the League, gentle pressure has been brought to bear on the stationmaster, postmaster, or gymnasium-director of the town, and has compelled him to take the initiative. In numerous cases such persons have, of course, come forward and founded branches of the League without any prompting, knowing well that their zeal would be in accordance with the " wishes of the Emperor," and would be rewarded by preferment when a suitable opportunity arose.

The Navy League is the only instrument the Emperor possesses for systematically and persistently propagating his ideas on world-policy and sea-power among the German people as a whole. It was founded in 1898, at his personal instance, but in all probability at Admiral von Tirpitz's suggestion, with the assistance of funds principally furnished by the Krupp family, which, as the chief material beneficiary from any increase in the German Fleet, could well afford to invest a little money in this way. Even in Bismarck's time the head of the Krupp firm had been induced to start a number of newspapers to advocate the augmentation of those armaments from which he had derived a considerable proportion of his vast wealth, and it is one of the least edifying features of modern Germany that those of its citizens who show the most bellicose spirit have a direct personal interest in the waging of war. The financial founders of the Navy League included other prosperous manufacturers who were anxious to deserve decorations or titles, and who, in some instances, went so far as to compel their employees to join the organization and so help to swell its membership.

Three weeks before the League was constituted, the first Navy Bill had already received the Emperor's signature, and the order of these events is a plain demonstration that even then the measure was intended to be merely the thin end of the wedge. It is an interesting and significant fact that almost all the ruling houses of Germany have been induced to identify themselves with the League, though it is nominally an absolutely independent and unofficial organization. The Emperor's brother, Prince Henry of Prussia, has assumed the general protectorate, and among the protectors of the affiliated State federations are Prince George of Bavaria, the Kings of Saxony and Württemberg, the Grand Dukes of Baden, Hesse, the two Mecklenburgs, Oldenburg, and Saxe-Weimar, the Dukes of Anhalt, Saxe-Altenburg, and Saxe-Coburg-Gotha, the Princes of the two Lippes, Waldeck-Pyrmont, and the two Reusses, the Statthalter of Alsace-Lorraine, the Regent of Brunswick, and the Burgomasters of Hamburg and Bremen. Thus the State governments have a direct interest in the League, are under a moral obligation to promote its work, and, it may be added, bear a certain amount of responsibility for the manner in which its agitation is carried on. The purposes of the organization are defined in the statutes as follows:

"The German Navy League regards a strong German Fleet as necessary—principally in order to ensure the sea frontiers of Germany against the danger of war, to maintain the position of Germany among the Great Powers of the world, and to support the general interests and commercial communications of Germany as well as the safety of her citizens at work in oversea countries. Accordingly, it is the aim of the German Navy League to awaken, cultivate, and strengthen the interest of the German people for the importance and functions of the fleet."

The members of the League are divided into two classes—"individual" and "corporative." The latter are members of branches of other societies which enrol themselves in the League *en masse*. The most fruitful sources of support of this kind are those kindred bodies, the Pangerman Federation and the Colonial Association. On December 31, 1911, the corporative members numbered 756,000, the individual members 298,000. The qualifications for individual membership are the attainment of the sixteenth year and a money contribution, which, if not fixed by the branch, is left for the member to determine for him- or herself. The pecuniary contribution of a corporation joining the League is fixed by special arrangement in each case. From the accounts published it would appear that the average annual member's subscription falls a good deal short of sixpence. A considerable number of the members are young persons of both sexes who send in their names because it is a cheap and easy method of gratifying the association instinct, so strong in Germans, or for the sake of the dances and other purely social entertainments which are arranged by the branches.

A monthly paper, *Die Flotte*, which is published in an edition of 350,000 copies, is the League's chief organ in the Press, but the Central Office also issues immense quantities of pamphlets and leaflets. These are largely distributed with newspapers owned or controlled by the iron and steel and shipbuilding industries—what the Socialists call the "armour-plate Press"—but naturally find their way to all quarters to which Government influence can give them access. Under the name of "Communications," items of naval news and controversial paragraphs are sent out about once a week to all the papers, and though little notice is taken of them in the metropolitan Press, struggling provincial journals are very glad to have their columns filled up with topical matter by expert and authoritative pens. The League also publishes a profusely illustrated *Naval Album*, of which the Emperor every year buys 600 copies for distribution as prizes in the schools of Prussia—a typical example of the interaction of the wheels of the naval agitation and the Government machine. Lecturing, too, occupies a prominent place in the League's activity, and the Central Office keeps a stock of magic-lanterns and slides, which it lends out free of charge to the local branches. It also supplies uniforms, badges, and bunting for local festivities.

By far the most effective department of the League's activity is, however, the excursions to the German naval ports, which it arranges for the benefit of schoolmasters and their classes. The participants in these outings are, as far as possible, selected from the inland states and districts, in which it is most difficult to arouse enthusiasm for the sea and the fleet. They are taken to Kiel or Wilhelmshaven, received with effusive courtesy by the naval officers delegated to look after them, and escorted through the streets by a ship's band to the dockyards or war vessels, over which they are conducted by amiable guides, who supply them with all the information likely to stimulate their interest in what they have seen. If the distance they have travelled makes it impossible for them to return home the same day, naval barracks or storehouses which happen for the moment to be vacant are placed at their disposal as night quarters. So much official complaisance and amenity, especially in a country where neither of these qualities is particularly common in the public services, arouses in those on whom it is expended a flattering sense of their own and their national importance, and schoolmasters thus captivated will naturally, in due time, convey their impressions to their pupils. Though the numbers of persons thus dealt with are inevitably somewhat limited, the League unquestionably gains more ground in this way than it can hope to win by pamphlets which are read and lectures which are listened to mainly by the already convinced.

In spite, however, of official patronage and assiduous labour, the League has probably failed to fulfil the anticipations of its founders. Three years after its incorporation it had already attained an "individual" membership of 240,000, and in the decade which has since elapsed it has added only 59,000 to that number. The fact seems to be that its influence has not extended far beyond that section of the population which is, directly or indirectly, amenable to official pressure, and the adherence of which could be counted upon from the outset. In the fluctuations of its membership we have a barometer of the League's own internal crises and of the tense phases of the international situation. Very soon after it had been founded, a handful of purists among its members felt compunction as to the manner in which it was being financed and administered. The substantial subscriptions which flowed into its coffers from the pockets of the Krupps and other industrial magnates with a business interest in the building of warships seem to have been the chief ground for their complaints; but it is evident that the entire management of the organization had got into a scandalously lax state in consequence of the inexperience of those to whom it had been entrusted. In fact, the League seems to have existed at that time principally for the benefit of two classes of people— the wealthy snobs who purchased honours by supplying its funds, and the overpaid lecturers from the ranks of the retired naval officers on whom those funds were spent. Though the actual facts were hushed up, a sufficient inkling of them got about to excite the misgivings of the public, and in the next two years the membership (individual) dropped by 70,000. It began to revive as soon as the scandal was forgotten, and, under the stimulus of the first stages of the Morocco imbroglio, reached in 1907 its record figure of 324,000. At this juncture, however, it became known that during the elections of that year, the League's manager, General Keim, had been so indiscreet as to issue pamphlets against the Centre (Catholic) party. The result was a great exodus from the League in Bavaria and other Catholic districts, and its membership gradually declined, till at the end of 1910 it stood at 291,000. The crisis of the summer of 1911 and disclosures made in England gave it another push forward, and, with a jump of 6,500, the membership reached the figure given above. Exactly how far the League's membership and the apparent success of its agitation have been the causes, and how far the effects, of the naval movements of recent years, it would be difficult to decide. Its most effective work has, however, unquestionably been done through the schools, and this has as yet hardly had time to bear tangible fruit, since the German citizen is enfranchised only at the age of twenty-five years.

To Germany's neighbours, the League's agitation is always valuable, because it affords some indication as to what the next development of the Imperial naval policy is likely to be. When the too impetuous General Keim committed the dangerous blunder of giving offence to the Catholics, he was deposed by official intervention, and Admiral Koester, a trusted confidant of the Emperor, placed in charge of the organization. The admiral is every year the monarch's guest at the Kiel yachting week and other maritime occasions, and it is obviously no mere coincidence that his most emphatic pleas for more armoured cruisers, or whatever it may be, have generally been uttered shortly after one of their meetings. There cannot, in fact, be the slightest doubt that the Emperor is the real director of the Navy League, and that it puts forward no demand that has not already received his approval, in principle if not in detail. The League is, in short, little more that a Government department, the function of which is to carry on an agitation for more warships. It must, however, always be remembered that the League's demands represent not what the Government desires or expects to get, but what it wants to be asked for. In order that it may keep up the pretence that it is an unofficial and independent organization, the League must naturally avoid too close a correspondence between its own programme and that of the Ministry of Marine, and it is also guided by the principle that it is necessary to ask much in order to get little. Occasionally it makes a show of hurrying and worrying the Naval Minister, and of being positively objectionable to the Government, but no one suffers less than Admiral von Tirpitz from these " attacks " upon him, and there is nothing he would like better to see than the satisfaction of the demands by which they are accompanied.

CHAPTER VIII

THE ECONOMIC BASIS OF GERMAN NAVAL POLICY

In order to form an opinion as to the probable development of the Anglo-German problem, it is of cardinal importance to know whether Germany has the ability and the will to continue her recent policy of naval expansion. Assuming that her present economic tendencies remain unchecked, there can be little doubt as to her ability to do this. Should her population, her industry, and her commerce expand in the future at anything like the same rate as in the past, she will, before very long, be in a position to build and arm warships with almost as great facility as the United Kingdom, and to pay for and man them with even greater ease than this country.

A nation's economic strength depends upon the numbers and character of its population and the position and natural resources of the country it inhabits. In the size of her population alone Germany's advantage over the British Isles is already enormous, and it is still growing steadily. In 1871, the year of the foundation of the German Empire, the populations of the two countries were:

Germany	41,000,000
United Kingdom	31,800,000
Germany's advantage	9,200,000

In 1911, the two populations were:

Germany	65,400,000
United Kingdom	45,400,000
Germany's advantage	20,000,000

Thus the advantage of Germany in mere numbers had increased since 1871 by nearly 11,000,000, or by one and a half the total population of Canada. How rapidly this advantage is progressing may be gathered from the subjoined comparison of the natural increase of the populations of the two countries in 1910, the latest year for which figures are available in both cases :

	Births.	Deaths.	Natural Increase.
Germany	1,983,000	1,104,000	879,000
United Kingdom ...	1,123,000	630,000	493,000
Germany's advantage	—	—	386,000

An annual gain upon the United Kingdom of nearly 400,000 souls by excess of births over deaths is not, however, the only factor by which Germany is increasing her numerical superiority. Especially in recent years, she has benefited further in this respect by the decline of her emigration. During the four decades which have elapsed since the foundation of the Empire, the excess of natives embarking over those disembarking in the two countries has been as under :

Years.	Germany.	United Kingdom.
1871-1880	625,968	1,678,919
1881-1890	1,342,423	2,558,535
1891-1900	529,875	1,742,790
1901-1910	279,645	2,841,464

In the individual years of the decade which closed with 1911, the emigration from the two countries was as below :

Year.				Germany.	United Kingdom.
1902	...	...	...	...	32,098	101,547
1903	...	...	...	...	36,310	147,036
1904	...	...	...	...	27,984	126,854
1905	...	...	...	...	28,075	139,365
1906	...	...	...	...	31,074	194,671
1907	...	...	...	...	31,696	235,092
1908	...	...	...	...	19,883	91,156
1909	...	...	...	...	24,921	139,693
1910	...	...	...	...	25,531	233,709
1911	...	...	...	...	22,690	261,858
Totals	...	...		280,262	1,670,981

It would be some compensation to the British Isles for the loss of these 1,670,000 emigrants if they had all gone to British dependencies, that might some day be united to the Mother Country by the bonds of immutable federation, but large numbers of them went to foreign countries, and so were lost to the British Empire. In the United Kingdom during the nine years 1902 to 1910, the emigration to exceeded the immigration from non-European foreign countries by 606,000 souls. During 1911, 121,829 British passengers shipped in the British Isles for the United States, and though a considerable proportion of them doubtless represented return business and tourist traffic, a large residue of genuine emigrants must still have remained over. Fortunately Canada, Australasia, and South Africa now attract an ever-increasing proportion of the emigrants from the United Kingdom, but it is still an open question whether those dependencies can be regarded as a British asset for all future time. During the last few decades the centrifugal forces within them have unquestionably developed more rapidly than the centripetal forces, and while there has been a good deal of sentiment in favour of closer union the actual facts have been in the direction of disruption. It is on the arrest of that tendency, and the substitution for it of a federative consolidation, that the whole future of the British Empire depends. For the present, it is inexpedient to regard the exodus from the British Isles as anything else than a sapping of the national strength, and it appears all the more strongly in that light when it is contrasted with the drying up of the stream of emigration from Germany.

It is also very significant that the decline in the drain on Germany's population, apparent from the figures set forth above, is due not merely to the reduction of her emigration, but also, to a considerable extent, to the return to her shores of many who had left them in earlier years. Some of these never intended to settle abroad definitively, but went to the United States to complete their industrial or commercial training. It is characteristic of modern Germany that many of her commercial leaders have spent several years in the States, studying the latest methods of making money quickly, and that their success in their native country has been largely owing to what they learnt on the other side of the Atlantic. American influences have, in fact, played a very large part in Germany's most recent development. But apart from these business students, Germany's rapid progress in material prosperity has drawn back to her many of her sons who had bidden her what they regarded as a final farewell, but who, having failed to find in the New World the Eldorado of their dreams, have been able to realize in their old home the hopes with which they once quitted it.

Moreover, besides ceasing to export her own people, Germany has commenced on a considerable scale to import those of other nations. In the last fifteen years her slight losses through emigration have been more than made good by the influx of foreign labourers required by her agriculture and industry. At the time of the professional census taken in June, 1907, no fewer than 766,000 foreigners were in employment in Germany. If the count had been made a little later in the year the number would

have been much larger, for the demand of German
agriculture for hands does not attain its maximum till
the season of the grain and root harvests. In the year
1911, between 350,000 and 400,000 aliens were taken
into Germany under contract to work on the fields.
Much of this seasonal labour would undoubtedly settle
permanently in the country if it were permitted to do
so, but in order to prevent an aggravation of the
Polish problem in Prussia—a majority of the seasonal
workers being Russian or Austrian Poles—the foreign
agricultural hands are compelled to recross the frontier
as soon as their contracts have expired. Even on
works of a military character, the details of which it
is desired to keep secret, it is found necessary to
employ foreigners, and from figures which have been
given in the daily press, it would appear that, in
spite of all the efforts of the authorities to eliminate it,
the alien element in the labour engaged in the widen-
ing of the Kiel Canal has varied from about 20 to
35 per cent. At the ordinary censuses which have
been taken since the foundation of the Empire, the
numbers of foreigners resident in Germany were as
under:

1871	...	...	...	...	...	206,755
1875	...	...	...	...	...	290,799
1885	...	...	...	...	...	372,792
1890	...	...	...	...	...	433,254
1895	...	...	...	...	...	486,190
1900	...	...	...	...	...	778,698
1905	...	...	...	...	...	1,028,560
1910	...	...	...	...	...	1,259,873

Among the million and a quarter foreigners counted
in 1910 were 635,000 Austrians, 144,000 Dutch, 138,000
Russians, 104,000 Italians, 68,000 Swiss, 32,000 Hun-
garians and Croats, 26,000 Danes, 19,000 French,
18,000 British, 18,000 North Americans, 14,000 Luxem-
burgers, 13,000 Belgians, and 10,000 Swedes.

At the present moment, there seems little prospect
of a substantial modification of the numerical relationship of the population of the British Isles and Germany,

in consequence of changes in their birth-rates. In
both countries human fertility has fallen off rapidly,
but it remains much greater in Germany than in the
United Kingdom. During the fifteen years ended with
1910 the birth-rate per thousand of population was in
the two countries :

Year.	United Kingdom.	Germany.	Germany's Advantage.
1896	29·0	37·5	8·5
1897	28·9	37·2	8·3
1898	28·7	37·3	8·6
1899	28·5	37·0	8·5
1900	28·2	36·8	8·8
1901	28·0	36·9	8·9
1902	28·0	36·2	8·2
1903	28·0	34·9	6·9
1904	27·7	35·2	7·5
1905	27·1	34·0	6·9
1906	27·0	34·1	7·1
1907	26·3	33·2	6·9
1908	26·6	33·0	6·4
1909	25·7	31·9	6·2
1910	25·0	30·7	5·7

It is true that Germany's advantage, which was
8·5 per thousand of population in 1896, had, by 1910,
sunk to 5·7, but simultaneously her death-rate declined
from 22·1 to 17·1 per thousand, while that of the
United Kingdom dropped only from 16·9 to 14 during
the fifteen-year period. In a recent newspaper article,
Professor Julius Wolf, of Breslau, an eminent
economist, pointed out that the birth-rate of Germany
exceeded that of England alone by only ·6 in the five
years 1851-55, whereas by 1881-85 its excess had risen to
3·5 and by 1908 to 5·5. While he apparently wished to
suggest that the fecundity of England was falling even
more rapidly than that of his own country, he at the
same time admitted the contradictory conviction that
the annual natural increase of the population of
Germany, which is at present between 800,000 and

900,000 souls, would, within measurable time, drop to 600,000, 400,000, or even lower.

It is only quite recently that the German authorities have shown signs of waking up to the decline in their country's human fertility, though it has been going on steadily since 1876, when the Empire's births numbered 42·6 per thousand of population. Early in 1912, the Prussian Government instituted an enquiry as to the causes of the phenomenon and the possibility of counteracting them, but it is very doubtful whether the investigation will lead to the discovery of an effective antidote. The tendency has been an invariable concomitant of the concentration of population in large towns, and is no doubt mainly of artificial rather than physiological origin both in the United Kingdom and Germany. In the latter country it has had a special cause in the extraordinarily rapid inflation of the cost of urban dwelling accommodation, which renders small families or overcrowding the only alternatives for the artisan classes. On the other hand, Germany possesses in her proprietary peasants and her Catholics a trustworthy bulwark against the danger of depopulation. Neither the incentives nor the opportunities for an interference with the natural law of multiplication exist in the rural districts in anything like the same degree as they do in the towns, and in no country in the world can the Church of Rome exact a more unquestioning obedience to its social decrees than it does in the Catholic areas of Germany.

Thus we find that, in 1909, whereas the birth-rate in Berlin was only 22 and in Hamburg 25·8 per 1,000, in the agricultural province of East Prussia it was 32·8, in Catholic Westphalia 38·8, and in Posen, where, it is true, it was assisted by the superior fertility of the Slav, as high as 39·5. It is, of course, unlikely that these safeguards will always retain their present effectiveness, but their operation will certainly be felt for a long time to come. Should the prediction of Leroy-Beaulieu and Professor Schmoller be verified, and the end of the century see the German nation swollen to 200,000,000 souls, it cannot be doubted that, other things remaining as they are, the disproportion between its numbers and those of the population of the British Isles will be much more pronounced than it is to-day.

Numbers alone do not, of course, count for everything, even as between nations living under similar economic conditions. Superiority of quality can make good almost any quantitative inferiority. The question must therefore be asked, whether the character, gifts and attainments of the Briton are, on the average, so much superior to those of the German as to compensate for the latter's enormous numerical superiority. And, undoubtedly, it can only be answered in the negative. While the German is slow, and lacks intuition, independence and initiative, he is, on the other hand, patient, industrious, thrifty, and sober. Though he has but little originality, he is a close observer, a diligent imitator, a laborious thinker-out of other men's thoughts. Indeed it is not infrequently he who thinks them out to their logical and their practical conclusions. If he fails where rapid improvisation is needed, and has difficulty in adapting himself to a sudden and unforeseen situation, he succeeds wherever faithful adherence to law, rule, regulation, prescription, discipline, organization, method, schedule, or pattern is the essential condition of success. Whatever is known by others he too will know ere long, and he may be the first to apply the knowledge to practical use. An invention or a fresh idea may give another nationality a momentary advantage, but the German will adopt it promptly, and will never remain far behind in the race. The whole history of German development during the last couple of centuries has been one long record of the adoption and adaptation of the ideas of other nations. Without Hume, as Professor Schulze-Gaevernitz has admitted, there would have been no Kant; without Louis XIV.,

Frederick the Great is unthinkable; without Napoleon, Moltke would never have planned his campaign of 1870. German industry has been copied stage by stage and process by process from that of Great Britain. In particular, both the ships and methods of Germany's Navy as well as of her mercantile marine have been based upon British models. The copying and the imitation have, however, been no mere apish mimicry, but the intelligent comprehension of principle and the sedulous application of scientific law; and in this way the German has frequently surpassed his master.

It would also be difficult to exaggerate the importance to Germany of her large infusion of Jewish blood. There are, indeed, those who regard the latest phases of the Empire's development as a specifically Semitic, and not at all as a Teutonic phenomenon. Germany's banks and financial houses are almost exclusively in the hands of Jews, and that race is the leaven of her commerce. Herr Ballin, the architect of the Hamburg-America Line, the biggest shipping concern in the world; Herr Rathenau, the organizer of the Allgemeine Electrizitäts-Gesellschaft, the leading electrical undertaking of Europe; and the Loewes, who have won international repute for German small arms and machine tools, are all Jews, and the list might be extended almost indefinitely. Jews throng the front ranks in Germany's law, medicine, art, music, literature, drama, and journalism. They are to be found everywhere exercising their unrivalled flair for the public's wants and their marvellous capacity for organization. Of the entire population of the Empire 111 out of every 10,000 are professing Israelites, whereas in the United Kingdom the ratio is only 20 to every 10,000. In some of the principal German towns the proportion of the Jews is, of course, much higher than it is on the average for the whole country; and practically the entire city of Berlin is their property. To some extent, at any rate, the partial removal of the disabilities which formerly weighed on this highly-gifted commercial race has contributed to Germany's rapid economic advance; and the merit is in no small measure theirs if it can be said that the qualities of the German mind are to-day as conducive to the creation and accumulation of material wealth as the characteristics of any other nationality.

On the other hand, a danger undoubtedly lies in the defects of the German's qualities. He inclines to formalism and rigidity, and his love of law and rule is already exposing him to the risk of being strangled by legislation. Moreover, there are unmistakable signs that his prosperity has been too sudden, and that his wealth is accumulating too rapidly. In the larger towns, and especially in the capital, the traditional thrift, frugality and idealism of the German have been replaced by a luxury, a self-indulgence, a crude materialism, and a delight in vulgar ostentation, which bode ill for the future of the race. The Lutheran religion is powerless, if not actually dead, and in its stead a scientific hedonism, which applies to pleasure and sensuality all the method and system which in other directions have done so much for Germany, is asserting its maleficent sway over the urban mind. Berlin is now the metropolis of European vice, and, strange though it may seem, there are many of its citizens who seem quite proud of this evil pre-eminence, regarding it apparently as a legitimate title to international fame.

It is not without significance that the article most widely advertised in Germany at the present day is champagne—either the French product or the inferior and deleterious native imitation known as "Sekt." This may indicate wealth, but it also points to a perilous habit of expenditure. It cannot be denied that the disposition to live for money and the luxuries it can buy has developed disquieting strength in the British Isles of recent years, but the Briton has an effective antidote in the bracing self-discipline of sport.

In Germany sport is still only the cult of coteries, and its stimulating principles cannot be said to play an appreciable roll in the national life. Whether they will, at some future date, impose an effectual restraint on the present inclination towards enervating amusements, is a question to which it is, at the moment, impossible to return an answer.

Strenuous efforts are being made by the Governments of some of the German States to awaken an interest in sports, and especially by that of Prussia, where the Emperor and the Crown Prince have placed themselves at the head of the movement. The monarch's encouragement of sailing and rowing, his regular attendances at the regattas at Kiel, on the Elbe estuary, and on the lakes round Berlin, have, of course, a more definite political purpose than the mere maintenance or improvement of the physique of the nation. It is here his outspoken purpose to direct the attention of his subjects to the water, on which he has told them that their future lies. The Emperor has, however, exerted himself to promote other types of sport—for instance, by the introduction of football into the Prussian Army; while the Crown Prince not only is himself a first-class all-round sportsman, but loses no opportunity of inciting others to follow in his footsteps. That both father and son have acquired their love of sport from English associations and English example is indisputable. Indeed, the former has repeatedly admitted as much. Addressing the troops about to embark on the expedition to China in 1900, he said: "The first care must be for the health of the men, and the principal thing is to keep them occupied with exercise, games, and races right round the deck. It is the experience of the English, too, that physical exercise is the main thing." Speaking to another batch of men setting out on the same errand, he said: "We can learn here from the English, who are very practical in these matters. Give your men plenty of running games." Similarly, the "path-finder" movement, which is making great progress in Germany under the active patronage of Field-Marshal Baron von der Goltz, was considered worthy of steady official cultivation only after the boy scout had become a popular figure in English life. The encouragement of sport in Germany is, in fact, but one more instance of Teutonic imitativeness. It has its origin in the conviction, that not only the Battle of Waterloo, but also Great Britain's commercial, industrial, and political position in the world was won on the playing-fields of Eton, and that to attain a like pre-eminence Germany must adopt similar methods. This cult has, however, still many obstacles to overcome, not only in the national habits of the German race, but also in the prejudices and traditions of its dominant classes. The feeling that Germany should follow the laws of her own national development, and close her doors to foreign influences, which seems to be growing in strength among one section of the population, finds expression in the complaints, uttered by members of the old Prussian nobility, that the Crown Prince would be better occupied in attending more closely to his military duties, and in mastering the intricacies of the bureaucratic machine, than in shooting elephants in India, playing tennis at Heiligendam, or toboganning in Switzerland. What will be the ultimate issue of this struggle of forces it is impossible to foresee.

Trustworthy data as to changes in the physical condition of the German people are not obtainable. German *laudatores temporis acti* lay much stress on the decline in the percentage of the young men due to enter the Army and pronounced by the doctors to be fit for military service, but the returns on this point are a very uncertain guide. Medical standards have changed and are still changing. Certain forms of nervous constitution which were formerly regarded as voluntary personal peculiarities are now classified as specific disease. Hereditary predispositions can now be detected at a much earlier stage than was possible twenty years ago. Moreover, it is certain that the Army doctors sound for political as well as physical disease, and that the medical examination is used to give preference to the rural recruits who are less likely than the young artisans of the towns to have been inoculated with the Socialistic virus. For it is felt that to give a military training to a Socialist may mean nothing more than to furnish an efficient fighter to the revolution which looms up menacingly in some Germans' dream of their Empire's future. Even if the diminution of military fitness were real it would not necessarily signify a depression of the national stamina, but might easily be accounted for by the advance of medical skill, which saves the lives of many persons of inferior vitality who at an earlier period would inevitably have perished in infancy.

The German people is undoubtedly passing through one of those phases of rapid development to which the word "transition" is generally applied, but it would be rash to assume that the outcome of it will be national degeneration or reduced efficiency in the contest for the commercial, industrial, and political supremacy of the world. Those whose position is threatened by Germany's challenge will do well to concentrate their attention on those factors which tend to make her strong rather than on those which appear to have the opposite tendency.

Having glanced at the human element in the problem, let us now, for a moment, consider the material element. The prime natural resources of a country are its area and the fertility of its soil, and in respect of these Germany again has a great advantage over the British Isles, in spite of the barrenness of those vast tracts in the north of the Empire which at present are covered only with heather and gorse, or with stunted fir-trees of little utility except as firewood. The total extents of the two countries and the areas under the principal types of cultivation in 1910 are shown in the subjoined table :

	United Kingdom.	Germany.
	Acres.	Acres.
Total area	77,716,992	133,585,000
Woods and forests	3,069,070	34,272,000
Total cultivated area	46,931,637	78,632,139
Wheat	1,857,671	4,842,196
Barley	1,899,130	3,879,090
Oats	4,116,137	10,594,341
Rye	57,004	15,280,235
Potatoes	1,144,465	8,141,323

The harvests yielded by these crops in 1910 were as below:

	United Kingdom.	Germany.
	Tons.	Tons.
Wheat	1,540,700	3,861,500
Barley	1,430,200	2,902,900
Oats	3,110,500	7,900,400
Rye	6,700	10,511,200
Potatoes	6,450,800	43,468,400

The numbers of the principal animals bred for human food in the two countries were in 1907, the date of the last German agricultural census, as under:

	United Kingdom.	Germany.
Cattle	11,630,142	20,630,544
Sheep	30,011,833	7,703,710
Pigs	4,055,793	22,146,532

In the consideration of the foregoing figures, allowances must be made for differences of national habit, the prominent place taken by rye, bread, and potatoes in the German's diet, and his preference for pork over mutton. It should further be mentioned that in 1909 Germany produced 12,684,874 tons of sugar-beet and 44,453,640 gallons of grape juice for the manufacture of wine. Moreover, while the tendency in the United

Kingdom is for land to go out of cultivation, in Germany it is the reverse. Till that problematical date when Germany possesses colonies in the temperate zone suitable for settlement by white men, her Government will do all in its power to restrain its subjects from emigration. For military and political reasons it is anxious to retain control over as large a number of people as possible, and it also desires to keep the Empire in a position to feed itself in case of need. Much attention has consequently been given of late years to the problem of repopulating the rural areas, which are being drained of their best blood by the call of the towns, and with this object in view great efforts are being made to reclaim the three-and-a-half million acres of waste, moor and marsh land which at present is put to no use whatever. Scientific opinion seems to encourage the idea that a considerable proportion of this might be brought under profitable cultivation if the proper methods were employed, and the probability is that before many years have gone by Germany will have largely increased her yield of agricultural products.

But if the agricultural resources of Germany are more productive than those of the British Isles, she has an even greater superiority over this country in her mineral treasures. In a recent lecture, Professor Engler, of Carlsruhe, estimated the total coal deposits of Europe at 700,000,000,000 tons, of which 416,000,000,000 tons or nearly three-fifths are situated in Germany, and only 193,000,000,000 tons in the British Isles. On the basis of the present rate of consumption, he calculated that the British stores of coal would last for 700, those of Germany for 3,000 years. A more cautious estimate of Professor Milch puts the life-time of the British coalfields at 300 years, and that of the Lower Rhenish and Upper Silesian beds, from which Germany draws the bulk of her supplies, at over a thousand years. In addition to these stores of solid fuel, Germany possesses beneath her own soil large reservoirs of petroleum, which already satisfy quite a considerable proportion of her requirements, and which every year yield more abundantly. In 1911 Germany's consumption of imported petroleum amounted to 925,000 metric tons, and her own production was 143,000 tons. As recently as the last lustrum of the nineteenth century she obtained from her wells no more, on the average, than 29,000 tons of oil annually, so that in ten years the output has increased fivefold. Germany also possesses in her voluminous and rapid rivers inexhaustible reserves of water-power, and the Bavarian Government is understood to be at present preparing a scheme for the exploitation on a large scale of the streams which rush down the northern slopes of the Alps for the generation of electrical energy. This project will possibly create in South Germany an industrial centre as busy and productive as those of the North and West of the Empire.

" The God who made iron grow " has likewise bountifully endowed the country, one of whose poets gave Him this name, with the cardinal metal of industry. A computation made by a Swedish committee for the International Geological Congress held at Stockholm in 1910 showed the utilizable supplies of iron ore in Europe and their metallic contents to be as under:

Country.	Ore.	Metallic Contents of Ore.
	Tons.	Tons.
Germany	3,607,000,000	1,270,000,000
France	3,300,000,000	1,140,000,000
United Kingdom	1,300,000,000	455,000,000
Sweden	1,158,000,000	740,000,000
Russia	864,000,000	387,000,000
Spain	711,000,000	349,000,000
Norway	367,000,000	124,000,000
Luxemburg	270,000,000	90,000,000
Austria	250,000,000	90,000,000
Greece	100,000,000	45,000,000
Belgium	62,000,000	25,000,000
Hungary	33,000,000	13,000,000
Italy	6,000,000	3,000,000
Switzerland	1,600,000	800,000

From this estimate it would appear that Germany possesses between two and three times as much as the British Isles of the principal metallic basis of all industries. The development of the production of the chief minerals in both countries during the last thirty years will be seen from the following tables:

COAL PRODUCTION.

Year.				United Kingdom.	Germany.
				Tons.	Metric Tons.
1880	...	...	...	...	146,969,000	46,974,000
1885	...	...	...	...	159,351,000	58,320,000
1890	...	...	...	...	181,614,000	70,238,000
1895	...	...	...	...	189,661,000	79,169,000
1900	...	...	...	...	225,181,000	109,290,000
1905	...	...	...	...	236,129,000	121,299,000
1910	...	...	...	...	264,433,000	152,828,000

Metric ton = 2,204 pounds.

IRON ORE PRODUCTION.

Year.				United Kingdom.	Germany (including Luxemburg).
				Tons.	Metric Tons.
1880	...	...	...	...	18,026,000	7,239,000
1885	...	...	...	...	15,418,000	9,158,000
1890	...	...	...	...	13,781,000	11,406,000
1895	...	...	...	...	12,615,000	12,350,000
1896	...	...	...	...	13,701,000	14,162,000
1900	...	...	...	...	14,028,000	18,964,000
1905	...	...	...	...	14,591,000	23,444,000
1910	...	...	...	...	15,226,000	28,710,000

Thus, whereas in the United Kingdom the production of iron ore declined substantially in the period dealt with, in Germany it increased nearly fourfold. The statistics with regard to the manufacture of pig-iron and steel tell a similar tale, and a few figures from

them may be inserted, though they properly belong
to a subsequent section of this chapter. During the
past thirty years the development of the production of
pig-iron in the two countries has been as under :

Year.				United Kingdom.	Germany.
				Tons.	Metric Tons.
1880	...	...	...	...	7,749,000	2,713,000
1885	...	...	...	...	7,415,000	3,673,000
1890	...	...	...	...	7,904,000	4,651,000
1895	...	...	...	...	7,703,000	5,455,000
1900	...	...	...	..	8,959,000	8,507,000
1903	...	...	...	...	8,935,000	10,018,000
1905	...	...	...	...	9,608,000	10,875,000
1910	...	...	...	...	10,012,000	14,794,000

It will be noticed that thirty years ago the United
Kingdom manufactured nearly three times as much
pig-iron as Germany, and that the latter country in
1910 had the advantage by approximately 50 per cent.
In the production of crude steel the relationship has
changed even more emphatically to the disadvantage
of the British Isles, as will be seen from the subjoined
table :

Year.				United Kingdom.	Germany.
				Tons.	Metric Tons.
1890	...	...	...	...	3,579,000	2,232,000
1893	...	...	...	...	2,950,000	3,163,000
1895	...	...	...	...	3,290,000	3,963,000
1900	...	...	...	...	4,901,000	6,362,000
1905	...	...	...	...	5,812,000	10,067,000
1910	...	...	...	...	6,515,000	12,281,000

In the two preceding tables special prominence has
been given to the year, inserted out of the quinquennial

series, in which Germany overtook the United Kingdom in these vital branches of industry. In addition to coal and iron Germany owns considerable deposits of the other principal metallic ores, from which she raised in 1910 the following quantities :

						Tons.
Copper ore	...	...	...	...	...	926,000
Zinc ore	...	...	...	...	...	718,000
Lead ore	...	...	...	...	...	148,000

Further, Germany is, in the words of one of her professors, "the richest country in salts that exists on earth," and among her saline treasures are vast deposits of soluble potash of a quality such as has, up to the present, been found in no other part of the world. She has, in fact, through a strange geological caprice, a natural world monopoly of a substance which is now practically indispensable to the manufacturer of artificial fertilizers, and this endowment not only is of inestimable value to her own agriculture, but has also been the origin of an important branch of her export trade. In the course of 1911 she shipped abroad nearly 2,000,000 tons of these potash salts, the bulk of it going to the United States.

It may well be asked why Germany, with her large, plodding and methodical population, her agricultural resources, and her inexhaustible mineral deposits, has been so tardy in taking her natural place in the ranks of the first industrial and commercial nations of the world. The answer will be found in those conditions of political division and confusion which have been either sketched out or indicated in earlier chapters. The lack of unity in government, administration, legislation, weights, measures, and coinage ; centuries of misrule, internecine strife, and foreign warfare ; a perpetual sense that the conditions were unstable and could not last, coupled with blank uncertainty as to the manner in which they might develop—these have been the causes which for so many centuries made Germany the Cinderella among the big nations of

Europe. Even in unbroken peace and under stable and uniform government the repair of the havoc wrought by the Thirty Years' War would have been the work of many generations, but these conditions were denied her till the closing quarter of the nineteenth century. The armies of the Great Elector could be maintained only by the help of foreign subsidies, and the wars of Frederick the Great so completely exhausted Prussia that he was compelled, in his extremity, to melt down the solid silver balustrade of the musicians' gallery in the Berlin Palace, and replace it with the plated woodwork which is still pointed out to tourists as a monument of kingly self-abnegation. Before the fruits of Frederick's conquests and administrative reforms could be reaped, the Napoleonic tempest burst upon Europe, and the industrial progress of Germany was again violently arrested. The French occupation and the exhausting indemnities exacted by the conqueror were not in themselves so debilitating as the consequences of Napoleon's attempt to ruin Great Britain by closing the Continent to her trade, and of the retaliatory blockade by which this measure was answered.

Under the conditions thus created, Germany's shipping languished and almost expired, and her export trade received a blow from which some branches of it have never been able to recover. The chronic distress among the weavers of the Erzgebirge, which has been so poignantly depicted by Hauptmann in his play, "Die Weber," is attributed by some writers to the closing of foreign markets to Silesian linen through the Continental blockade, and in Germany there is a curiously illogical tendency to blame Great Britain rather than Napoleon for this calamity. The flag of Prussia practically disappeared from the seas ; at the commencement of the Napoleonic wars the ship-owners of that State possessed an aggregate fleet of 1,100 vessels, but when the conclusive peace arrived the number had sunk to 700, and these were for the most part antiquated and of little value. While the blockade was in force the prices of exotic commodities, such as sugar, coffee, rice, tobacco, and cotton, rose in Germany to three, four, and even five times their former level, and in its impoverishment the population was all the less able to pay the higher rates. In Hanover, according to an official computation, the consumption of some of these articles was reduced during the blockade to a hundredth part of what it had previously been.

The War of Liberation, by which the Napoleonic yoke was shaken off, was financed largely by voluntary contributions. In the principal centres the Prussian Government opened subscription offices, to which, in default of money, noblemen and their wives brought their family plate and their personal jewellery, and members of the poorer classes any trinkets or trifles made of the precious metals they might possess. To such straits had Germany been reduced by the Napoleonic era.

The repartition of Europe carried out by the Congress of Vienna left 'n Germany no sense of finality. How deeply the population was imbued with the feeling that further changes in the direction of national unity were inevitable, was shown by the spontaneity with which the Revolution of 1848 blazed forth simultaneously in a score of different places. But so long as that feeling of suspension and uncertainty prevailed, the fundamental conditions of industrial and commercial progress were lacking. The country recovered so slowly from the convulsions of the first fifteen years of the nineteenth century, that a careful and conscientious investigator like Professor Sombart calculates that the economic condition of its people in 1830 was lower than it had been in 1802.

The Zollverein, by which Germany became a Customs unit, only partially removed the hindrances to trade and traffic which had arisen from the multiplicity and multifariousness of her systems of government.

Though, for the purposes of trade, the internal frontiers were abolished, and it was no longer necessary, as it had been at the close of the eighteenth century, to pay sixteen separate Customs dues on a journey from Dresden to Magdeburg, a great variety of restraints on traffic continued to impede the exchange of commodities for many decades to come. Moreover, the Zollverein was only of gradual growth. As formed in the years 1834 and 1835, it included Prussia, Bavaria, Württemberg, Saxony, the two Hesses, Baden, Nassau, the Thuringian States, and the town of Frankfort-on-Main. Ten years more were to elapse before it took in the large territories of Hanover and Brunswick; and the two chief Hanse towns, Hamburg and Bremen, did not accept Customs membership of the Empire till 1888. And while the first Customs Union Treaty of 1833 bound its signatories to aim at uniformity of weights, measures, and coinage, this ideal was not actually realized till the metric system was made compulsory throughout the Empire in 1872. At the outbreak of the great war of 1870 no fewer than seven different systems of currency still obtained in Germany.

Another bond which had to be burst before Germany could freely extend her limbs was the serfdom of the peasantry. Under the agrarian system generally prevailing in the country at the commencement of last century, the entire peasant population was tied fast to the soil by innumerable allodial obligations to the larger landowners. All the work on the estate of the junker was performed by the peasant proprietors of the vicinity, who, with their own horses or oxen, ploughed his land, sowed his seed, and reaped and threshed his crops. That they might not escape these labours, they were legally bound to the places of their birth. Until this modified enslavement was done away with, and the rural population was permitted to migrate to the towns, the modern industrial development of Germany was impossible through lack of labour, if for no other reason. Attempts at agrarian reform were made by Stein and Hardenberg from 1807 to 1821, but it was not till the second half of the century that the *adscriptus glebi* was fully and finally abolished. Meanwhile the United Kingdom had passed completely over to factory and machine manufacture, with the assistance of workmen drawn from the rural districts.

Yet another impediment which shackled German industry in the earlier part of the nineteenth century was the guild organization of her trades. For hundreds of years the guilds had followed the selfish and short-sighted policy of restricting output and smothering enterprise in the interests of their members. They imposed regulations limiting the number of apprentices who could be indentured by the individual master, controlling his output, and fixing the times, prices, and methods both of the purchase of his raw materials and of the sale of his finished commodities. This entire system had to be swept away before Germany could adapt herself to cosmopolitan trade.

It has been seen how the opposition of Hanover to the construction of a railway through her territory made it necessary to convey building material for the naval base of Wilhelmshaven by the long and circuitous sea-route; and this was but a crowning example of the purblind and petty policy by which German Princes had long obstructed the provision of those channels of communication that are the arteries and veins of a country's commerce. In consequence of political division and princely jealousy, Germany was, at the beginning of last century, almost entirely devoid of highways. Especially in the northern districts, traffic had to be carried on along rough tracks that were hardly passable in the winter and after rainy weather. It was only in the forties of the nineteenth century that the construction of highways was systematically taken in hand. By 1857 Germany had nearly 20,000 miles of good roads; ten years later a further 10,000 miles had been added; and by the close of the century the aggregate length had increased to over 80,000 miles. The state of the roads naturally reacted on the speed of travel and transport. In the early decades of the nineteenth century twenty-five miles was considered a good day's journey, and it was little less than a revolution when, in 1824, the Prussian Minister of Posts introduced the English mail speed of forty-five miles, and so reduced the distance between Berlin and Magdeburg from two days and a night to fifteen hours. Even then, owing to the multiplicity of authorities, the postal service was very slow in developing. In 1842, two years after the adoption of national penny postage in England, the annual epistolary correspondence of Prussia amounted to only a letter and a half per head of population, and ten years later this proportion had not more than doubled. By the Prusso-Austrian postal agreement of 1850 the number of independent post-offices in Germany was reduced to seventeen, but even the postal tariff of the North German Confederation was a volume of 300 printed pages. It was not till 1868 that Germany received the blessing of unified postal rates.

Railways, too, came a little too soon for Germany. If that great transformation in locomotion had succeeded instead of preceding her unification, she would have adopted it with less doubt and hesitation, and have been quicker in reaping the benefits of it. The prophetic eye of Friedrich List at once recognized the enormous importance of the iron road, and he employed his most eloquent persuasions in favour of a plan for " raising Germany by a great net of railways to the rank of the industrial countries, and so uniting the severed limbs of the German nation to a sound and vigorous body." But this keen-visioned seer was far in advance of the bulk of his countrymen, and especially of those governments which had imprisoned and banished him, as they had so many of the truest of German patriots. Stephenson's " Rocket " made its first triumphant journey in 1829, and it was ten years later before Dresden and Leipzic were linked up by the first railway of any importance to be constructed in Germany. In the meanwhile, two short local lines had been laid down between Nuremberg and Fürth (1835), and between Berlin and Potsdam (1838). The subsequent development of German railways may be seen from the appended table:

Year.						Length of Line in Kilometres.
1845	...	...	...	...	...	2,131
1850	...	...	...	...	...	5,822
1855	...	...	...	...	...	7,781
1860	...	...	...	...	...	11,026
1865	...	...	...	...	...	13,821
1870	...	...	...	...	...	18,560
1875	...	...	...	...	...	27,795
1880	...	...	...	...	...	33,865
1885	...	...	...	...	...	37,572
1890	...	...	...	...	...	41,818
1895	...	...	...	...	...	45,203
1900	...	...	...	...	...	49,878
1905	...	...	...	...	...	54,680
1910	...	...	...	...	...	59,031

Kilometre = ⅝ mile.

Here, too, it was the removal of political uncertainty by the foundation of the Empire which imparted the decisive stimulus, for 15,305 kilometres of line, or more than a quarter of the whole, were completed in the decade from 1870 to 1880. The development of railways in the United Kingdom may be compared with that in Germany by a glance at the subjoined table:

Year.				United Kingdom.	Germany.
				Miles.	Miles.
1840	...	...	...	843	293
1870	...	...	...	15,239	11,600
1900	...	...	...	21,826	31,173
1910	...	...	...	23,387	36,894

It should, of course, be remembered that Germany does not build railways solely for the purposes of general traffic, but has constructed many hundreds of miles with the main object of being able to fling her armies with the utmost possible rapidity on to a threatened frontier.

Of the many secondary causes which have contributed to give Germany to-day what must be considered her natural place in the front rank of the industrial States, none has been more effective in its operation than the adoption of steam locomotion. England owes her industrial supremacy very largely to her insular structure and the situation of her mineral resources. Iron ore, coal, and limestone were found on English soil in close proximity to one another, and in no case very far removed from the coast or navigable water. Iron and steel could thus be produced, manufactured, and shipped to either home or foreign ports without being burdened with heavy charges for land transport. In Germany the conditions were the very reverse of these; though coal and iron abounded they lay at great distances from one another, and could, as a rule, be brought together only by overland routes. It has been calculated that even to-day transport accounts for as much as 28 to 30 per cent. of the cost of producing pig-iron in Germany, whereas in England the corresponding proportion is only 9 to 10 per cent. It may easily be imagined how serious a handicap this geographical separation of her mineral stores was to Germany in the days before the horse had been ousted by the locomotive. By the nationalization of the railways the State was provided with a valuable instrument for stimulating industries which were considered of vital importance, and by the manipulation of the transport tariff economic miracles have been worked.

Moreover, it was not till Germany's political future was assured by her victory over France that she properly developed the capacities of her 6,000 miles of natural and artificial waterways. The channels of the rivers were then dredged out and their banks

protected by buttresses and groins; new and improved locks were constructed; and a way to the
interior was thus opened out to vessels of much larger
draught.   On the Rhine, the barges, which had
averaged about 100 tons displacement in the first
half of the nineteenth century, gradually increased in
size to 200, 400, and, finally, 1,500 and even 2,000 tons.
During the last quarter of the century the traffic on
these waterways expanded from 2,900,000,000 to
11,500,000,000 kilometre tons.   It would be difficult
to exaggerate the importance of these improvements
in methods of communication to that process of "moving things," which, according to Mill, constitutes the
whole of industry and commerce.

A salient feature of modern Germany is the prominent part played by the big banks in the industrial
life of the nation.   Credit has thus become not so
much a means as one of the chief causes of industrial
expansion.   As Professor Sombart says, "The banks
have actually become promoters of the spirit of
enterprise, the pacemakers of industry and commerce."   But here, again, we have to do with a quite
modern development.   Until the second half of last
century, commercial credit in Germany was in a most
primitive condition.   There was a time between 1830
and 1840 when the Lübeck Private Bank was the
only institution in the country which issued notes.
In 1851 the Prussian State Bank, finding its deposits
accumulating and not knowing what to do with them,
gave its customers notice to withdraw them.   Bill
discounting has become general in Germany only
during the last hundred years.   It is also certain that
the great increase in the savings bank deposits, so
often cited as proof of Germany's prosperity, has been
very largely due to the abandonment of the habit of
hoarding, which had been the natural outcome of a state
of political uncertainty.   Even to-day certain features
of banking are but imperfectly developed in Germany.
The settlement of tradesmen's bills by cheque is

almost unknown, and any day the head offices of the chief banks of Berlin may be seen crowded with customers patiently waiting till receipts for the money they have paid in have been signed by two members of an overworked directorate. It is no uncommon experience to have to wait a quarter, or even half an hour for the cashing of a small cheque on a substantial account of long-standing. The quick passage of money across the counter of an English bank would take away the breath of a German cashier.

Nearly all the great financial undertakings which have capitalized the successive advances of German industry have come into existence since the middle of last century, and it is worthy of note that more than one of them were admittedly modelled on the Crédit Mobilier, which commenced operations in 1852. The Schaafhausenscher Bankverein was founded in 1848, the Disconto-Gesellschaft in 1851, the Darmstädter Bank in 1853, the Berliner Handelsgesellschaft in 1856, the Deutsche Bank in 1870, and the Dresdener Bank in 1872. Just as it is now impossible to imagine Germany's business life without these financial houses, so it is easy to appreciate how difficult it must have been for her industry to get on to its feet in the days when nothing corresponding to them existed. As a matter of fact, it seems to have been with English capital that the larger reticulations of Germany's network of railways were constructed, just as it was English capital which introduced gas-works and water-mains into some of her principal towns, and inaugurated the earliest line of regular steamers on the Elbe between Hamburg and Berlin.

When the long-looked-for moment actually arrived, and Germany found herself for the first time a real national unit, the pent-up forces burst forth with such violence as to cause a grave momentary catastrophe. In his great German History, Professor Lamprecht says of this period : " With extraordinary rapidity, new factories, mines, iron foundries, railways sprang up on every hand. To deal first with the most important of all undertakings—railways—there were in Prussia, in 1872, besides 1,800 miles (German mile = 7·42 kilometres) completed, 700 miles under construction and 1,200 miles projected. From 1871 to 1874 as many blast furnaces, iron foundries, and machine works were established as had come into existence from 1800 to 1870." The flotations in the lustrum following the declaration of the Empire at Versailles far surpassed in their aggregate capital, if not in their number, those of any equal period of the century, as will be evident from the subjoined figures:

Five Years.				Number of Companies Floated.	Capital in Million Marks.
1871-1875	...	...	...	1,073	2,932
1876-1880	...	...	...	270	224
1881-1885	..	...	...	620	596
1886-1890	...	...	...	1,061	1,100
1891-1895	...	...	...	635	586
1896-1900	...	...	...	1,390	1,997

In the single year 1872, no fewer than 479 companies, with an aggregate capital of M. 1,477,730,000, were got together. Economists will probably always differ as to how far this reckless speculation and the crash which succeeded it were, respectively, caused by the indemnity of £200,000,000 that Bismarck extorted from France. The bulk of this money was spent almost immediately, £130,000,000 of it being devoted to the rearming and remunitioning of the German land forces, while a further large sum went to build strategic railways on the Western Frontier.

It is not proposed to consider here the influence which a protective commercial policy has had upon Germany's industrial expansion, but it may be pointed out that Bismarck's abandonment of free trade in 1879 coincided with another event from which the Empire has incidentally reaped inestimable benefits—namely,

the invention of the Thomas-Gilchrist process of
making steel.   Up to that time the inexhaustible supplies of iron found in Lorraine had been practically
useless for the manufacture of steel owing to the high
percentage of phosphorus contained in the ore.   The
Thomas-Gilchrist process, however, turned this drawback into a positive advantage, for the conversion of
Lorraine ore into steel leaves a valuable bye-product
in the form of phosphoric acid.   Profiting by this English invention, Germany now obtains more than half
her iron and three-quarters of her agriculture's requirements of phosphoric acid from the previously
despised and neglected ore-beds of Lorraine.   It was
a singular dispensation of Providence that the native
land of Liebig, the father of agricultural chemistry,
should, in its potash salts and its phosphoric ores,
be so richly endowed with the two substances which
he showed that it was necessary for the farmer to
restore to the soil after gathering his crops.   In the
opinion of Professor Sombart, "the dominant position
which the German iron industry occupied at the close
of the nineteenth century is to a large extent to be
ascribed to the blessings that have fallen to it from the
invention of the basic process of casting iron."

In past ages Germany suffered immeasurably from
the mutual jealousies and animosities of her rulers,
and from their selfish territorial ambitions, but their
emulation in the fields of science and art at any rate
conferred upon her one great blessing from which she
has benefited enormously in her industrial ascent.
This rivalry set up in the region now united as the
German Empire numerous centres of culture, and,
in course of time, led to the establishment of the
twenty-one universities, where, at the present day,
between fifty and sixty thousand matriculated students
drink at the purest springs of knowledge.   To these
institutions it is due that the transition from empirical
to inductive industry found the Germans better
equipped, as a whole, with scientific and technical

information and training than the people of any other country. It was a particularly fortunate circumstance for Germany that her political renaissance should have coincided with the birth of an entirely new industry—the electrical—and the fundamental regeneration of another—the chemical. These two now absolutely vital industries differ from all previously existing branches of manufacture in this, that they are the offspring of science and not of empirical practice, of laboratory experiment and not of workshop experience. With the help of her large class of scientifically trained minds Germany was able to grapple with them from the outset, and she rapidly took the lead in both. A hundred years ago Germany had no chemical industry whatsoever; she now holds the place of chemist to the world. In 1911 her exports of chemicals, drugs, dyes, colours, and artificial manures, were worth £35,500,000, those of the United Kingdom only £20,000,000. In the preceding year Germany exported electrical machinery and apparatus to the total value of £10,000,000, the United Kingdom only to the value of £5,700,000.

It seems hardly necessary to dwell on the rapid forward strides that have been made by Germany's export trade within recent years, so frequently and fully has this theme been dealt with in English publications; but a few figures may serve to revive the essential facts in the reader's memory. Since the statistics of the Empire were placed on something like their present basis, the value of its exports has leapt up from decade to decade by the following gradations:

Year.					£
1880	...	...	...	...	... 144,800,000
1890	...	...	...	...	... 166,400,000
1900	...	...	...	...	... 230,000,000
1910	...	...	...	...	... 367,000,000

Of more importance for our present purposes than the mere bulk is the composition of that trade, and here it is highly significant that, step by step with the transformation of the battleship into a huge and complex mechanical contrivance, an ever and rapidly increasing proportion of the value of Germany's exports has been accounted for by the products of the engineering industries. Ten years ago she sent abroad machines of all kinds to the total value of £9,800,000, and that was 4·1 per cent. of the value of her aggregate export trade. In 1911 the value of her exports of machinery was £27,500,000, and its proportion to that of her total export trade 6·7 per cent. A clearer idea of this tendency of German industry will be obtained if a glance is cast at the subjoined figures from the three occupation censuses that have been taken in the Empire. They show the proportions of the persons engaged in certain occupations to the totals of those earning a livelihood by industry or commerce :

Industry.	1882.	1895.	1907.
	Per Cent.	Per Cent.	Per Cent.
Agriculture	50·12	43·13	39·54
Mining	2·72	3·00	3·91
Metal working	3·26	4·56	4·82
Machinery	1·76	2·04	3·68
Chemicals	0·36	0·54	0·65
Textiles	5·25	5·00	4·29
Building	5·84	7·16	7·74
Commerce	5·20	6·37	7·07

When the great fiscal project was under consideration by the Reichstag in 1908, the Imperial Finance Minister submitted to that Chamber a vast mass of statistical material, the purpose of which was to show that Germany was well able to bear the additional burden that it was proposed to place on her shoulders. A special series of tables was devoted to the progress of German industry during the ten years immediately preceding the introduction of the Government scheme. One of these tables demonstrates the changes which had taken place during the decade in question in the number of persons employed, and in the aggregate horse-power of the engines at work, in the leading manufacturing industries. As compared with the figures for the period 1894-1896, those for the years 1904-1906 showed the following increases:

Industry.				Employees.	Horse-power.
				Per Cent.	Per Cent.
Mining and iron	...	...	...	71·96	157
Potteries	...	...	...	37·84	138
Chemicals	...	...	...	63·95	167
Paper	...	...	...	41·36	160
Leather	...	...	...	39·66	36
Wood	...	...	...	72·75	115
Food, etc.	...	...	...	6·78	70
Clothing	...	...	...	92·30	148

Equally striking is the progress made by the export trade of these industries during the ten years under consideration. Comparing the two periods 1894-1896 and 1904-1906, we get the following percentual increases:

Industry.				Values of Exports.	Quantities of Exports.
				Per Cent.	Per Cent.
Mining and iron	...	...	...	104·00	70·84
Potteries	...	...	...	74·27	23·71
Chemicals	...	...	...	50·68	113·43
Paper	...	...	...	34·41	42·09
Leather	...	...	...	7·54	58·96
Wood	...	...	...	30·11	11·75
Food, etc.	...	...	...	2·11	1·96
Clothing	...	...	...	30·84	15·51

It will be noticed that the industries which are most highly technicalized went ahead much more rapidly than the others. A vivid picture of the advancing activity of Germany in manufacture is also afforded by the appended figures of the horse-power of the stationary steam-engines used at various periods in the industry in Prussia:

Year.					Horse-power.	Percentage.
1878 ...	...	...	...	...	887,780	100
1885 ...	...	...	...	...	1,221,884	137
1895 ...	...	...	...	...	2,358,175	269
1907 ...	...	...	...	...	5,190,417	585

A multitude of other conclusive proofs of the prosperity of the nation were also adduced by Herr Wermuth. It has already been pointed out that the increase in the savings bank deposits in Germany has been largely due to a change of habit; but even with this qualification, it is sufficiently remarkable that they should have augmented, between 1875 and 1907, from M. 1,869,200,000 to M. 13,889,100,000. Between 1883 and 1907, the deposits in the ordinary German banks rose from M. 813,000,000 to M. 7,050,000,000, or, expressed in percentages, from 100 to 867.

Concurrently with the accumulation of savings, it was shown that an enormous increase in the consumption of articles of food had taken place. In the case of the two principal bread grains, the annual consumption per head of population was :

Average of Years.					Wheat.	Rye.
					Kilos.	Kilos.
1878-1882	...	...	...	...	61·4	128·0
1883-1887	...	...	...	...	65·4	118·7
1888-1892	...	...	...	...	67·9	109·7
1893-1897	...	...	...	...	87·2	151·5
1898-1902	...	...	...	...	92·7	149·6
1902-1906	...	...	...	...	96·5	151·1

A particularly noteworthy feature of this table is the evidence it affords that the consumption of wheat is advancing more rapidly than that of the cheaper rye. In many parts of Germany, and especially in the north, where wheat cannot be profitably grown, white bread is still regarded as one of the luxuries of life, and its increased consumption is, therefore, doubly a proof of growing wealth. The increase in the *per capita* consumption of other articles of food bears similar witness, as will be seen from the appended figures:

Average of Years.		Barley.	Oats.	Potatoes.	Sugar.	Tobacco.
		Kilos.	Kilos.	Kilos.	Kilos.	Kilos.
1879-1883	...	46·8	82·3	34·1	6·3	1·2
1884-1888	...	52·8	85·7	401·7	7·7	1·5
1889-1893	...	57·9	84·8	434·3	9·8	1·5
1894-1898	...	69·8	113·3	545·0	11·4	1·7
1899-1903	...	73·0	120·7	633·6	13·5	1·6
1902-1906	...	77·9	120·6	608·0	15·5	1·6

Unfortunately, no trustworthy statistical data with respect to the consumption of meat in Germany during the latter part of the nineteenth century are available. In the Treasury publication, from which the above figures have been taken, the ascertainable facts are carefully weighed, and the conclusion is drawn from them, that the German, on an average, now eats as much meat as the Englishman. That the consumption of meat has increased enormously in Germany of recent years is incontestable.

Still more notable than the *per capita* consumption of articles of food is that of the chief raw materials of industry. From 1879 to 1909, the consumption of coal per head of population rose from 0·86 of a ton to 2·153 tons; of iron from 48·94 kilograms to 191 kilograms. The annual average consumption of cotton per head of population was, in the years 1871 to 1875, only 2·84 kilograms; in the years 1906 to 1910 it was 6·64 kilograms.

Further convincing evidence of the rapid accumulation of wealth in Germany is afforded by the taxation assessments. Between 1896 and 1907 the aggregate income of individuals assessed for taxation in Prussia rose from M. 10,148,000,000 to M. 15,874,000,000, or by 156 per cent. Few things are more difficult to calculate than the actual total wealth of a nation, and German

economists differ widely in their estimates of that of
their own country.   Many of them are of opinion that
Germany is already richer than France, some that it
has even outdistanced England in point of wealth.
Steinmann-Bucher, who takes the most optimistic
view of the Empire's riches, calculates that, by the
year 1930, they will have attained the sum of
M. 600,000,000,000, and that those of Great Britain
will then amount to no more than M. 424,000,000,000.
These and similar German computations are, no
doubt, unduly sanguine.   They are based, for one
thing, on an arbitrary and misleading definition of
wealth, and sometimes entirely ignore the important
item of domestic appurtenances and personal orna-
ments, which, after land and hard cash, are the most
enduring of all forms of property.

The casual visitor to Berlin is, as a rule, deeply
impressed by the pretentious plaster façades of that
mushroom city, which he usually takes to be stone,
and he compares them with London's monotony of
grimy brick, very much to the disadvantage of the
latter.   Let him, however, wander in the environs of
the two capitals, and what does he find?   Within a
radius of fifty miles around London the country is
dotted with ancient mansions, each filled with the
masterpieces of the goldsmith's, the jeweller's, the
cabinet-maker's, and the potter's craft, many of which
have an artistic value almost beyond price.   Five or
six miles from Berlin he enters a region where he can
walk for hours through forests of stunted fir-trees or
flat expanses of sandy soil, without encountering a
trace of the material refinements of civilization.   The
contrast is just as sharp if the surroundings of the
towns of second-class magnitude in the two countries
be compared.   Germany is beyond all doubt heaping
up wealth at an amazing rate, but an observant eye
will divine, much more truly than the computations of
the economists, that she has yet much way to make
up before she can get level with Great Britain.   At

the same time, it must ever be borne in mind how much larger both her area and population are than those of this country, and though Steinmann-Bucher's estimate assuredly exaggerates the prosperity of Germany, it cannot be doubted that, if present tendencies remain unchanged, the Empire will, before the end of the century, have become by far the richest country in Europe.

Long before that point is reached, Germany will be able without an effort to bear the weight of much heavier armaments than those she now carries. It is often said that she cannot maintain both the strongest Army and the strongest Navy in Europe. The statement sounds plausible, but it is in reality an unreasoned begging of the question. Whether or not she can do this thing depends entirely upon her resources in men, money, and manufacturing power, and in respect of these three taken together she is probably already much more favourably situated than any other European State—that is to say, if we leave colonies out of the question. And though she is rightly regarded as essentially the military State of the world, she as yet has neither absolutely nor relatively spent so much on national defence as some of her neighbours. *Nauticus*, the naval annual issued indirectly by the German Ministry of Marine, gives the expenditure of the principal Powers of the world on national defence in the year 1912 as under :

State.	Army.	Navy.	Together.
	Thousand Marks.	Thousand Marks.	Thousand Marks.
Great Britain	568,340	899,342	1,467,682
Russia	1,067,684	354,956	1,422,640
Germany	947,825	461,983	1,409,808
United States	647,708	533,943	1,181,651
France	736,399	338,623	1,075,022
Austria-Hungary ...	455,801	118,794	574,595
Italy	338,049	173,509	511,558
Japan	196,259	194,643	390,902

Per head of population this expenditure works out as below :

State.	Army.	Navy.	Together.
	Marks.	Marks.	Marks.
Great Britain	12·46	19·72	38·18
France	18·55	8·53	27·08
Germany	14·23	6·94	21·17
Italy	9·66	4·96	14·62
United States	6·80	5·61	12·41
Austria-Hungary ...	8·72	2·27	10·99
Russia	6·86	2·28	9·14
Japan	3·76	3·73	7·49

So that both absolutely and relatively Great Britain spent more than any other country on national defence, whereas Germany, the military State *par excellence*, stands only third on the list in respect both of aggregate and *per capita* expenditure.*

Similarly, the financial burden which Germany has to bear is not, at any rate in its immediate incidence, as great as that which presses on some other countries. The German official publication, already quoted, gives the following as the total *per capita* incidence of taxation, local and municipal as well as national, in the eight chief countries of the world :

	Marks.
United Kingdom (1904-05)	95·80
France (1908)	82·70
United States (1906-07)	80·80
Italy (1906-07)	48·40
Germany (1907)	48·17
Austria-Hungary (1906)	41·70
Japan (1906)	20·50
Russia (1908)	18·40

Even if the twenty to twenty-five millions sterling of additional annual taxation, which the German nation has since that time been called upon to pay were to be

* This survey takes no account of the German Army scheme of 1913, which at the moment of writing had not yet been laid before the Reichstag.

included in the above figures, the Empire would still stand in a very favourable position. It is, of course, true that the additional taxes imposed in Germany of recent years have been very sorely felt and very bitterly resented. But that by no means implies that the country has reached the limit of its taxable capacity. It is rather the result of the combined action of a number of other causes. In the first place, the prosperity of Germany is of so recent a date that it has not yet had time to penetrate to all classes of the population. While manufacturers, merchants, and certain categories of skilled artisans have benefited largely by it, the salaried classes generally and the vast body of unskilled labourers have hardly yet begun to feel its effects. Moreover, a considerable proportion of the German revenue is obtained from protective duties on necessary articles of food, the prices of which are raised accordingly. The consumer pays the amount of the duty not only on the imported but also on the home-produced portion of his food, though the latter yields nothing to the public revenue.

German financial policy has also been exceedingly improvident, unsound, and injudicious, for till the great finance reform of 1908 the Empire carried on its military and naval expansion largely on borrowed money. Up to that date the Imperial funded debt had grown, in times of peace be it noted, in the following manner:

March 31.				Million Marks.	Marks per Head.
1878	...	...	...	...	72·2	1·66
1881	...	...	...	...	267·8	5·90
1886	...	...	...	...	440·0	9·36
1891	...	...	...	...	1,317·8	26·56
1896	...	...	...	...	2,125·3	40·46
1901	...	...	...	...	2,395·7	42·29
1906	...	...	...	...	3,543·5	58·14
1907	...	...	...	...	3,803·5	61·48
1908	...	...	...	...	4,003·5	63·78

At the close of the financial year 1907, the national debt comprised the undermentioned items of expenditure :

		Marks.
Army	1,670,100,000
Navy	768,400,000
Kiel Canal	109,000,000
Colonial administration	24,000,000
South-West Africa Expedition ...	379,000,000
East Africa Expedition	1,800,000
China Expedition	287,000,000

For some years Government and Reichstag cheerfully committed the country to vast expenditure for the Navy and other purposes without troubling themselves as to where the money was to come from. In the Memorandum to the Navy Bill of 1900 Admiral von Tirpitz had enunciated the principle : " If new sources of income cannot be opened up, all that will remain will be to increase the amount of the loan." This principle was unquestioningly adopted by the Reichstag, not with the cool calculation of the Naval Minister, but in the blindness of the Anglophobia which the Boer War had engendered. Naturally the limits to such a policy are quickly reached. In 1906 a half-hearted attempt was made to recover the lost financial equipoise, and the German nation was saddled with additional taxation to the amount of about 10 millions sterling annually. This, however, proved totally inadequate, and, a couple of years later, further imposts, expected to yield 25 millions sterling annually, were demanded from the Parliament. Thirty-five million pounds of fresh taxation within three years after nearly forty years of still unbroken peace ! It is not surprising that the taxpayers raised a howl of protest, and gave more support to the only party which had consistently opposed this expenditure—namely, the Socialists; nor that, even after the renewed outburst of Anglophobia over the Morocco Question in 1911, it was the Socialists who, at the expense of all other parties, enormously increased their holding of seats in the Chamber. The other parties were at length thoroughly alarmed by the consequences of their prodigality, and the military and naval measures of 1912 would have had but small chance of acceptance had it not been a perfectly understood thing, even before they were presented, that the increased outlay they involved would not be covered by additions to the fiscal burdens of the masses of the population.

A less reckless and improvident naval policy might very easily have attained the same ends at a somewhat later date without involving these inconveniences; for, as has been seen above, the taxation borne by the German people, in comparison with that paid by other nations, is by no means excessive, and all sources of public revenue have the tendency to yield more abundantly as a country grows richer, which, as must also have become apparent, Germany is doing very rapidly.

If it could be assumed that Germany had, during the last ten or fifteen years, been governed only by shrewd and far-sighted statesmen, thoroughly aware of all the bearings of their actions, it would be safe to conclude that the Empire was preparing for a naval war which either they had determined upon or considered immediately inevitable; for such an hypothesis is the only satisfactory explanation of the manner in which Germany has pushed her naval armaments beyond her momentary financial strength. Fortunately this assumption cannot be made. Germany's policy in these respects has been the result, not of clear, but of clouded thinking—that is, if we except one man, Admiral von Tirpitz, who conceivably calculated that the opportunity presented by the Boer War might never recur, at any rate during his tenure of the Ministry of Marine, and that if he did not get his ships then he never would do so.

As to the immediate future of German finance it would be dangerous to prophecy. The increased quantity of foodstuffs now imported into the country has the effect of swelling the public revenue, and the present apparently satisfactory condition of the Empire's finances is, by an odd paradox, very largely due to the partial failure of the harvest in 1911. But augmented import of food means higher prices in a protected country, and the urban population, which is growing by leaps and bounds by the absorption of ambitious rustics, is already up in arms against the agrarian tariff. It is quite conceivable, nay, even probable, that its discontent may ere long rise to such a pitch as to force a change in the Empire's commercial policy. That would mean a dislocation of the Imperial finances, and some time would have to elapse before it would be possible to establish them on another footing.

CHAPTER IX

PARLIAMENT AND GERMAN NAVAL POLICY

THE question whether Germany will continue to enlarge her Fleet concurrently with her economic expansion is not easy to answer, for the reply to it depends upon political considerations, both foreign and domestic, of a somewhat complex character.

When we speak of Germany, or any other country, having certain "determinations" or "intentions," all we can mean is the effective will of the nation as it has been, or is likely to be, manifested in legislative or administrative acts. This effective will is not necessarily synonymous with the popular will—indeed often is diametrically opposed to it—and it is liable to modification both by intrinsic change and by alterations in governmental forms. Both nations and parliaments are, too, swayed by waves of emotion and fits of passion, which are frequently followed by reactions just as sudden and violent, so that what was the effective will one day ceases to be so on the morrow. Such considerations have an important bearing on the attitude of Germany towards the naval question.

It is sometimes quite falsely assumed that the Germans are to an exceptional degree a homogeneous, contented, united, and harmonious people, of which all the members concentrate their energies primarily on the attainment of specifically national ends. No notion could be farther from the truth. Germany is, on the contrary, with the possible exception of Austria-Hungary, the most heterogeneous, dissatisfied, disunited, and discordant nation in Europe. In no other country do the divisions of class, creed, and party cut so deep; in none other are they so complicated by cross-lines of territorial cleavage. Professor Hans Delbrück has justly said: "How small is at bottom the number of those Germans who, in the true and higher sense of the term, form the German nation and represent the German idea—a small, very small minority." And nowhere does the remark more accurately apply than in respect to naval policy, though it must be admitted that, owing to a combination of circumstances, the number of Germans who are fascinated by the idea of sea-power has very largely increased of recent years.

In past ages particularism was the bane of Germany, and to-day it is still her most serious weakness. But it is a particularism of a new type. The old form of particularism has ceased to exist as a vital force. True, the other German rulers regard the Hohenzollern ascendancy with a certain amount of jealousy and distrust, and resent the apparent desire of the Emperor William to encroach still further upon their already sadly diminished prerogatives. True, many of the inhabitants of Hanover and Hesse-Cassel still describe themselves as "must-Prussians," to indicate that their adherence to the predominant German State is not a voluntary one. True, the people of Munich hate those of Berlin as sordid and unfeeling barbarians, and the people of Berlin despise those of Munich as idle and emotional sots. But these are merely the little bickerings and frictions that exist in all large families without seriously imperilling the ties of kinship, and the Germans as a whole are far too keenly alive to the blessings of national unity ever to risk them for the gratification of traditional grudges. Still less would they allow their tranquillity and security to be staked on dynastic squabbles. The particularisms of to-day spring, not from historical traditions and local sentiments, but from the two most powerful agencies in human society—spiritual ideals and material interests.

The Germany of the days of the Holy Roman Empire

has often been likened to a mosaic of loosely-cemented pieces. Modern Germany rather resembles a plate in which a series of cracks cross one another, thus increasing the probabilities of a breakage. The main cleft is that which separates the Protestants from the Roman Catholics, and it is all the deeper because it is to a large extent geographical as well as denominational. Thus, in Bavaria, Baden, Alsace-Lorraine, and the Prussian provinces of Westphalia, the Rhineland, Silesia, Posen, and Hohenzollern, Catholicism largely predominates ; while in Württemberg and Oldenburg it is strongly represented. According to the census of 1910, the two creeds were territorially distributed as under :

			Roman Catholic.	Evangelical.
Prussia :				
West Prussia	...	...	844,566	764,719
Posen ...	...	...	1,347,958	605,312
Silesia ...	...	...	2,765,394	2,120,361
Westphalia	...	...	1,845,263	1,733,413
Rhineland	...	...	4,472,058	1,877,582
Hohenzollern	...	...	64,770	3,040
Bavaria ...	...	...	4,612,920	1,844,736
Württemberg	...	...	696,031	1,582,745
Baden ...	...	...	1,206,919	769,866
Oldenburg	...	...	96,067	339,916
Totals	...	...	17,951,946	11,641,690

Thus out of the twenty-two million Catholics counted at the census, close upon eighteen millions are concentrated on two continuous belts of land, one of which extends from Westphalia up the Rhine and across the south of Germany, the other from Silesia through Posen to West Prussia. Moreover, the denominational concentration is really much more intense than appears from the figures given above, the population being Catholic almost to a man over large tracts of territory.

Now, two features of this religious segregation are deserving of special attention. In the first place, it is

noteworthy that the Catholic belts are composed
either of those States of Germany where the traditional antagonism to Prussia is strongest, or of
provinces which have been conquered by the sword
of the Hohenzollerns.   In the second place, it should
be observed that they are of a specifically inland
character, have no historical associations with the
sea, contain no port of any significance, and have little
direct contact with the Empire's maritime interests.
The bearing of these facts will be apparent when it is
realized that Catholicism is in Germany, not only
a political force, but the most homogeneous, constant,
and stable of all political forces, though it has been
momentarily eclipsed in mere numbers by Socialism.

It was Bismarck's Kulturkampf—perhaps the greatest
mistake of the Iron Chancellor, who, like Napoleon,
failed to understand the character of the Church of
Rome—which forced German Catholicism into political
consolidation.   His attempt to undermine the influence
of the Papacy on its German adherents failed, and at
the same time called into existence that solid and
compact element in the Reichstag, which is indiffer-
ently called the Centre, or Catholic, or Clerical, or
Ultramontane party.   This party is the foundation on
which the German Empire in its existing form rests.
At the present moment, it completely dominates the
Parliamentary situation, for without its consent no
legislation and no budget can be passed, and so far as
the eye of the mind can penetrate into the future, it is
likely to become more rather than less indispensable
to the Government as time goes on.   In particular, its
acquiescence is, and will be, necessary for any further
additions to the German Army or Navy, and for this
reason it is desirable that its character should be fully
understood.

In the present Reichstag, the Centre occupies of its
own right ninety seats out of a total of 397, so that it
holds the balance between the Socialists, who are
110 strong, and the other non-Socialist groups.   Its

Parliamentary representation now stands lower than it has ever done since the election of 1874, which followed the inauguration of the Kulturkampf, but, on the other hand, it has never been higher than 106, and these facts in themselves indicate clearly its remarkable stability. This characteristic, however, appears in a much more striking light when we find that out of its ninety seats the Centre has held no fewer than seventy-three uninterruptedly since 1874, and fifty-one since 1871. In other words, it has for nearly forty years successfully defied all challenge in three-quarters of the constituencies which may be regarded as its normal Parliamentary holding. The causes of this steadiness are not far to seek. The ratios of the Catholics to the entire population in the ninety Centre constituencies are as below :

Over 60 per cent. in 86 constituencies.
,, 70 ,, in 75 ,,
,, 80 ,, in 66 ,,
,, 90 ,, in 45 ,,
,, 95 ,, in 24 ,,

Until some decided change takes place in the religious sentiments of either Protestants or Catholics, at least these eighty-six constituencies seem certain to remain Centre strongholds. The degree of the Centre ascendancy over the minds of the Catholic electorate may be illustrated by a few extreme instances from the results of the last (1912) elections :

	Centre Poll.	Poll of all other Parties.
Bergheim (Rhine)	17,138	894
Daun	20,657	452
Gelsenkirchen	22,606	915
Paderborn	17,108	519
Kelheim	11,161	737

Though the above are extreme cases, they may be taken as typical of the general tendency. It is, in fact, only in the large towns, where the Catholic masses have been exposed to the corrosion of urban scepticism and materialism, that the Church of Rome has substantially lost control over those who nominally acknowledge its sway. The 145 constituencies in which Catholics are in a majority returned at the 1912 elections members of the following parties:

Catholics:

Centre	90
Poles	18
Alsace-Lorrainers	9
Bavarian Peasants' League	2
	— 119

Non-Catholics:

Socialists	11
National Liberals	8
Radicals	3
Imperial party	2
Conservatives	2
	— 26
	145

These twenty-six Catholic constituencies with non-Catholic representation, included the towns of Mülheim (population 53,000), Metz (68,000), Freiburg (83,000), Wurzburg (84,000), Mühlhausen (95,000), Saarbrücken (105,000), Strasburg (179,000), Duisburg (229,000), Düsseldorf (358,000), Cologne (516,000), and two divisions of Munich (595,000). It is such towns as these that account for the difference between the percentage of the Catholic population of Germany (37), and that of the Centre voters to the total electorate (21). Essen is the only town of first-class business importance with a predominantly Catholic population which now remains in the hands of the Centre. It is an anomalous feature of the religious structure of Germany that in certain big towns situated in the heart of pronouncedly Catholic districts, the Evangelical population is in a majority, and of these Elberfeld, Barmen, Nuremberg, and Mannheim may be cited as examples. It may also be mentioned in passing, that in 1912 not a single Conservative was returned in Westphalia, the Rhine Province, or Baden, and that the two candidates of this party who were successful in Bavaria were both chosen by Evangelical divisions.

The geographical concentration of the Centre may be further illustrated by the fact that, of the 1,990,700 votes which its candidates secured at the 1912 elections, no fewer than 1,680,600 were cast in the three Prussian provinces of Silesia, Westphalia, and Rhineland, the Kingdom of Bavaria, and the Grand Duchy of Baden ; and that seventy-nine out of its ninety Reichstag seats were won in the same regions. Votes and seats were distributed as below :

	Votes.	Seats.
Prussia :		
Silesia	154,100	9
Westphalia	262,000	8
Rhineland	664,000	27
Bavaria	471,400	29
Baden	129,000	6
Totals	1,680,600	79

We must now briefly consider the political principles of the Centre, and the motives which usually determine its actions. And here it must first be emphasized that the party stands on a purely denominational basis. All the temporal interests and political principles which usually go to the making of parties play a secondary and quite subordinate rôle with its leaders. It is there to safeguard the spiritual interests of the Roman Catholics of Germany, and for the sake of these interests all other considerations are allowed to sink into the background. Catholicism is in a minority in Germany, and would necessarily be on the defensive, even if it had not passed through the ordeal of the Kulturkampf, and was not continually being warned by the invectives of the Evangelical majority of the possibility of a fresh attack upon its position. While the Protestant denomination has lost practically all its spiritual force, it has retained, as an inheritance of the Thirty Years' War and of the territorial division with which that struggle ended, an intense and virulent antipathy to the Church of Rome, and the feeling is especially strong among the urban, and consequently Liberal, classes. It is the manifestations of this sentiment which make German Catholics fear for their faith, and, sinking all temporal differences, hold together, as they consider, in its defence. The Centre party comprehends all ranks, classes, and occupations. On its block of benches in the Reichstag, Princes and priests sit side by side with university professors, farmers, manufacturers, butchers, publicans, and trade union secretaries. These men have only one thing in common—their religion—and when this is not at issue their line of action is determined by compromise and opportunism.

On one main point the views of the Centre harmonize with those of the Conservatives : both are in favour of denominational teaching in the schools and of State support of religion in general. It might be thought that there would rather be risk of conflict here, but such is not the case. Where the Conservatives prevail, Protestantism is as predominant as is Catholicism in the Centre districts, and consequently the danger of proselytism is not serious in either. But there is yet another force which brings the two parties together— both are mainly dependent on a rural electorate, and for this reason favour a protective tariff on agricultural products. Conservatives and Centre, therefore, form the most intimate and enduring of the opportunist party combinations, without which Parliamentary action is impossible in Germany. On the other hand, the south and west, whence the Centre draws its chief strength, are—apart from questions of religion— distinctly Liberal in spirit, and the Clerical party is also compelled to pay some heed to the temporal claims of the tens of thousands of Catholic artisans who are employed in the coalmines of Silesia and the ironworks of Rhenish Westphalia. Consequently the Centre is always somewhat democratic in professions, though seldom so in practice, and, for example, consistently advocates the adoption of universal suffrage in Prussia, while never taking any serious steps to enforce its demand.

But, for our present purposes, most weight must be attached to another feature of Centre policy. The gravamen of the attacks made upon that party by the Liberals and Radicals lies in the contention that its real allegiance is to Rome, that it pursues aims which are cosmopolitan rather than German, and that, accordingly, it cannot be relied upon to safeguard the interests of the Empire, especially in matters of foreign policy, where the Wilhelmstrasse and the Vatican sometimes do not see exactly eye to eye. This charge of lack of patriotism tells very heavily against the Centre, and has even drawn away from it some who, in other respects, can claim to be unimpeachable Catholics, and it makes the party very cautious when it is called upon to deal with Army, Navy, or colonial votes. In such a situation its practice depends much more upon adventitious circumstances than upon the intrinsic merits of the case. If nothing is to be obtained by special bargaining, it may be relied upon to play the popular card, or what it believes to be the popular card.

The Navy Bills of 1900 and 1912 furnish excellent illustrations of Centre policy and tactics. The party had offered considerable opposition to the earlier naval project of 1898, principally on the ground that it constituted an infringement of the budget rights of the Reichstag, and a handful of Catholics actually voted with the Noes in the decisive divisions. When the 1900 Bill was announced, however, something very significant happened — the Catholic press raised a clamour for the repeal of the Jesuit Law. This statute, which was one of the fruits of the Kulturkampf, at that time consisted of three clauses. The first forbade settlements of, and activity by, the Society of Jesus and kindred congregations within the German Empire. The second empowered the Government to expel members of these Orders from the country if foreigners, and to exclude them from particular places or districts if natives of the Empire. By the third clause the Federal Council was invested with the power to issue regulations for the execution of the law. The general belief has always been, and probably rightly, that it was no mere accidental coincidence when, as soon as a decent interval had elapsed after the promulgation of the 1900 Navy Bill, the Imperial Government laid before the Reichstag a measure repealing the second clause of the Jesuit Law. That no causal connection existed between the two events seems all the more improbable when we consider that a renewed agitation for the repeal of the remnant of the Jesuit Law set in simultaneously with the preparation of the Defence Bills of 1912. It is impossible to demonstrate with the conclusiveness of legal proof that these sequences and coincidences were really connected in the manner suggested. The German has a great faculty for keep-ing secrets, and the contemporary world seldom hears the details of the confidential negotiations which are the essential process of so much of the legislation that passes through the Reichstag. But that the Catholics are not accustomed to give their support for nothing if they can obtain a price for it is beyond all doubt.

However, another motive entered into the Centre's calculations in the session of 1912. A new Reichstag had been elected, and it presented an almost exact balance between the Conservatives, Centre, and Poles on the one hand, and the National Liberals, Radicals, and Socialists on the other. The country was ringing with the cry, "More soldiers and more ships," raised, it is true, by a comparatively small number of people, but uttered with such persistency and vehemence as to produce the impression that a strong popular feeling was inspiring it. It had been declared by the Government that the chief task of the new Parliament would be the closing up of the gaps in the Empire's armour. If under such circumstances the Centre had placed obstacles in the way of the Defence Bills it would have exposed itself to the charge of having left the country imperfectly armed in the hour of its need, and would have tempted the Government to repeat Prince Bülow's experiment, so disastrous to himself, of ruling with the Conservatives and Liberals. In spite of the recent triumph of the anti-militarist Socialists, the Centre no doubt calculated that it would stand to lose if a General Election were taken on the Defence Bills as the result of its opposition to those measures. That is why, having a year before declared itself emphatically against any further naval expansion, it accepted Admiral von Tirpitz's latest project without a murmur.

Moreover, the feeling was widely diffused among all the monarchical parties that it was necessary to demonstrate to the outside world that the victories of the Socialists at the elections had not weakened Germany where national questions where concerned, and could not prevent her from adopting such military and naval measures as were considered by the responsible organs of Government to be necessary for her protection.

It is by considerations such as these that the Centre, though less directly affected by maritime interests than any other party, and though pledged to strict economy and sound finance, has always been persuaded to vote Army and Navy Bills, and will probably always go on being persuaded to vote them in the future whenever the Government can bring forward a "purely defensive" pretext, and the temper of the patriots is in a purely aggressive state. No one, however, will pretend that the peasants of the Bavarian Alps and the Black Forest have much understanding for the problems of "world-policy," or that the Catholic artisans of the Black Country of the Ruhr are more avid of sea-power than their Protestant colleagues who are Socialists to a man.

The second main line of cleavage across the German

plate is that which divides the Socialists from the Monarchists. The antithesis can best be put thus, for the effective barrier which separates the Socialists from the remainder of the population is not so much their communism as their rejection of the monarchy. This crack has extended and deepened with alarming rapidity, and there is at any rate some slight ground for the fears of the nervous politicians who believe that it will one day culminate in an absolute breakage. Since the formation of the Empire the development of the German Socialist party has been as below:

Election.				Socialist Votes Cast.	Socialist Seats in Reichstag.
1871	...	...	...	124,000	1
1874	...	...	...	352,000	10
1877	...	...	...	493,000	12
1878	...	...	...	437,000	9
1881	...	...	...	312,000	12
1884	...	...	...	550,000	24
1887	...	...	...	763,000	11
1890	...	...	...	1,427,000	35
1893	...	...	...	1,787,000	44
1898	...	...	...	2,107,000	56
1903	...	...	...	3,011,000	81
1907	...	...	...	3,259,000	43
1912	...	...	...	4,250,000	110

This is the bane. The antidote we have already dealt with—it is the Roman Catholic Church. So long as that institution retains anything like its present influence in Germany the Socialists can never hope to obtain a clear majority in the Reichstag, and till they can do that they are powerless for legislative purposes. On the other hand, there is real danger in the absolute control which they have secured over the artisan classes in the urban Evangelical districts of the Empire. They are particularly strong in and around the capital and the other chief centres of industry and commerce, as will be seen from the appended table, showing the present representation of those districts in the Reichstag:

District.	Total Members.	Socialist Members.
Berlin	6	5
Brandenburg	20	7
Province of Saxony	20	10
Kingdom of Saxony	23	19
Saxon duchies	8	5
Hanse towns	5	5
Totals	82	51

Thus five-eighths of the seats of these districts are in the possession of Socialists, and it is not a little remarkable that the only two seaports of the Empire which count for anything—Hamburg and Bremen—and one of its two chief naval bases—Kiel—should be Parliamentarily represented by a party which has persistently and energetically opposed the Government's colonial and maritime policy. A better idea of the territorial concentration of German Socialism will perhaps be afforded if we examine the 1912 poll for the central area of the Empire. If, following state and provincial divisions, we take the compact block of territory, bounded to the north by Schleswig-Holstein and Mecklenburg, to the south by Bohemia, to the east by the River Oder from the point where its course turns due northward, and to the west by the Weser, we get the following figures :

District.	Total Poll.	Socialist Poll.
Prussia :		
Berlin	408,600	307,800
Brandenburg	853,100	418,800
Province of Saxony	622,700	266,000
Hanover	588,800	187,200
Saxony	933,500	513,200
Saxon duchies	228,800	111,800
Brunswick and Anhalt	167,200	79,700
Minor principalities	134,200	56,600
Hanse towns	318,400	187,600
Totals	4,255,300	2,128,700

Within this area, therefore, more than half of the votes cast in 1912 were given to Socialist candidates, and it is thus the heart of Germany that is coloured red on the electoral map. The Socialist predominance in this central mass of the country would have appeared in an even more striking form if the frontiers of states and provinces had been disregarded, and, attention being paid only to geographical compactness, the region under consideration had been clipped a little here and extended a little there. In the principal towns of this area the total and Socialist polls were as under:

District.	Total Poll.	Socialist Poll.
Berlin	408,600	307,800
Berlin suburban divisions ...	453,700	277,800
Stettin	35,000	18,000
Madgeburg	56,700	30,900
Halle	51,500	27,300
Erfurt	44,500	23,200
Osnabrück	38,200	8,000
Hanover	82,500	43,800
Dresden	105,100	54,700
Leipzic	158,300	94,100
Chemnitz...	65,500	42,000
Brunswick	46,600	25,900
Lübeck	25,400	13,400
Bremen	67,100	35,900
Hamburg	65,900	46,900
Totals	1,704,600	1,049,700

Thus in the fifteen principal towns of the central area of Germany the Socialists failed to obtain an absolute majority over all other parties in the first ballots of 1912 only in Osnabrück, where close upon one-half of the population is Roman Catholic. Their aggregate majority in these fifteen towns was nearly 395,000.

As tendencies are at present it would be rash to attempt to lay down limits for the future growth of Socialism in Germany, and especially in this area. The urban proletariat of the Protestant regions of the Empire is already completely dominated by the doctrines of Marx, and it is likely to continue under this obsession as the process by which Germany is being transformed from an agricultural into an industrial State progresses. How rapidly this transformation is being accomplished will be evident from the appended figures, showing the proportions of the total population of the Empire engaged, respectively, in agricultural and in industrial and commercial pursuits at each of the last three professional censuses :

Census.				Agriculture.	Industry and Commerce.
				Per Cent.	Per Cent.
1882	...	...	... ...	42·51	45·57
1895	...	...	... ...	35·74	50·64
1907	...	...	... ...	31·31	56·16

A necessary concomitant of this process of transformation is the steady drain of human energy from the country districts and its concentration in the towns. In the subjoined table are shown the proportions of the total population residing, respectively, in the towns of over 20,000 and over 100,000 inhabitants at each of the last five ordinary censuses :

Census.				Towns of over 20,000 Inhabitants.	Towns of over 100,000 Inhabitants.
				Per Cent.	Per Cent.
1880	...	...	... ...	16·1	7·2
1885	...	...	... ...	18·4	9·5
1895	...	...	... ...	24·6	13·9
1900	...	...	... ...	28·8	16·2
1910	...	...	... ...	34·79	21·2

Already we find that the infection of Socialism has spread from the artisan classes to large numbers of persons dependent upon them for their livelihood. In the chief Protestant towns the artisan districts are so entirely Socialist, that doctors, lawyers, and tradesmen cannot exist in them without at any rate a lip service to the prevailing political creed. Consequently it would be unsafe to assume that Socialism will stop short in Protestant Germany at any particular point, for the possibilities of industrial expansion are not limited by those physical laws which set a term to the multiplication of peasant ownership of the soil, the one solid bulwark against Utopian experiments that at present exists north of "the Main line." On the contrary, so long as the general political conditions of the country remain unchanged, and its industrialization continues, Socialism is likely to go on extending its sway. It is true that the Socialist vote is not a precise measure of the prevalence of communistic conviction, for large numbers of monarchists support "red" candidates as the only means of entering an emphatic protest against the manner in which Germany is ruled. At the same time, the strength of genuine Socialism in Germany should not be underestimated. The numbers of those actually enrolled in the Socialist organization and pledged to propagate communistic principles by word, deed, and pecuniary contribution, have grown during the past few years as under :

Year.				Total Membership.	Female Members.
1906	...	...	...	...	384,327	—
1907	...	...	...	...	530,466	10,943
1908	...	...	...	...	587,336	29,458
1909	...	...	...	...	633,309	62,259
1910	...	...	...	...	720,038	82,642
1911	...	...	...	...	836,562	107,693
1912	...	...	...	...	970,112	130,371

It may be doubted whether any other political cause in the history of the world has ever had at its disposal a permanent organized army of nearly a million workers, but even these do not exhaust the standing forces of communism. The federated "free" trade unions, which have a total membership of nearly two and a half millions, are an outcome of the Socialist propaganda, and are entirely Socialistic in spirit. Their chairman, who represents Kiel in the Reichstag, is a prominent member of the Socialist party there. It is an arguable point whether the "free" trade unions are not a safer index than the purely political organization of the true strength of Socialism in Germany.

This is not the place for a searching analysis of the causes which have given Socialism its strong hold upon the German people, but it may be pointed out that it has more than doubled its poll since the inauguration of the Tirpitz era in 1898; that it attained its present high-water mark, with four and a quarter million votes, or nearly 35 per cent. of the total number cast, in the midst of the most violent Chauvinistic agitation which the country had experienced since the war with France; and that this agitation was directed almost exclusively against Great Britain as "the tyrant of the seas." Yet the Socialists have not merely opposed every vote for the colonies, the Army and the Navy, but have always given a most prominent place in their propaganda to denunciations of militarism, "marinism," and schemes of oversea expansion. That they should, nevertheless, have flourished so abundantly indicates that very large sections of the German people have yet to be converted to the principles of "world policy" and sea-power, or at any rate do not desire them on the present terms of increased taxation.

A third line of cleavage separates agriculture from industry, the rural from the urban population, and it is all the wider because the German Government, in its recent commercial policy, has favoured the products of the soil at the expense of those of the factory. Agrarianism finds its parliamentary expression in the Conservative party, and here again we have one of those curious segregations of political force which are so characteristic of modern Germany. At the 1912 elections, the Conservatives obtained 1,508,700 votes and 58 seats, and of these 1,038,200 votes and 53 seats came to them from those provinces of Prussia which lie almost entirely to the east of the Elbe and from Mecklenburg. They were distributed as below:

District.	Votes.	Seats.
Prussia :		
East Prussia	133,500	9
West Prussia	83,800	7
Brandenburg	199,300	8
Pomerania	148,500	10
Posen	96,900	3
Silesia	189,800	10
Province of Saxony	138,300	4
Mecklenburg	48,100	2
Totals	1,038,200	53

Not a single Conservative was returned in the Prussian provinces of Schleswig-Holstein, Hanover, Westphalia, Hesse-Nassau, and Rhineland, or in Württemberg, Hesse, the Saxon duchies, Oldenburg, Brunswick, the minor principalities, the Hanse towns, and Alsace-Lorraine. Of the five seats which fell to the party west of the Elbe, two were in Bavaria, two in Saxony, and one in Baden.

In spite of their trifling parliamentary representation (58 out of 397 seats), and their slight hold on the electorate (they secured only 12·4 per cent. of the total poll in 1912), the Conservatives are more nearly a dominant party in Germany than any other of the Reichstag groups. This position they owe in part to the large representation which, under a curious system of franchise, they possess in the Prussian Legislature, and in part to the support of the Centre, which, as has been indicated, looks at religious and agrarian questions very much from their general point of view. It is this Conservative-Catholic domination on which German domestic politics turn. The German people is, as a whole, essentially Liberal in character, and it resents that laws and regulations should be dictated to it by what is little more than a tenth of the electorate. As the industrialization of Germany continues, the Conservative rule will become less and less tolerable, and some inevitable day the Empire will be plunged into a constitutional crisis of the severest kind, from which it will eventually emerge with its political institutions considerably modified. Nor can the change be long postponed, except by a war or a period of acute international tension.

Whether a constitutional change in Germany would be followed by any appreciable alteration in her attitude towards the rest of the world is a question on which there is plenty of room for differences of opinion. The Conservatives, as a whole, have never been particularly enthusiastic on behalf of "world policy." It is generally conceded that Germany already has enough tropical territory, and what the colonial party clamours for is areas on which she can settle the surplus population that she will no doubt one day have to find new homes for. But where white men can become acclimatized grain grows and cattle flourish, and the Conservatives have unpleasant visions of colonial agricultural produce pouring into Germany and narrowing their margin of profit. That is why they have never lent much encouragement to the proposal that the Empire should direct its attention to the acquisition of Asia Minor, and why they have watched the construction of the Bagdad Railway with ill-disguised uneasiness.

It is also probably quite clear to the Conservative leaders that immigration colonies would be a death-blow to their domination in Germany. As soon as such colonies became at all thickly populated they would demand self-government with such insistence that it would be impossible to ignore their wishes. No new country inhabited by people of European race would long consent to be ruled by the rigid formulas of the German bureaucracy. But what was granted to the colonist could not well be refused to the German at home, and the agitation for a reform of the Prussian franchise, already sufficiently vigorous, would acquire such strength as to be irresistible. That, however, would mean the destruction of the Conservative power, which the junkers value much more highly than the hypothetical benefits of colonies populated by men and women of German stock.

Moreover, it is from Conservative elements that the officers' corps of the German Army is mainly drawn. This body has always looked upon the Navy with a jealous eye, and has frequently uttered the complaint that the land force was being dangerously neglected in order that the sister service might be disproportionately encouraged. For these reasons there are many Conservatives who have all along regarded Admiral von Tirpitz's policy with distrust, and have only voted for the Navy Bills because it is the tradition of their party to grant what the Government declares to be necessary for the purposes of the national defence.

These remarks do not, however, apply to the "Empire party," or Free Conservatives. This small group — its members are at present but thirteen — forms a narrow and unsteady bridge between the Conservatives proper and the National Liberals, and comes nearer to being a "Government party" than any other in the Reichstag. It is qualified to hold this place in virtue of its compromise character. But just as the Government, though nominally "standing above parties," is essentially Conservative in spirit, so this group always inclines strongly to the Right, and for all general purposes may be treated as one with the main Conservative mass. On matters of colonial, military, and naval expansion, however, the Empire party takes the lead, and it usually criticizes the official policy, if at all, on the grounds of alleged insufficiency. Among its leading members are to be found several personages who play prominent parts in the coulisses of German politics : for example, Prince

Hatzfeldt, who, in character and standing, occupies a position in the public life of the Empire not unlike that held for so many years in England by the late Duke of Devonshire ; Prince Ernest Hohenlohe, who administered the colonies for a brief period before they were raised to the dignity of an independent department under Herr Dernburg ; Prince Lichnowski, the Imperial Ambassador in London, who, however, is, in many respects, in but imperfect correspondence with his party environment ; and the ex-Governor of East Africa, General von Liebert, who is now a leading spirit in the Pangerman Confederation, and the chairman of an extensive organization that issues millions of leaflets and otherwise displays a laudable activity without, so far as can be seen, in any way attaining its object, which is to check the spread of Socialism. The present Chancellor, Dr. von Bethmann-Hollweg, sat among the Free Conservatives during his very short occupancy of a representative seat in the Reichstag.

It is a curious trait of the Empire party that it should be closely connected with the newspaper *Die Post*, which is conspicuous alike for its rabid Anglophobia and for its occasional virulent and personal attacks on the Government. Always in a condition of frenzy, this journal does not even spare the Emperor himself when its fits are in what may be called " the critical phase." It is quite in harmony with the character of *Die Post* that the Marine Minister should have obtained from among the ranks of the Empire party the most cordial support for his policy, and this group is the only one in the Chamber which can be regarded as favouring as a whole and in principle the Admiral's ambitious schemes. But just as the Socialists have prospered in spite of their consistent and vehement opposition to these projects, so the Empire party has drooped and languished in spite of its championship of them. At the 1912 elections it lost eleven out of twenty-four seats and 106,000 votes, or 23 per cent. of the number which had been given in its favour at the contest of 1907—again a strange commentary on the boasted eagerness of the German nation to make a bid for sea-power.

The parliamentary representation of the bourgeois urban interest is in the feeble hands of what calls itself Liberalism, as exponents of which two parties contest the palm for incompetency and ineffectiveness. Of these the National Liberals attempt to compensate for their lack of a domestic policy by the loudness of their professions of patriotism and their readiness to pass military and naval votes. They are, in fact, much more concerned to be "national" than Liberal, and are the only other main party besides the Free Conservatives in which Admiral von Tirpitz has really convinced and enthusiastic disciples. As a class representation, they stand for industry and a portion of Liberal professionalism, and they are consequently to some extent subject to Semitic influence. Recently they have made strenuous, but not very successful, efforts to draw the peasant land-owners out of the Conservative camp and into their own.

Jewish influence plays a much more important rôle in the counsels of the " People's Party of Progress," as the German Radicals now call themselves. This group derives its main strength from finance, commerce, minor industry, the residue of the professional classes, and the diminishing section of small townsmen who ardently desire sweeping changes but cannot bring themselves to vote for a Socialist candidate. Whereas the National Liberals in principle favour protection for both agriculture and industry, the Radicals are divided upon this point. Until recently, indeed, they were split up into three separate groups as the result of this difference of opinion, and it was only because the question was not at the moment a burning one that they were able to reunite their forces. It would seem that Free Trade doctrines have gained ground among the Radicals of recent years, in consequence mainly of the rise in the prices of the staple articles of food.

278 PARLIAMENT AND NAVAL POLICY

Apart from the Socialist, this is the only party in which pacificism and other derivatives of " Manchesterdom " make much progress. As a parliamentary group it is contemptible both in numbers and character, but it paradoxically has behind it the best and most largely circulated papers that exist in Germany.

Side by side with the Liberal and Radical parties, and in intimate association with them, is the Hanse League, which was founded at the time of the last finance reform to safeguard the interests of industry and commerce in general, and to combat the agitation of the Agricultural League in particular. Both organizations have memberships running into hundreds of thousands, and they form, respectively, the standing armies of urban and rural occupation, which in Germany are practically synonymous with Liberalism and Conservatism. In fact, the tendency is for these two political forces to become divorced from general constitutional principles, and to concentrate on the purely material interests of the two great sections of the population from which they proceed. And herein lies yet another of the causes why German Socialism, with its noisy advocacy of democratic rights and franchises, has gained so strong a hold on the masses of the people.

For all practical purposes, German party politics are limited to the four forces which have just been enumerated — Catholicism, Socialism, Conservatism, and Liberalism. All these forces pull different ways, and the effect of their efforts is to neutralize one another, and to render it easy for the Government, when it wishes, to follow a line of its own. The maxim, *Divide et impera*, has never been more effectively put into practice than in the German Empire of to-day.

Of the minor groups in the Reichstag, the Poles, Alsatians, and Lorrainers are *au fond* separatist. Prussia has never succeeded in reconciling foreign races to her rule, and she never will succeed in doing it so long as she retains her present spirit and methods.

Her theory of government is that the peoples subject to her are her children, that discontent with her rule is naughtiness, and that the only means of correcting naughtiness is the rod. Nothing could be more characteristic of the difference between the two countries than the contrast between the Irish policy of Great Britain and the Polish policy of Prussia. Great Britain has attempted to solve her problem by placing the Irish on the land; Prussia is exacerbating hers by trying to turn the Poles off it. Through their community of religion, the Poles and Alsace-Lorrainers have a strong affinity for the Centre party, and on matters not touching their specific aims frequently accept its leadership. As, however, they wish Germany to be weak, they always oppose any measures intended to increase her strength.

The various groups of Anti-Semites may for all general purposes be counted to the Conservatives. They are composed of dreamers, unpractical idealists and cranks, who are completely out of touch with the realities of life, and especially with that gross manifestation of it which we call politics. Among them are to be found the people who hope to maintain and extend German influence in the world by adhering to the use of Gothic type and expunging from their language all words of foreign origin. Some of them will tell you with a grave face that Germany will never be a healthy State till she has purged herself of her Jews, her Socialists, and her Catholics. That is much the same as if a doctor should advise a patient to part with his brain, heart, and muscular tissue. Yet the Anti-Semites who would divest Germany of her vital organs are among the loudest in clamouring that she should be in a position to call all the world into the lists, and they demean themselves on every opportunity as if they were in a special sense the guardians of their country's honour. In their ranks stand many of the stalwarts of Admiral von Tirpitz, frenzied fanatics whom the coolly adroit Naval Minister

can at any moment plunge into paroxysms of patriotic
fervour. The Anti-Semites find much sympathy among
the Conservatives and some among the Catholics, but
their force in the Reichstag is recruited principally
from those portions of the Empire where Jewish usury
still presses hard upon the agricultural population.

It is from this strange medley of discordant elements that the effective national will of Germany must
be evolved, and the fact that it sometimes differs
considerably from any of their individual intentions
is the result of their number and their discordancy.
At the election of 1912, the 397 seats in the Reichstag
were distributed among these groups as below :

```
Conservatives:
    Conservatives proper  ...   ...   ...  45
    Empire party   ...   ...   ...   ...  13
    Anti-Semites   ...   ...   ...   ...  11
                                              —  69
Catholic group :
    Centre   ...   ...   ...   ...   ...  90
    Poles   ...   ...   ...   ...   ...  18
    Alsace-Lorrainers, Guelphs, etc.   ...  15
                                              — 123
Liberals :
    National Liberals   ...   ...   ...  43
    Radicals ...   ...   ...   ...   ...  42
                                              —  85
Socialists   ...   ...   ...   ...   ...  110
Nondescript ...   ...   ...   ...   ...   10
                                              ——
        Total   ...   ...   ...   ...  397
```

As has been indicated, the only three of these sub-
groups which can really be said to favour in principle
a forward naval policy are the Empire party, the
Anti-Semites, and the National Liberals. It may well
be asked how, in such circumstances, a small body
of zealous patriots can, time after time, make their
own aspirations the effective will of the nation. The
main cause of this phenomenon has already been
pointed out in those fits of national passion or jealousy
to which Germany is at least as prone as other
countries. But this cause could not produce its effects
if it were not helped by the simplicity and ignorance

of the German politician. It is the commonest thing in Germany to come across persons of high literary and artistic culture to whom politics are a sealed book into which they have no desire to look, and a large section of the population is profoundly indifferent alike to the questions of the domestic legislation and to those of the foreign relations of their country. These people look upon the acts of the Government as the dispensations of a minor providence, inscrutable and unchallengeable. The members of the Reichstag are not of course in this frame of mind, but many of them are extraordinarily lacking in political acumen and aptitude. It is, in fact, here more than anywhere else that the defect of the German's mind and intellectual training manifests itself. Where there are hard-and-fast rules and regulations to follow, he may be depended upon to follow them. But that science of applied psychology which is called politics knows no such rules and regulations, and there he fails, and fails miserably. The politician of no other country is so fast bound as he in the thraldom of his own phrases, and the history of modern German naval legislation has been one long exploitation of specious catch-words.

The average German politician declares that the Empire is building its fleet " for purely defensive purposes," and is genuinely astonished that this assurance does not set the whole world at rest. He absolutely fails to realize that the defensive relationship of two States resembles a pair of scales: that if one pan is raised the other must be depressed; that the enhancement of the safety of one country can only be secured by the diminution of the safety of another. And he persists in regarding every addition to his own fleet as a defensive, every addition to the British Fleet as an aggressive measure, oblivious of the patent fact that it is his own country and not Great Britain that has altered its policy, and thereby modified the naval relationship of the two countries very considerably to its own advantage. He protests that Germany is building her fleet "according to the measure of her own needs and without reference to the naval strength of other States," though it is self-evident that the measure of the naval needs of one country can only be the naval strengths of others. He urges that Germany's Fleet is intended merely "to protect her coasts, commerce, and colonies," and apparently fails to recognize that exactly in proportion that this purpose is fulfilled Great Britain will be unable to protect her only frontier line, her much larger and more vital commerce, which is literally a matter of life and death to her, and her vastly more extensive and more valuable colonies. He argues that "each nation has the inalienable right to fix for itself the dimensions of its armaments;" but if he were to reflect for a moment, he would be compelled to admit that Germany would not remain unmoved or idle if France and Russia were largely to augment their land forces, and were to mass the new corps on his country's frontiers; and, making the necessary allowances for the different conditions of naval warfare, that is precisely what Germany is doing by Great Britain.[*]

Even within the narrow limits of their possible meanings these phrases are not true, for the entire modern naval agitation in Germany has from first to last been carried on with reference to Great Britain and to that country only. It was British naval supremacy which the German was called upon to break; British "arrogance" and "tyranny" on the sea, by which his pride was wounded and the feeling of resentment stimulated, without the existence of which Admiral von Tirpitz could never have been so successful with his schemes.

But the crowning example of German political inconsequence is the argument, frequently employed,

---

[*] Something of the character actually happened early in 1913, when a marked improvement in the fighting efficiency of the Russian Army led Germany to embark on a policy of military expansion. France, of course, followed suit.

though never, of course, precisely in these terms: "The increase of the German Fleet has involved us in the danger of war; therefore we will diminish that danger by increasing it further." This argument can have validity only on the assumption that Great Britain is prepared to abdicate her position in the world and exist on sufferance like the smaller States, for otherwise it is perfectly evident that every addition to the German Navy necessarily aggravates the risk of war, which would come, if at all, at a date before Germany was able to engage in it with much chance of success.

Nevertheless, to those who have closely followed the debates in the Reichstag on naval topics, it must appear at least exceedingly probable that the great majority of the members of that Parliament are quite sincere in their expressed convictions that Germany has no intention of rivalling the naval power of Great Britain, and is actuated in her shipbuilding policy by the desire to attain a position which, to put it in the terms of its true significance, will alter her naval relationship to other nations without changing theirs to her.

Another of the phrases with which considerable sections of the Reichstag and of the German nation confuse their brains and disturb their judgments is this: "England fears our commercial rivalry, and has resolved to destroy us before it is too late." Yet but a very slight acquaintance with the leading facts of international trade is required to show that by "destroying" Germany Great Britain would deprive herself of the best foreign customer she has, and it may well be doubted whether any sane mind has ever believed that any diminution of Germany's competition in neutral markets that could be brought about by a naval war could compensate for the corresponding loss from her purchases of British products, which have an annual value of between thirty and forty millions sterling.

However, as already indicated, the phrases which

have helped so much to carry succeeding Navy Bills through the Reichstag attain their maximum and effective force only in moments of popular excitement over affronts or dangers, real or imaginary, to the Fatherland. External pressure has made the German Empire, and the same force holds it together in its present form. Napoleon's service to Germany was not confined to the destruction of the mouldy framework of the Holy Roman Empire; he also made the nation realize vividly what dread possibilities its political particularism involved. And to-day, at the slightest semblance of a threat from without, the Germans incline even more strongly than other nations to forget their own domestic quarrels and to place themselves unreservedly at the disposal of their Government, the only power that can do anything for them against a foreign foe. This characteristic, which has been cleverly exploited by Admiral von Tirpitz, involves no small peril to the peace of the world. The most clamorous of the various sections of naval enthusiasts in Germany is that school of thinkers who hold that war is in itself a good thing, and the only tonic by means of which nations can shake off their social and political ailments. They openly proclaim that the maladies of which Germany is sickening —Socialism, materialism, and hedonism, for instance— have been allowed to spread too far, and that a big war should be prescribed for their cure.* There is this much in favour of their theory—that a successful war would undoubtedly impose a check, temporarily at any rate, on the dissemination of communistic doctrines, and therein lies a temptation and a risk. On the other hand, it is by no means improbable that an unsuccessful war, with the sufferings that it would inflict upon the people, would so aggravate the prevailing dissatisfaction with the Government as to precipitate a revolution. This possibility is recog-

---

* This view is held, and held very vehemently, by the Admiralstab —that is, by the officers mainly responsible for Germany's naval policy.

nized in Government circles, and in this recognition lies the safeguard. Should Germany, however, some day find herself in a position to declare war with strong prospects of success, the temptation to draw the sword would be very great indeed.

Should the international horizon clear, German politicians may, in spite of the insidious counsels of Admiral von Tirpitz, recover from their mental agitation, and awake to the facts that British distrust is the effect and not the cause of the increase of their fleet ; that their recent naval policy, however " defensive " in theory and intention, is aggressive in effect ; that it has not diminished the risks of war between the two countries but increased them ; that it has not, in the sum total of its consequences, strengthened Germany but weakened her, internally and externally, politically, militarily, and financially, by raising up opposition to her abroad and encumbering her with debt, taxes, and Socialism at home. They may, in that event, once again become preoccupied with their own internal affairs, and concentrate their energies on the great struggle which will have to be fought out before German democracy can assert its claims to an equal share in the government of the Empire. How long that struggle would last, or what forms it would take, it is impossible to predict ; but there are no sufficient reasons for supposing that its issue would permanently impair Germany's position in the world, or render her at all less formidable as a possible opponent. On similar provocation a democratic German Parliament would probably act in precisely the same way as did the National Assembly in Frankfort when it decided to build a navy in a hurry, and sweep the Danes off the sea. And a Germany in which the effective will of the nation represented the views of a majority of the population would for all genuinely national purposes be stronger than one in which that will is the product of the adroit exploitation by a determined few of panics, party jealousies, and religious dissensions.

The mere removal of some of the many political grievances which are rampant in Germany would of itself liberate for larger national objects a vast force of interest and energy which is at present consumed in futile protests against the existing régime. A sense of full partnership in the business of the Empire would awaken a new pride in its institutions, and diminish the present large number of political fatalists, who, feeling that they have no real influence on the destinies of their country, stand aside from the party struggle, and watch its progress with the indifference of strangers.

Above all, a democratization of Germany would stay the advance of Socialism, and reduce the risk of an eventual plunge into perilous communistic experiments.

On the other hand, the school of blood-letters and prescribers of prophylactic wars would have but little influence in a democratic Germany, which, in normal times, would, on the whole, be of a peaceable disposition, for it is undoubtedly true that a vast majority of the nation intensely dislikes the idea of war, and has no more fervent wish than to live in peace and concord with its neighbours.

In any case, however, the rapidly progressing industrialization of Germany, which renders a change in the form of her government inevitable, also makes it highly probable that she will, before many generations have elapsed, outstrip all the other purely European nations in wealth and national energy, as she has already far surpassed them in population. When that day arrives it will be difficult for the United Kingdom alone to keep pace with her in the building of warships, as in other manifestations of national activity, and the future of the British race will then depend on the result of the efforts now being made to knit together into one indivisible political whole the diverse regions of the earth which it now inhabits.

CHAPTER X

GERMANY'S MARITIME INTERESTS

PASSING mention has already been made of Germany's maritime interests—her colonies, her oversea trade, and her shipping—which, it is urged, compel her from motives of self-preservation, to build up a powerful fleet for their defence. It will be well to look a little closer into the nature and scope of these interests.

When the record of Germany's colonies is examined, it is difficult to understand how she can either wish to add to their number, or be anxious to spend millions of pounds on their defence against hypothetical dangers. The general belief among patriotic Germans is that the Empire's colonies have provided agreeable homes and remunerative employment for its surplus population, large and profitable markets for its trade, and abundant supplies of raw materials for its industry. In no singular particular is this belief well-founded. Germany's colonies have so far been merely a source of weakness and impoverishment to her: they have not been occupied to any appreciable extent either by her own or by any other white people, their trade is of quite insignificant dimensions, they have supplied her with no mentionable quantities of the raw materials of her staple industries, and they have cost, and are costing, her immense sums of money, which can only be recouped, if at all, at a very remote date.

In mere area the German colonies are a very imposing mass, for their superficial extent is five times as large as that of the Fatherland, but in all other respects their value has been a negative one. Let us first of all consider to what extent they have furnished fresh fields for the activities of German emigrants. In 1911 the total white population of the one million square miles which the Empire then owned in oversea lands (certain tracts of swampy jungle on the Congo have since been added to these estates) was 25,758 souls, of whom 20,966 were Germans. But if we wish to ascertain the genuine German colonial element, we must deduct from these latter 8,856 official individuals— officials, protectorate troops, missionaries, wives of officials and missionaries, nurses, and school teachers, and 3,431 children.

In this way we get an adult German population of 8,679 spread over a million square miles of territory, practically all of which has been in the possession of the Empire for nearly thirty years. The detailed figures, which are taken from official returns, are appended, and it should be mentioned that the Navy Department, which administers Kiauchow, restricts its enumeration of official personages to the white garrison, and does not distinguish children from adults, so that the numbers stated above really afford too favourable a view of the situation :

Colony.	Total White Population.	Germans.	Official Persons.	Children.
East Africa... ...	4,227	3,113	1,414	617
Cameroons... ...	1,455	1,311	594	66
Togo	363	327	202	4
South-West Africa	13,962	11,140	3,424	2,579
South Sea Colonies	1,660	1,056	584	165
Kiauchow	4,091	4,019	2,638	—
Totals	25,758	20,966	8,856	3,431

By way of comparison, it may be mentioned that, within the German Empire, there are some 230 towns, each of which contains more persons of Teutonic race than all these colonies taken together. The German population of the Imperial oversea possessions is, in fact, just about equal to that of insignificant places like Passau and Kempten, which might disappear from the map to-morrow without causing a perceptible dislocation of the world's affairs.

It will, perhaps, be objected that Germany's colonies, though unsuitable for settlement by white men, may nevertheless be of substantial benefit to her trade. Let us see. In 1910 the value of the total trade of Germany's colonies, and of her share in it, were as under :

IMPORTS.

Colony.	Value of Total Imports.	Value of Imports from Germany.
	£	£
East Africa	1,932,000	983,000
Cameroons	1,274,000	999,000
Togo	573,000	314,000
South-West Africa	2,217,000	1,722,000
New Guinea	194,000	84,000
East Carolines	15,000	3,000
West Carolines, etc.	36,000	14,000
Marshall Islands	65,000	11,000
Samoa	173,000	42,000
Kiauchow...	3,501,000	109,000
Totals	9,980,000	4,281,000

EXPORTS.

Colony.	Value of Total Exports.	Value of Exports to Germany.
	£	£
East Africa	1,040,000	629,000
Cameroons	996,000	862,000
Togo	361,000	226,000
South-West Africa	1,734,000	1,433,000
New Guinea	181,000	118,000
East Carolines	10,000	9,000
West Carolines, etc.	72,000	31,000
Marshall Islands	468,000	109,000
Samoa	176,000	86,000
Kiauchow	2,369,000	17,000
Totals	7,407,000	3,520,000

In the same year in which Germany's aggregate imports from the whole of her own colonies were worth £3,520,000, she took from British West Africa alone goods to the total value of £5,401,000. In the same year in which Germany's aggregate exports to the whole of her own colonies were worth £4,281,000 she sent to the British East Indies goods to the total value of £5,165,000. From these figures it is clear that all Germany's colonies taken together have not yet so great an importance for her trade as single colonies of the United Kingdom. The total external trade of the German colonies is approximately equal to that of the British West Indies, which in area are not much more than a hundredth part of their size. In 1910 only two of Germany's colonies sent her as much as $\frac{1}{10}$ per cent. of her total import trade: they were the Cameroons and East Africa, and their joint contribution amounted to $\frac{2}{8}$ per cent. of her aggregate imports. Three of her colonies—South-West Africa, East Africa, and the Cameroons—each took as much as $\frac{1}{10}$ per cent. of her outward trade, their aggregate purchases amounting to $\frac{3}{8}$ per cent. of her total exports.

But here again it should be borne in mind that nearly one-half of the German population of the German colonies consists of officials and their dependents, so that a considerable proportion of the imports of these possessions is composed of stores for the administration and commodities for the consumption of its employees. Thus we find that Germany's exports to her colonies in 1910 included railway material to the value of upwards of £250,000, silver coin to the value of nearly £300,000, beer to the value of £42,000, and preserved foods to the value of £43,000.

Nor is there the slightest ground for the idea current in Germany that her colonies supply her with any considerable proportion of the raw materials which she requires for her manufactures, or of the articles of food which she cannot produce herself. The Year-Book issued by the Imperial Statistical Office gives special tables, showing all articles of which the export from or the import into Germany had an annual value of at least £150,000, and the countries of destination or origin which took from or sent to her such commodities to the annual value of at least £25,000, together with the detail values in both cases; and for 1910 her colonies appear under only eight separate headings as sources of raw materials or foodstuffs. These eight commodities and the value of her colonies' contribution to Germany's total import of them were as below:

Commodity.	Total German Imports.	Share of German Colonies in Imports.
	£	£
Agave fibres	176,000	54,000
Uncut jewels	305,000	152,000
Coffee	8,823,000	26,000
Cocoa beans	2,270,000	50,000
India-rubber	11,112,000	1,366,000
Copra	4,125,000	228,000
Palm kernels	4,420,000	119,000
Phosphate of lime	1,808,000	143,000

From these figures it would appear that the only raw materials of which Germany draws any considerable proportion of her consumption from her own colonies are agave fibres and rough diamonds. She derives from none of her oversea possessions either cotton, silk, tobacco, wool, hides, tea, or metallic ores, to the annual value of even so much as £25,000.

During recent years great efforts have been made, and much money has been spent, by the German Government on the promotion of cotton culture in the East Africa Protectorate and Togo. Mainly as the result of this State encouragement, the two colonies named placed upon the market in the year 1911 raw cotton of a total weight of 2,750 metric tons. In the same year Germany's aggregate import of cotton was 444,017 tons, so that she was then in a position to cover from her own territory only the one hundred-

and-sixtieth part of her own requirements of this raw material. Cotton growing in the German colonies can so far be regarded only as an interesting experiment, and is otherwise entirely without present significance for the industries of the Fatherland.

The plain facts are that, up to the present, Germany's colonies have been practically worthless to her, whether for the settlement of her own people, as markets for her manufactures, or as sources of supply of raw materials and tropical food-stuffs. On the other hand, they have placed large tracts of her territory at the mercy of any enemy who can sweep her shipping off the seas, and have thus exposed her to a risk which never threatened her so long as she remained a purely Continental State. It may be argued that they have, at any rate, provided her with a convenient pretext for building a fleet which she really wishes to have for other and more general purposes of "world-policy"; but the incontestable bulk and importance of her oversea trade, so little of which goes to her colonies, has always been, and will, so far as can be foreseen, always remain a much more effective argument in favour of her naval policy.

So far, however, only the credit side of the balance-sheet has been considered, and we have yet to see what Germany's colonies have cost her. Here we find much more imposing figures. The bill which had been incurred up to the year 1908 was as under:

		£
Cost of central administration ...	...	14,500,000
Purchase of Caroline Isles	... ...	830,000
Loans to colonies	...	1,170,000
Subsidies to balance deficits of local administration :		
East Africa	...	5,384,000
Cameroons	...	1,564,000
Togo	...	85,000
South-West Africa	...	7,446,000
South Sea Islands	...	452,000
Kiauchow	...	6,514,000
South-West Africa war loan ...	...	18,955,000
East Africa war loan	...	90,000
Total	...	£56,990,000

For all the German colonies, with the exception of Samoa and Togo, the Imperial subsidies still continue, and their aggregate amount for the year 1913-14 was estimated in the budget at upwards of a million and a half sterling. In the immediate future they are likely to be substantially increased through the acquisition of a portion of the French Congo under the Morocco Treaty of 1911. The proportion of the large and ever-increasing cost of the Empire's Fleet which must be written down to the debit of this account, cannot, of course, be computed; but if the part which the colonies, present and future, play in the naval agitation can be taken as a guide, it must be a very large one.

Altogether it can be said that a very considerable measure of ignorance or optimism must be available before it is possible to look at the results of Germany's colonial policy with enthusiasm or confidence. There was clearly much truth in the exclamation of Caprivi: "No greater misfortune could befall us than to be presented with the whole of Africa." Yet many members of the Reichstag have been so completely hypnotized by the colonial legend that they go on year after year talking as if Germany's colonies were a source of wealth and power, instead of, as they really and obviously are, a drain on her finances, and a weak spot in her defences. To the meanest intelligence it should be quite evident that up to now Germany would have been considerably richer and much stronger if she had never possessed a square inch of oversea territory.

The development of Germany's shipping and ship-building has a double bearing. On the one hand, the growth of her mercantile marine increases the stake which she has floating on the water, already very large in the shape of the 70 per cent. of her total foreign trade that is sea-borne; on the other hand, the evolution of her shipbuilding industry touches

very closely the question whether she can place herself in a position to defend those maritime interests
against all possible foes, and so become the dominant
naval Power of the world.

When the development of German ship-owning
during the last hundred years is examined, it will be
noticed that at the outset of that period it was suffering
from artificial retardation, that it made its decisive
step forward under the influence of a morbid stimulus,
and that in its most recent phase it can hardly be
regarded as quite normal and healthy.

Like all other forms of industrial and commercial
activity in Germany, shipowning was, until the
foundation of the new Empire, most prejudicially
affected by the territorial divisions and political convulsions which for centuries had hampered every
manifestation of the national life. Passing mention
was made in an earlier chapter of the operation of the
Napoleonic wars and the Continental blockade upon
the German mercantile marine. No port was hit
harder by these events than Hamburg, which is now
the chief shipping centre on the European Continent,
and owns nearly three-fifths of the sea-going tonnage
of Germany. From 1804 to 1813 there is a gap in the
official returns of the sea traffic to and from the Hanse
town, and in the place of the usual figures the following
note appears : "During these years there was no shipping traffic, as the French occupied the left bank of
the Elbe, and the blockade on the part of England
came into force. Only on June 8, 1814, was shipping
reopened." It is also very significant of the low ebb
to which the mercantile marine of Prussia had sunk,
that, when Further Pomerania was handed over to
that State at the general peace, a number of vessels
belonging to the ports of the transferred province
continued to fly the Swedish flag, as affording them
greater security than that of their new country against
the ravages of the Barbary pirates.

In fact, German shipping had lapsed into a condition

of coma, from which recovery was possible only by slow degrees. A certain amount of stimulus was imparted by the Treaty of 1824, under which Prussia secured exemption from the provisions of the British Navigation Acts. The policy embodied in these statutes, which had been borrowed from the Venetians by the Hanseatic League and copied from the latter by England, had long, by a curious irony, proved a great obstacle to the progress of German shipping. Treitschke goes so far as to describe the Treaty of 1824 as the "first real blow struck at the bulwark of British sea supremacy since the restoration of peace."

It is, however, in the emigration of her people to the United States that the main cause of the recent development of Germany's mercantile marine is to be sought. In the individual decades from 1820 to 1870 the number of persons who left what is now German territory for North America were :

1821-1830	6,761
1831-1840	152,454
1841-1850	434,626
1851-1860	591,667
1861-1870	822,007

In the early days of this migration the settlers crossed the Atlantic almost exclusively in British ships, and this necessitated a voyage over the North Sea and a railway journey from one side of England to the other. The advantages of direct shipment from German ports were too obvious to be overlooked, but it is a significant fact that it was a man of English birth who first clearly appreciated in Germany the latent possibilities of the passenger traffic from the Continent to the United States. Robert Miles Sloman was born at Yarmouth in 1773, and as a boy of ten years settled at Hamburg, where he was destined to become, and long remain, the most enterprising and far-seeing pioneer of German shipping. It was he who, in 1836, started the first regular line of German sailers between the Elbe and the Hudson ; and in 1850 he made another new departure by placing a steamer in this service. The vessel, however, did not remain afloat very long, and her loss seems for a time to have discouraged him from further experiments with mechanical propulsion.

In 1847, a year in which, as has been seen, the German emigration to the United States had already assumed colossal dimensions, a number of Hamburg firms decided to make an attempt to capture and exploit this rapidly growing traffic. With the modest capital of £15,000 was formed what is now the biggest individual shipping undertaking in the world—the Hamburg-Amerika Paketfahrt Gesellschaft. It is a curious fact that the original partners in this concern were not individuals but firms, and that at the outset practically the entire business of the line, both passenger and freight, was placed in the hands of brokers.

The Hamburg-America line did not venture on the purchase of a couple of steamers till 1856, so that the field was still fully open for enterprising competition when, in 1857, the Norddeutscher Lloyd was started at Bremen as a purely steam line, for the purpose of disputing with the older company the profits of the emigrant traffic. By a bold and far-sighted policy, the Bremen concern succeeded in attracting to its boats a very large proportion of the German emigration. Further, by accepting return cargoes at merely nominal freights, and treating cotton and tobacco substantially as ballast, it made Bremen the chief Continental emporium for these articles, and thus deprived Liverpool and London of much of their transit trade. Half a century ago the spinners of Chemnitz obtained the entire supply of their raw material from Liverpool, but now that Bremen ranks second among the world's cotton-importing towns, they have become quite independent of the English middleman. The development of the importation of cotton by Liverpool and Bremen respectively during the last quarter of a century is shown in the appended figures :

				Liverpool.	Bremen.
				Bales.	Bales.
1885-86	...	...	...	2,558,798	530,451
1895-96	...	...	...	2,090,123	918,955
1905-06	...	...	...	2,485,686	1,612,066
1911-12	...	...	...	3,690,800	2,792,000

The tobacco manufacturing trade of Bremen shows to this day traces of its origin, for its products are packed in the English fashion, bear English names (sometimes of an unintentionally grotesque character), and are sent out under labels and wrappers printed in the English language. It may be mentioned in passing that in American tobaccos, as in jams and biscuits, German manufacturers have hitherto failed completely in their attempts to reproduce British samples.

Hamburg had been the pioneer of the German transatlantic passenger traffic, but now found itself in danger of being outdistanced by Bremen. This menace spurred the shipowners of the Elbe to fresh efforts, and the subsequent history of the German mercantile marine has been practically synonymous with that of the two leading lines of Hamburg and Bremen respectively. A separate book would be needed to tell the tale of their rapid growth, their mutual emulation, and the ultimate agreements under which, in amicable compromise, they divided up the traffic on those ocean routes where they had no native rival to fear. Nor does the space available here allow the presentation of details of the numerous bargains of the same kind which they have from time to time concluded with the leading lines of other countries.

A few figures will suffice to give an adequate idea of what these two concerns mean to the German mercantile marine, and of the dislocation which their immoderate growth has brought about. In 1912 the capital of each of them stood at M. 125,000,000 (in round figures £6,000,000), exclusive, in both cases, of debentures to the total amount of about £3,500,000. At the beginning of that year the gross register tonnage of the vessels belonging to the two companies was as under:

Hamburg-America Company	...	...	1,160,424
Norddeutscher Lloyd	...	...	...	739,740
Total	...	...	...	...	1,900,164

This total is not far short of half the aggregate tonnage of the entire mercantile marine of the German Empire, which at the same date was 4,513,191 gross register tons.

The concentration of so large a share of the German merchant navy under the management of these two concerns has aggravated the disproportionate development of the two Hanse towns in which they have their respective headquarters at the expense of the other German ports. Up to 1854, the mercantile tonnage of the German ports on the Baltic was larger than that of those on the North Sea, but after that date the positions were reversed, and the tendency which produced the change has continued with gathering force ever since. It has manifested itself not only in a greater rapidity of growth on the part of the merchant fleet of the North Sea, but also in the actual absolute decline which that of the Baltic experienced for many years. In 1875 the shipowners of the German Baltic ports owned 2,109 vessels, of an aggregate of 470,914 tons net, but by 1900 these numbers had sunk to 840 vessels and 218,750 tons. In the thirty years which had elapsed since the foundation of the Empire the German Baltic littoral had actually lost more than half of its merchant shipping. On January 1, 1912, German shipping was distributed between the two seas as under :

	Vessels.	Net Register Tonnage.
North Sea	3,730	2,594,353
Baltic	945	309,217
Totals	4,675	2,903,570

There is obviously this much justification for Germany's new policy of naval distribution, that in so far as her merchant navy and sea-borne commerce are concerned, she is ceasing to be a Baltic, and becoming a very important North Sea, Power. And it is noteworthy, that of the 2,903,570 net tons of mercantile shipping registered in the Empire at the commencement of 1912, no fewer than 1,604,415 tons, or considerably more than half the total, were owned at Hamburg, and 859,064 tons at Bremen. In fact these two free towns between them contribute very nearly 85 per cent. of the total tonnage of the German mercantile fleet.

But the concentration of German merchant shipping is even greater than appears from the foregoing figures. At the close of 1911, the composition of this shipping was as is shown in the appended table, in which once more we return to gross tons, as the net figures necessary for comparison are not available in all cases :

	Gross Register Tonnage.
Steamers	3,949,759
Sailing vessels	452,996
Sea-going lighters	110,436
Total	4,513,191

Included in this tonnage were the following individual merchant fleets:

	Gross Register Tonnage.
Hamburg-America	1,160,424
Norddeutscher Lloyd	739,740
Hansa Company	289,873
Hamburg-South America Company ...	221,859
German-Australian Company	199,757
Kosmos Company	153,324
Levant Line	121,243
East Africa Line	103,703
Woermann Line	98,134
German-American Petroleum Company	84,219
Total	3,172,276

It thus appears that 70 per cent. of the total merchant tonnage of Germany, and 80 per cent. of her steam tonnage are in the hands of ten companies, and considerably more than half of the latter in those of the two leading concerns. In fact, the recent remarkable growth of German mercantile shipping has been almost entirely due to the development of a few big lines of steamers plying regularly along fixed routes.

The concentration of Germany's shipping at Hamburg and Bremen is, however, not only natural, but in many ways exceedingly advantageous. A glance at the map will show that the Elbe, in conjunction with the Oder, with which it is linked up into one system of waterways by a couple of junction canals, is the natural entrance into Germany from by far the greater part of the outside world. Dividing the Empire diagonally into two approximately equal parts, this mighty stream is navigable right through the heart of the highly industrialized Kingdom of Saxony and beyond that deep into Bohemia, where it serves as the channel of transport for a considerable proportion of the Austro-German trade. By way of the Oder, it permits unbroken water traffic between the North Sea and the busy mining district in the extreme south-east of Silesia. Barge-loads of cheap manufactured articles are brought down from Breslau to Hamburg, there transhipped on board sea-going vessels, and landed in the London docks without having traversed an inch of railway line, and it is this exclusively water transport that chiefly accounts for the lowness of the prices at which many German articles can be sold in England.

The busiest point on this vast system of waterways is, however, Berlin, with its manufacturing suburbs, which is connected with the Elbe by the Spree and the Havel. It is to the Elbe alone that the German capital owes its present position as the chief manufacturing and trading centre of the Empire. The Rhine, while serving districts of even higher industrial development than those traversed by the Elbe, has not nearly so central a course as the latter river, and is, for the moment, of comparative unimportance from the point of view of the German mercantile marine, because its mouths are in the possession of other countries.

It may be mentioned incidentally that a movement is now on foot with the object of providing the Rhine with a German mouth by means of a canal from Cologne to Emden. The proposed waterway would include stretches of the Ems and Ruhr, and would tap the coal-mining and iron industry district which takes its name from the latter stream. This project would, if carried out, have the additional significance of assisting the efforts now being made to transform Emden into that first-class commercial port on the North Sea which Prussia at present lacks. It has been suggested that the canal would yield large surpluses, which might be employed in the construction of the much-talked-of strategic waterway between the Ems and the Jade, to enable German warships of the largest size to pass at will, under cover of the land, from Wilhelmshaven to Emden, and so baffle the vigilance of a blockading squadron.

The great importance which Hamburg has recently

acquired as a trading port was rendered possible only by the introduction of steam-shipping. Prior to that event the harbour was frequently frozen up and in-accessible during a considerable portion of the winter. For instance, in the five years, 1826 to 1830, the Hamburg water-traffic was, on an average, suspended for seventy-two days annually by accumulations of ice. The constant coming and going of powerful tugs and ice-breakers now prevents the water in the basins from congealing, and keeps the traffic of the actual port open right through the winter. On the other hand, the German canals are generally closed by ice for a few months every year, and though the period of unnavigability naturally varies with the severity of the weather, traffic upon them is usually suspended during the whole of the period which experience has shown brings with it a risk of being frozen in. The goods which arrive at Hamburg during this period *en route* to an inland destination find it cheaper, except in cases of urgency, to remain warehoused at the Elbe port till the spring than to finish their journey by rail.

It is the geographical idiosyncrasies of Hamburg, which, to some extent, are shared by Bremen, that form the main justification for the massing of the bulk of Germany's shipping at these two ports, but there are also other respects in which this concentration possesses undeniable advantages. For example, it has provided the two Hanse towns with the financial basis for a bold and comprehensive harbour policy, and they have developed their channels, docks, wharves, warehouses, cranes, and all the appurtenances necessary for the rapid loading and unloading of ships to the highest point of efficiency. Concentration also means considerable economy in administration, and though the aggregate sums spent at Hamburg and Bremen on harbour improvement and management have been large, they will, in the long run, prove to have lightened the proportional burden of dues and costs falling on each ton of merchandise handled.

What Bremen lacks in natural facilities, it has partially made good by a superior spirit of enterprise and emulation, and it thus affords a valuable illustration of what can be effected by these two ideal motives. In many respects it has led the way, and Hamburg, though much more prodigally endowed by Nature, has merely followed in its footsteps. It is a common and pardonable boast of Bremen business men that, if they had been at Hamburg, the great port and emporium at the mouth of the Weser would never have been allowed an opportunity of developing.

There are, however, unquestionable risks and drawbacks in the manner in which German shipping has evolved. For one thing, it has prospered through the long and general upward movement of the world's trade consequent on the opening out of fresh markets in Asia, Africa, and South America, and though it will, no doubt, continue to flourish whilst that movement lasts, it might find it very difficult to survive an extended period of universal depression. The brief commercial crisis of 1908 hit the Norddeutscher Lloyd exceedingly hard. For that year, even after reducing the sum due to be written off, the company's accounts showed a loss of £800,000, which absorbed the entire renewal and reserve funds, and left only the insurance fund of £800,000 untouched. It was 1910 before the line was able to resume the payment of dividends, and the rate was only 3 per cent.

It is obvious that the large liners of such companies cannot adapt themselves to the fluctuations of trade so easily as tramps of moderate size, which can tide over bad times by picking up an odd freight here and there. It is another weak spot in the constitution of the big lines, that they are, to a very large extent, dependent for their profits on agreements of the nature of international trusts. No one is likely to contend that such agreements are as sound a basis to stand upon as the unrestricted competition on which the enormous British tramp trade has been built up.

The crisis of 1908 was so acutely felt in German maritime circles that leading Hamburg owners seriously advocated the joint purchase and scrapping by the big lines of a million tons of shipping, or, as an alternative, a mutual undertaking to abstain from building, except to replace losses, for a period of two or three years. Such fits of compunction are quickly overcome, however, and there were building for Hamburg's account alone at the beginning of—

1910, 16 steamers of a total of   66,000 gross register tonnage.
1911, 35   „   „   198,000   „   „
1912, 51   „   „   412,000   „   „

Nor can it be said that the principal German shipping companies have so far proved a bad investment for the original shareholders. There are three of these companies which each have a capital of over a million sterling, and during the past ten years their dividends have been as under:

Year.	Hamburg-America.	Norddeutscher Lloyd.	Hansa.
	Per Cent.	Per Cent.	Per Cent.
1903	6	6	6
1904	9	2	9
1905	11	$7\frac{1}{2}$	9
1906	10	$8\frac{1}{2}$	6
1907	6	$4\frac{1}{2}$	8
1908	0	0	6
1909	6	0	10
1910	8	3	10
1911	9	5	15
1912	10	7	20
Totals ...	75	43·5	99
Averages ...	7·5	4·35	9·9

During these ten years the average annual dividends of the four German shipping companies which rank next in point of capital were as under:

Company.	Annual Average.
	Per Cent.
Hamburg-South America	8·7
Kosmos	7·1
German-Australian	8·5
German-East African	3·6

At the same time, it cannot be maintained that the mercantile marine of the United Kingdom is as yet seriously threatened by that of Germany. The progress of the two merchant fleets during the past forty years has been, from decade to decade, as under:

Year.				United Kingdom.	Germany.
				Net Register Tonnage.	Net Register Tonnage.
1870	...	...	...	...	5,690,789	982,355
1880	...	...	...	...	6,574,513	1,181,525
1890	...	...	...	...	7,978,538	1,433,413
1900	...	...	...	...	9,304,108	1,941,645
1910	...	...	...	...	11,555,663	2,903,570

Included in these figures are the following quantities of steam shipping :

Year.				United Kingdom.	Germany.
				Net Register Tonnage.	Net Register Tonnage.
1870	...	...	...	...	1,112,934	81,994
1880	...	...	...	...	2,723,468	215,758
1890	...	...	...	...	5,042,517	723,652
1900	...	...	...	...	7,207,610	1,347,875
1910	...	...	...	...	10,442,719	2,396,733

These figures are, no doubt, capable of being twisted in such a way as to bear a very ominous aspect. It is, for instance, perfectly true that, in the forty years under consideration, the shipping of the United Kingdom merely doubled, while that of Germany increased nearly threefold. In some circumstances this might mean a great deal, but percentage growths cannot alter the essential fact, that whereas in 1870 the United Kingdom owned only 1,031,000 tons more steam shipping than Germany, her superiority had increased by 1910 to over 8,000,000 tons.

Nor does it signify very much that the share of the United Kingdom in the world's steam mercantile fleet sank in the ten years 1901 to 1911 from 53·3 to 49·8 per cent., while that of Germany rose simultaneously from 10·6 to 11 per cent. If all the factors of the economic history of the past fifty years are taken into consideration it must astonish, not that the British proportion has declined, but that its downward movement should have been so insignificant in extent. It is really, when we come to think of it with unbiassed minds, an astounding phenomenon, that a State with forty-five million inhabitants should own half the merchant shipping in a world with two thousand millions.

The essential question from our present point of view is, however, how far Germany's water-borne trade and mercantile marine have reacted on her shipbuilding industry; for if a nation hopes to take the first place among the naval Powers of the world—and this is the destiny which some Germans prophesy for their country—it must be able not only to pay for the biggest fleet, but to construct it in its own yards. As to whether Germany is likely ever to be in a position to do this it is impossible to make positive predictions, but it is incontestable that the progress of her shipbuilding has, in some respects, been hardly, if at all, less remarkable than that which she has made in other branches of industry, and at present there are no obvious reasons for supposing that it will be brought to a standstill.

What Germany has accomplished in the art of shipbuilding appears all the more remarkable if we consider the disadvantageous circumstances in which she was overtaken by those two great revolutions of navigation —the transition from sails to steam as a means of propulsion, and the substitution of iron for wood as construction material. When the American watchmaker, Fulton, fitted his first vessel with Watt engines, in 1802, Germany was on the eve of the ordeal of the French occupation. In 1807, the year which saw the first line of paddle-boats plying on the Hudson River between New York and Albany, that hard probation had already commenced ; and Europe was only just beginning to recover from the effects of the Continental blockade as the *Savannah* opened a new area of transoceanic traffic by crossing the Atlantic under mechanical power.

A steam engine had been built in a German workshop as early as 1785, but the general adoption of machinery in the country was very slow, and it was 1822 before it was put to any other use than that of pumping, the Royal Porcelain Works at Berlin leading the way in applying it to other purposes. In 1840 it was estimated that there were only 500 stationary engines in the territories belonging to the German Customs Union. Six years later, 196 engines of an aggregate of 2,446 horse-power were known to exist in Saxony, and 1,139, of an aggregate of 21,716 horse-power, in Prussia. In England 5,000 steam engines had been at work as early as 1810. Of the 245 locomotives which were in service on the German railways in 1840, only 38 were of home manufacture, 166 having been made in England, 29 in the United States, and 12 in Belgium. These facts will make apparent how heavily handicapped Germany was in the great international competition of the machine age.

Moreover, at the commencement of that epoch, German shipbuilding was still comparatively in a very primitive stage of development. The Hanseatic Federation, always more concerned about commerce

and carrying trade than about industry, severely discouraged the building of ships by its members for
other countries.   Repeatedly it issued prohibitions
against the sale of vessels to foreigners, and it was
only after much trouble that Dantzig, which was
favoured through its geographical situation with an
abundant supply of wood suitable for shipbuilding,
secured the final abolition of these restrictions.

During the eighteenth century several states of the
German littoral, and especially Prussia and Hamburg,
endeavoured to stimulate shipbuilding by the offer of
premiums, and in other ways, but their efforts availed
little against the short-sighted selfishness of the trade
guilds, which arbitrarily fixed wages and opposed
the opening of new yards as well as the extension
of old ones.   Nothing could have been better calculated to prevent an industry from keeping pace
with the times, and the advent of steam found
German shipbuilders for the most part confining their
activities to the rule-of-thumb construction of small
coasters.

The first marine engine to be built in Germany seems
to have been that supplied by the works of Egells
of Berlin (which subsequently developed into the
Germania yard, at Kiel, now in the possession of
the Krupp firm), for a small paddle passenger boat
for use on the Elbe; and it was not till 1852 that
Fürchtenicht and Brock, now the Vulcan Works of
Hamburg and Stettin, launched what appears to have
been the first sea-going steamer of German construction.

For the transition from wood to iron as the material
of ships' hulls, Germany was also very badly prepared.
Her builders found it exceedingly difficult to break
with their traditional empiricism, and asked sceptically
how iron was to float.   Many of them paid dearly for
their lack of adaptability, and were eventually obliged
to close their yards.   Even if they had been willing to
change with the times, they would have been unable to

procure the necessary technical instruction in their own country. A school of shipbuilding was opened at Grabow, near Stettin, in 1831, but both its teaching and its equipment were of a very rudimentary character, and it was only after it had been transferred to Berlin (1861) and staffed by the naval constructors of the Ministry of Marine, that it can be said to have done much towards the fulfilment of the purposes with which it was inaugurated. Meanwhile German students who wished to acquaint themselves with the shipbuilding art were accustomed to attend the courses at the School of Naval Construction at Copenhagen.

Another drawback under which German shipbuilding suffered much at that time, and to some extent still suffers, was the distance of her mineral fields and iron works from the sea-coast. The addition to the cost of the raw materials thus incurred goes far to explain why the German yards found it so difficult to compete with their rivals on the Tyne, Wear, and Tees, who obtained their plates at their very doors. At a later period, when the Government had opened its eyes to the importance to the Navy of a strong shipbuilding industry, the materials required by the yards were granted special rates on the railways; and in 1879, when Germany adopted protection, they were admitted into the country free of Customs duty. On the other hand, the policy of the trusts in selling abroad at lower prices than at home has done something to counteract the effects of these measures, and Holland has been able to develop her shipbuilding industry with the aid of German materials supplied to her at cheaper rates than those charged to the home consumer.

Germany was also under a disadvantage through her poverty in the industries auxiliary to shipbuilding. A large modern steamer, whether battleship or trans-atlantic liner, is the most highly developed product of industry that exists, many of its component parts being the finished articles of special trades. Several of these special trades did not exist in Germany when she first seriously turned her attention to the cultivation of her shipbuilding, whereas they had been firmly established in England for generations. For many years after they had acquired the ability to construct hulls and engines, the German shipbuilders were entirely dependent upon British manufacturers for boilers, anchors, chains, windlasses, and many other important features in the equipment of their vessels. It was in England, too, that most of the machines now used in the building of ships were invented and first brought into use; and here, again, Germany was, and still is, though not to anything like the same degree as a couple of decades ago, in the position of a pupil who has yet to obtain full command over his implements.

But the Germans are clever and assiduous imitators, and nowhere have they shown that more distinctly than in their shipbuilding. The engineers who were sent over to British yards to supervise the construction of vessels for German firms kept their eyes open and took back with them to their native land much precious knowledge of British methods. It happened time and again that German shipowners ordered a new type of vessel, or engine, or boiler, from British builders, and had another constructed on this model in Germany. Several of the technical high schools in various parts of the Empire now have special chairs of naval construction, and none has ever equalled the German professor in the patient accumulation of all the available information on his particular subject.

If the advocates of the combustion motor are to be believed, we are at present on the threshold of another new era in marine engineering, and in that event the United Kingdom may easily lose much of the advantage which her old-established mechanical industry gave her when steam displaced sails for the propulsion of ships. Germany is quite awake to the potentialities of the new power-generator, and several of her leading shipbuilding firms and engineering works have vigorously grappled with the problem of the marine oil motor.

At the beginning of August, 1912, the Howaldt Yard, at Kiel, completed for the Hamburg-South America Line a 6,500-ton vessel, the *Monte Penedo*, fitted with engines of this type, and ships of the same class have also been built in Germany for the Hamburg-America and the German-American Petroleum Companies. It is further understood that the Augsburg-Nuremberg Engineering Company has constructed a set of oil motors of 6,000 horse-power for the Imperial Ministry of Marine. Should the oil motor prove universally victorious on the sea, Great Britain will, of course, derive no further benefit from her unique deposits of smokeless steam coal, and will become even more dependent on foreign countries for her motive power than she already is for her food.

Though of doubtful advantage from the point of view of the immediate interests of the German Fleet, General von Stosch's rule that all the Imperial war vessels should be constructed in home yards and of native material unquestionably did a great deal to stimulate shipbuilding in Germany. Another measure which contributed much to the same end was the subsidization of the mail lines to the Far Orient, Australia, and East and South Africa. It has always been maintained by German authorities that the sums paid by the Government under the postal contracts are not really subsidies, and that they had neither the intention nor the effect of promoting shipping. Their sole purpose, it is contended, was to establish a regular mail service between Germany and portions of the globe where she had important commercial interests. The Norddeutscher Lloyd, which has almost monopolized the mail-carrying under these contracts, professes to have had no initial benefit from them, but rather to have lost heavily at the inauguration of the service; while the

Hamburg-America Line renounced participation in the subsidies after a very brief experience.

That the Government was not exclusively concerned for the carrying of letters when it proposed these contracts was shown by the clauses providing for the transformation of the mail steamers into auxiliary cruisers in time of war. All the fastest steamers of the German lines are now constructed with a view to such a contingency; their engines are protected against lighter shell fire, platforms are provided for the mounting of quick-firers, and the guns themselves are kept in readiness, if not actually on board, so that the change from merchant-ship to warship can be accomplished with a minimum of delay. A large number of the officers of these liners belong to the Naval Reserve, and the Emperor, here again taking a leaf out of the British book, allows them to bear the iron cross, the German war emblem, on their flag. As is the case with the reserve officers of the British Navy, they also derive various other privileges from their connection with the Imperial sea service.

For nearly twenty years after the general adoption of iron construction, practically every important addition to the German mercantile marine came from the United Kingdom. The seventies witnessed the first considerable spurt in German shipbuilding, which in the succeeding decade finally broke with its old traditions and passed over to the use of iron as building material. The Imperial yards at Kiel and Wilhelmshaven laid down their first ironclads in 1869, and in 1875 the works at Dillingen, now a branch of the vast Krupp establishment, commenced the manufacture of armour plating, for which they were subsequently to become famous. About the same period the Vulcan works secured orders from China for two armoured vessels and three protected cruisers, and the Schichau yard, at Elbing, made its name by the construction of torpedo craft, which it subsequently supplied to

practically every navy in the world, with the exception
of those of Great Britain and France. (One of these
vessels is actually in the British service at the present
moment, having been captured from the Chinese at the
time of the Boxer rising.)

Simultaneously the German yards came to the front
with the construction of large passenger liners. The
first vessels of this class to be built in Germany were
ordered by the Hamburg-America Company from the
Vulcan and Reiherstieg yards in 1882, and they were
soon followed by the first half-dozen mail-boats of the
Norddeutscher Lloyd. An attempt to rival the swift
British liners was made in 1888 with the *Augusta
Viktoria*, and less than ten years later the same
owners and builders captured the blue riband of the
Atlantic with the *Kaiser Wilhelm der Grosse*, which,
with its 22½ knots speed, remained unchallenged till
the Cunard Line, with the assistance of substantial
and direct State subsidies, won it back with the
Mauritania and *Lusitania*. It is claimed that the
Kaiser Wilhelm der Grosse was completed in the record
time of eighteen months, but rumour has it that this
was only rendered possible by the employment of
English material in her construction. It must be
admitted, however, that, considering that German
shipbuilding can be said to have been still in its
infancy at that time, the vessel bears very eloquent
testimony to its quickness in learning and its skill in
applying its lessons.

With the 50,000 - ton and 70,000 - horse - power
Imperator, built for the Hamburg-America Company
by the Vulcan Works, and the two sister ships which are
being constructed by Messrs. Blohm and Voss for the
same line, Germany hopes once more to take the lead in
the transatlantic passenger traffic in size and comfort
if not in speed. It can hardly be pretended that either
in design or workmanship she is any longer sensibly
behind the British Isles in turning out steamers of this
type, and her shipyards are equipped with the very

latest and most efficient appliances for saving labour
and handling heavy castings. Thus Messrs. Blohm and
Voss have erected a crane to lift weights up to 300 tons,
while the Germania yard has two (one floating and
one stationary), and the Vulcan Works one, of only
fifty tons less raising power.

For various reasons the amount of capital sunk in
the German shipbuilding industry cannot be precisely
ascertained. The great Schichau works at Dantzig
and Elbing are, for instance, a private concern, which
publishes no accounts, and the proprietors of which owe
the fortune of six millions sterling they are reputed to
have accumulated at least as much to their agricultural
machinery and locomotives as to their torpedo craft
and dredgers. The Germania yard at Kiel is part of
the immense Krupp undertaking, which, though, for
purposes of convenience, worked as a public company,
is, with the exception of the qualifying directors' shares,
a family property, and allows no insight into the details
of the financial adjustments between its manifold departments. It is, however, estimated by Herr Lehmann-
Felskowski, a well-informed writer on the subject, that
an aggregate sum of M. 200,000,000 (say £10,000,000) is
at present invested in German shipbuilding. Something like one-half of this is administered by ordinary
limited liability companies, and of the numbers, capital,
and profits of these during recent years, the appended
figures will afford an adequate idea:

	1907.	1908.	1909.	1910.
Number of companies ...	18	19	19	18
Share capital in M. 1,000 ...	63,660	68,739	64,363	59,726
Debentures in M. 1,000 ...	23,927	31,056	31,884	34,187
Dividend in M. 1,000 ...	3,867	2,594	2,189	1,852
Dividend per cent.	6·09	3·77	3·4	3·1

The companies included in these statistics have, however, worked with very unequal results, as will be

seen from the subjoined details of the dividends of the chief of them :

	1903.	1904.	1905.	1906.	1907.	1908.	1909.	1910.	1911.
Vulcan ...	14	14	14	14	14	14	12	11	11
Blohm and Voss	7	9	9	9	7	7	4	6	4
Weser ...	5	5	0	0	0	0	0	0	4
Howaldt ...	0	4	0	0	0	0	0	0	0
Reiherstieg ...	10	5	6	7	10	10	7	5	6
Tecklenborg ...	12	10	10	4	9	0	0	0	4
Oderwerke ...	3	3	5	6	6	6	6	5	6
Neptun ...	8	7½	5	6	7	4	4	0	0
Seebeck ...	10	5	4	5	0	0	4	0	0
Bremen Vulcan	0	6	10	10	10	0	0	7½	10
Nordseewerke	—	—	—	0	0	0	—	—	—

It is impossible to survey these figures and the facts explanatory of them without a faint suspicion that the efforts of the German Government artificially to stimulate shipbuilding have not been an unmixed blessing to the yards whose services to the Navy were to have been rewarded by extended business and increased profits. Before the Howaldt works received an order for a cruiser in 1901, and, by the promise of more important naval commissions, was encouraged to lay down expensive special plant for the construction of large warships, they had never paid a smaller dividend than 5 per cent. What the subsequent results of their operations have been is indicated in part by the foregoing figures, which, however, give no sufficient idea of the severity of the crisis of 1910, when the company was driven to desperate financial devices in order to complete the battleship *Helgoland*, and at one time actually contemplated the sale of the greater portion of its site at Kiel as the only sure method of staving off irretrievable disaster. Its difficulties were ultimately surmounted by a combined condensation of old and issue of new capital, the existing shareholders supplying the funds necessary to save the situation. It is not known to what extent, if any, the Imperial

Ministry of Marine contributed to the rescue of the establishment, the disappearance of which would have seriously interfered with its plans.

It was, however, to some degree through the intervention of this department that the Weser yard was kept on its feet. This concern had, on the whole, paid very well up to the inauguration of the new naval policy of the German Empire. But in 1904 it undertook a considerable extension of its premises and plant, to enable it to take full advantage of the increased construction for the German Fleet, and from that date up to the moment of writing its shareholders have received nothing. Miscalculations and strikes caused delays in the carrying out of the new works and consequent losses, and by 1907 the company was shaken to its foundations. Its shares fell from 130 to 45, and its position was all the more critical because its buildings and other structures were erected on rented land. At this juncture the Ministry of Marine took over the half-finished ships which the yard was building to its order, and in the following year the shareholders were persuaded to contribute an additional three and three-quarter million marks to save their investments from annihilation.

These have not been the only untoward incidents in the recent history of German shipbuilding. In 1903 an attempt was made to establish a big yard at Emden, where, with the assistance of the municipality, the Nordseewerke were founded. The original capital was M. 2,100,000; but this proved altogether insufficient, and in 1907 a committee appointed to advise what could be done to keep the undertaking going recommended that an additional M. 2,200,000 was absolutely necessary. This was raised by shareholders' contributions and the renunciation by the creditors of a portion of their claims; but these efforts to place the yard on a sound footing were unavailing, and it was sold by auction for M. 53,000 to the big coal-dealing firm of Hugo Stinnes. Another shipbuilding undertaking which has been unable to keep its head above water was the Eider yard, of Tönning, which, after various abortive attempts to amalgamate it with the Howaldt and other companies, went into liquidation in 1909.

In the summer of 1912, when a distinct revival had already set in, it was complained in the German Press that shipbuilding was altogether in a parlous state, and that companies like the Vulcan,* of Stettin and Hamburg, which continued to pay substantial dividends, were enabled to do so only by the profits of their general engineering business. It was urged that the only means by which German shipbuilding could be saved was a comprehensive trust, or, at any rate, an amalgamation into several large groups, which would have no difficulty in coming to agreements, as necessity arose, to prevent underbidding in the home market. Rumours of secret rebates granted to the German shipbuilders by the manufacturers of their materials suggest also that the yards do not work under the same economic conditions as other branches of industry, but are rather privily favoured at their expense.

If it cannot be said that Germany as yet seriously menaces the oceanic carrying trade of the British Isles, even less dangerous seems her rivalry in general shipbuilding. The variations from year to year in the output of this industry are very great, a period of high freights invariably leading to over-production, and this, in its turn, being followed by a term of restricted activity, while the building of one or two vessels more or less of the largest type will cause considerable discrepancies between the construction figures of successive years. For these reasons quinquennial periods have been taken in the appended table, showing the

---

* While this book is in the press it is announced that, in consequence of a loss of £100,000 on the construction of warships for the Imperial Navy, the Vulcan Company will divide profits for 1912 (a record year for German shipbuilding) at the rate of only 6 per cent.

progress of shipbuilding in the two countries during the past thirty years :

Quinquennium.				United Kingdom.	Germany.
				Tons Built.	Tons Built.
1881-1885	...	...	...	3,313,431	248,504
1886-1890	...	...	...	2,950,040	242,793
1891-1895	...	...	...	3,512,841	307,829
1896-1900	...	...	...	4,145,396	439,545
1901-1905	...	...	...	4,624,642	574,403
1906-1910	...	...	...	4,126,093	612,112

Here again, by the use of percentages and multiples, the figures can be given an appearance very threatening to the United Kingdom's predominance in the shipbuilding industry. It is obvious at a glance that while her output of tonnage in the quinquennial periods under review increased by only about 30 per cent., that of Germany became twice and a half as great as it was; further, that from being more than thirteen times as large as that of Germany, the output of the United Kingdom declined in comparison till it was less than seven times as large. These relationships are, however, of little significance in comparison with the facts that the excess of British over German shipbuilding rose during the period dealt with from 3,064,927 tons to 3,513,981 tons. So far, indeed, is Germany from seriously imperilling the United Kingdom's position as shipbuilder to the world that, in spite of all the pressure and inducements brought to bear on her shipowners, they still purchase large quantities of tonnage abroad. In the quinquennial periods of the last thirty years the amounts of these foreign purchases were :

Quinquennium.					Tons.
1881-1885	...	...	...	...	... 217,004
1886-1890	...	...	...	...	... 275,382
1891-1895	...	...	...	...	... 273,928
1896-1900	...	...	...	...	... 515,486
1901-1905	...	...	...	...	... 450,258
1906-1910	...	...	...	...	... 334,007

A great deal of this shipping was not, of course, built to order, but was transferred to Germany by British firms, who had exhausted its utility so far as their purposes were concerned. During the three years 1909, 1910, and 1911, the vessels built in the United Kingdom on German account were of the following aggregate tonnage :

Year.				Vessels.	Tons Gross.
1909	...	...	...	2	8,179
1910	...	...	...	5	26,507
1911	...	...	...	3	20,527

As clinching evidence of the overwhelming pre-dominance which British shipbuilding still maintains, the following figures, showing the number and tonnage of vessels of all kinds launched in the United Kindom and elsewhere, respectively, during the year 1911, may prove interesting :

	Number.	Tonnage.
United Kingdom	822	2,034,630
British Colonies and foreign countries	946	1,384,379
Totals	1,768	3,419,009

By the exclusion of warships these figures become :

	Number.	Tonnage.
United Kingdom	772	1,803,844
British Colonies and foreign countries	827	846,296
Totals	1,599	2,650,140

It is, however, our special present object to enquire how far Germany is equipped for rivalry with Great

Britain in the building of a war navy, and here it must be admitted that her situation is much more favourable than it is in respect to the mercantile marine. To demonstrate this it is only necessary to state that the warships of over 100 tons launched in the United Kingdom in 1911 had a total displacement of 221,430 tons, while those launched in Germany had a total displacement of as much as 128,340 tons. If the extreme possibilities of construction were not attained on the side of the United Kingdom, no more were they on that of Germany. In the winter of 1905-06— that is to say, just before the era of the Dreadnought battleship—Count Ernst Reventlow, the well-known writer on naval topics, circularized the German yards that up to that time had built capital warships, with an enquiry as to the speed at which they could construct such vessels and the number they could complete annually. The replies received may be summarized as under:

Yard.	Period of Construction in Months.	Could be Completed Annually.
Germania	24-30	2
Howaldt	24	1
Vulcan	24-30	4
Blohm and Voss	24-30	2
Schichau	30-36	2
Weser	24-30	2
Total	—	13

Up to the present Germany has never laid down more than four capital warships in one year, so that at the date of Count Reventlow's investigation, without the co-operation of the Imperial yards at Wilhelmshaven, Kiel, and Dantzig, her private industry would, as was stated in the reply of the Schichau firm, have been able to turn out such vessels at a rate which would have been three times the Empire's past maximum production.   It could, in fact, according to these figures, which must, however, be accepted with some reserve, have kept up a speed of construction twice as great as that which Great Britain would be compelled by the German Navy Law to maintain for all future time if the two-keels-to-one standard were to be observed. It should, however, be mentioned that the undertakings given to Count Reventlow by some of the yards were conditional upon the prompt delivery of armour plating and heavy guns by Krupps, who so far have furnished the German Navy with its entire requirements of these two essential articles of warship equipment.

This Krupp monopoly is undoubtedly a weak spot in Germany's warship-building arrangements, and especially since the able race which developed the great works at Essen has become extinct in the male line and the undertaking is managed solely by what are in fact, if not in name, salaried officials.   As yet, however, there is no reason to doubt the quality of Krupp workmanship or the capacity of the establishment, in case of need, to supply guns and armour for a much larger number of battleships and large cruisers than Germany has any immediate intention of building ; and the intimate friendship which has long existed between the Emperor William and the Krupp family is possibly an even more important factor than it was, now that the ordinary share capital of the undertaking is entirely in the hands of a woman.

There can be no doubt that Krupps were taken into the confidence of the Government before the Navy Bill of 1900 was drafted, and that the subsequent extensions of the works were then agreed upon in principle. These extensions took the form of the acquisition of the Germania shipbuilding yard in 1901, and of enormous additions to the ordnance and armour plate works a few years later.   To carry out these developments debentures were issued to the amount of M. 20,000,000 in 1901, and to the amount of M. 25,000,000 (out of a total of M. 50,000,000, for which rights were obtained) in 1908. On neither side is the relationship of the German Government to Krupps an ordinary business one, and in all probability its basis is an undertaking to the effect that, if the works would lay down the plant necessary to supply a certain quantity of big guns and armour plate annually, the Government would do its best to see that the orders required to keep that plant remuneratively employed were duly forthcoming.

Since the replies to Count Reventlow's enquiries were penned, the building of the *Dreadnought* has brought about a positive revolution in the dimensions of capital warships. A sudden jump of five thousand tons in displacement, and then a further advance of nearly as much, together with the corresponding increases in length and beam, must have been very unwelcome to the German shipyards; but if the builders have not fully kept pace with these changes, at any rate it may be assumed that they have not been left very far behind, and that their powers of production have not been substantially reduced since they sent in the estimates in question. Besides, the completion of the new Vulcan yard at Hamburg, from which the company anticipated an increase in efficiency of from 50 to 75 per cent., took place subsequent to the launch of the *Dreadnought*, and naturally arrangements were made to comply with the fresh standard.

This establishment was decided upon in 1905, and was formally opened in the presence of the Emperor William on June 21, 1909. It contains three slips, respectively, 305, 259, and 207 metres in length, for the construction of liners; while a fourth, which provides accommodation for vessels of up to 41 metres beam, was specially designed for warships of the largest dimensions. The 1912 edition of *Nauticus* gives a useful table (of which the essential features are reproduced as an appendix to this book), showing, among other details, the slip accommodation at all the principal German shipyards. From this it would appear that the yards which have already had experience in the building of battleships and large cruisers have at their disposal the following slips for vessels of the larger types :

Yard.	150 to 200 Metres.	Over 200 Metres.
Vulcan, Hamburg	—	2
Vulcan, Stettin	3	2
Schichau	3	2
Blohm and Voss	5	4
Weser	1	3
Germania	4	—
Howaldt	2	1
Totals	18	14

In addition to these private slips, there are five of unspecified length at the Imperial yards at Wilhelmshaven, Kiel, and Dantzig, and it would certainly be no exaggeration to state, that, in an emergency, this accommodation would suffice for the construction of at least twice as many large armoured ships as are specified in the Fleet Law, other conditions—the supply, in particular, of guns, armour, torpedo equipment, and engines—being of equivalent capacity. But, as already stated, Germany is handicapped by the inability of her shipyards to manufacture their own heavy ordnance and armour plates and their dependence for these articles on the one firm that at present produces them in Germany. And so long as that firm is, in its turn, dependent solely, or nearly so, on home orders for the utilization of its plant and the remuneration of its capital, it will never be in a position to respond to the exigencies of such an emergency.

German naval legislation was not, however, dictated exclusively by political motives ; one of its objects was to establish an industry which should break the British shipbuilding monopoly, and become not merely a broad and stable foundation for the erection of the Empire's war fleet, but also a valuable national economic asset. The Navy Act of 1900 gave the German shipbuilders the assurance of future orders, which was necessary to induce them to run the risk of laying down the plant required for the construction of ships of the largest classes. From the date of the passing of that measure, it was known that for all future time the Imperial Ministry of Marine would require the annual delivery of at least three capital warships, and the yards had a definite justification for large capital outlay. What was hoped, and what is hoped, is that, with the aid of the experience thus gained, they will be able to enter more successfully into competition with the United Kingdom for the naval orders of those States that cannot build their war vessels for themselves. On the degree of the fulfilment of these hopes will depend to a very large extent the issue of the struggle for the supremacy of the seas.

The German Government will assuredly leave no stone unturned to assist its shipbuilders to obtain foreign contracts. It was undoubtedly with a view to securing orders that the *Von der Tann*, as soon as she had passed through her trials in such a way as, on the published figures, to warrant the boast that she was the fastest battle-cruiser afloat, was despatched to South America at forced speed for a tour of the Republican ports, and similar motives will in the future frequently have to be looked for behind German naval movements. For the first time in modern history, the German Navy is now equipped with a large number of vessels approximately equal in size, speed, and strength to the best in the world, and what it has effected in this respect during the twelve years which have elapsed since the change in the Empire's naval policy was clearly formulated has been little less than astounding.

The approach which in that short period has been made to Great Britain has involved not only the size and number of the vessels, but also their quality, and it is not improbable that in a few years' time Hamburg, Bremen, Kiel, and Dantzig may be able to secure a considerable proportion of those foreign orders for large armoured ships, which now go almost exclusively to the Clyde, the Tyne, and Barrow.* This is an ambition which has played an important part in German naval legislation, and should it ever be realized it will have a very decisive bearing on the chances of the Empire in a naval war.   With her slips and her finishing docks regularly occupied by vessels building for foreign States, Germany would have an invaluable reserve of material on which to fall back in case of need, and which might easily decide in her favour the fortunes of a campaign against an enemy of anything like equal strength.

Up to the present the only German yard which has to any considerable extent executed foreign orders has been that started by Ferdinand Schichau in 1837, and now owned by his son-in-law, Herr Karl Ziese.   It is not without interest that the founder of this undertaking made prolonged investigations in England before embarking on his venture, though the mention of this must by no means be taken to imply that he was not an engineer of great and original gifts.   The Schichau yard can boast the distinction, unique for a German shipbuilding concern, of having done pioneer work in at least one branch of naval construction.   In turn it has been able to claim for the Russian 28·4-knot torpedo-boat *Adler* (1880), the four Chinese destroyers built in 1898 (36·7 knots), of which one, it may be recalled, is now in the British service, the Russian cruiser *Nowik* of the same year (26 knots), and the Argentine torpedo-boat destroyers, *Cordoba* and *La Plata*, finished in 1911, that they were the fastest vessels

* Since these words were written a first-class battleship has been commenced at the Vulcan yard at Hamburg for the Greek Government at, it is reported, an unremunerative price ; and at the moment of going to press the same establishment has strong hopes of securing the order for a sister vessel to the one under construction.

of their respective classes afloat, though the details of the conditions under which the trials that yielded these results took place have not been published. The two last-named boats belonged to a series of twelve, of which four each were placed in the United Kingdom, France, and Germany, and in their trials they attained a speed of 36·8 knots ; whereas, according to the reports in the German Press, the stipulated 32 knots was reached neither by the British nor the French boats. Up to 1912 the Schichau yards had delivered the following torpedo craft (torpedo-boats, destroyers, and torpedo cruisers):

To—						Number.
Germany	...	...	...	...	...	179
Russia	...	...	...	...	...	39
Italy	...	...	...	...	...	36
China	...	...	...	...	...	21
Japan	...	...	...	...	...	19
Austria	...	...	...	...	...	18
Turkey	...	...	...	...	...	9
Brazil	...	...	...	...	...	5
Norway	...	...	...	...	...	4
Argentine	...	...	...	...	...	2
Sweden	...	...	...	...	...	1
Denmark	...	...	...	...	...	1
		Total ...	...	...	...	334

A few foreign orders have also been executed by the Vulcan Works and the Germania yard. Up to the end of 1911 the former had completed the following war vessels :

For—			Battle-ships.	Large Cruisers.	Other Cruisers.	Torpedo Craft.
Germany	...	...	10	—	14	38
China ...	...	...	2	2	4	16
Japan ...	...	...	—	1	—	—
Russia ...	...	...	—	—	1	2
Uruguay	...	...	—	—	1	—
Greece	...	...	—	—	—	10

The Germania yard, which, it should be noted, is the only shipbuilding establishment that up to the

present has applied itself to the construction of submarines, had, at the commencement of 1912, supplied
the following war vessels :

To—	Battle-ships, etc.	Large Cruisers.	Other Cruisers.	Torpedo Craft.	Sub-marines.
Germany	12*	1	9	32	16
Turkey	1†	—	—	14	—
Russia	—	1	—	4	4
Brazil	—	—	—	3	—
Argentine	—	—	—	3	—
Spain	—	—	—	1	—
Norway	—	—	—	—	4
Austria	—	—	—	—	2
Italy	—	—	—	—	1

* Including one armoured coast-defence ship.
† Armoured coast-defence ship.

The yards of the Weser Company, Messrs. Blohm
and Voss, and the Howaldt Company, the only three
other German undertakings which up to the present
have occupied themselves seriously with the construction of warships, seem to have executed no orders for
foreign Governments.

APPENDIX I

GERMAN NAVAL LEGISLATION

ACT RELATING TO THE GERMAN FLEET OF APRIL 10, 1898

WE, Wilhelm, by the grace of God, German Emperor, King of Prussia, etc., order in the name of the Empire, with the consent of the Federal Council and of the Reichstag, what follows:

I. SHIP ESTABLISHMENT.

Clause 1.

1. The ship establishment of the German Fleet is, apart from torpedo craft, school-ships, special service ships, and gunboats, fixed as below:

(*a*) Ready for use—

    1 fleet flagship,
    2 squadrons each of 8 battleships,
    2 divisions each of 4 armoured coast-ships,
    6 large cruisers ⎱ as scouts of the Home Battle Fleet,
    16 small cruisers ⎰
    3 large cruisers ⎱ for foreign service.
    10 small cruisers ⎰

(*b*) As material reserve—

    2 battleships,
    3 large cruisers,
    4 small cruisers.

2. Of the ships existing or under construction on April 1, 1898, there shall be reckoned on this establishment—

as battleships	12,
as armoured coast-ships	8,
as large cruisers	10,
as small cruisers	23.

3. The provision of the means for the new ships necessary for the attainment of the establishment (Clause 1) is subject to annual determination by the Imperial Budget, with the standard, that the completion of the legal establishment, in so far as the means stated in Clause 7 suffice, can be attained by the end of the financial year 1903.

Clause 2.

The provision of the means for the necessary replacement construction is subject to annual determination by the Imperial Budget, with the standard that, as the rule—

> battleships and armoured coast-ships can be replaced at the end of 25 years,
> large cruisers at the end of 20 years,
> small cruisers at the end of 15 years.

The periods run from the year of the granting of the first instalment for the ship to be replaced to the granting of the first instalment of the replacing ship.

To a prolongation of the replacement period the consent of the Federal Council is required in the individual case, to an abbreviation that of the Reichstag. Any grants of replacement ships before the expiry of the statutory life-time—acts of God, such as the sinking of a ship, excepted—are to be compensated for, within a period to be agreed upon with the Reichstag, by the postponement of other replacement construction.

II. Maintenance in Commission.

Clause 3.

The provision of means for maintaining the Home Battle Fleet in commission is subject to annual determination by the Imperial Budget, with the standard that there can be kept in commission :

(a) For the constitution of active formations—

> 9 battleships,
> 2 large cruisers,
> 6 small cruisers.

(b) As nucleus ships of reserve formations—

> 4 battleships,
> 4 armoured coast-ships,
> 2 large cruisers,
> 5 small cruisers.

(c) For rendering a reserve formation active for a period of two months—

2 battleships or armoured coast-ships.

III. Personal Establishment.

Clause 4.

Of warrant officers, petty officers, and men of the seamen's divisions, and of the dockyard and torpedo sections, there shall be:

1. $1\frac{1}{2}$ crews for the ships on foreign service.
2. Full complements for—
   the ships belonging to active formations of the Home Battle Fleet,
   half of the torpedo craft,
   the school-ships,
   the special service ships.
3. Nucleus crews (engine-room personnel $\frac{2}{3}$, remaining personnel $\frac{1}{2}$ of the full complements) for—
   the ships belonging to reserve formations of the Home Battle Fleet,
   the second half of the torpedo craft.
4. The necessary shore requirements.
5. An addition of 5 per cent. on the total requirements.

Clause 5.

The strengths required according to the standard of these principles for the seamen's divisions and dockyard and torpedo sections are subject to annual determination by the Imperial Budget.

IV. Other Expenditure.

Clause 6.

All recurrent and non-recurrent expenditure in the Naval Estimates with regard to which no provisions are made in this law are subject to annual determination by the Imperial Budget according to the standard of the requirements.

V. Cost.

Clause 7.

During the next six financial years (1898 to 1903) the Reichstag is not bound to provide for all non-recurrent ex-

penditure of the Naval Estimates more than M. 408,900,000—
viz., for building and arming ships more than M. 356,700,000,
and for other non-recurrent expenditure more than M. 52,200,000
—or for the recurrent expenditure of the Naval Estimates more
than an average increase of M. 4,900,000 annually.

In so far as the law cannot be carried out in accordance
with this provision before the end of the financial year 1903,
its execution will be extended beyond the year 1903.

Clause 8.

In so far as the total of the recurrent and non-recurrent expenditure in any financial year exceeds the sum of M. 117,525,494
marks, and the proper revenue of the Empire does not suffice
to cover the excess, the extra amount may not be raised by
augmenting or adding to indirect Imperial taxes on articles
consumed by the masses.

Legally attested under our own signature and Imperial seal.
Given at Homburg vor der Höhe, April 10, 1908.

WILHELM.
FÜRST ZU HOHENLOHE.

ACT RELATING TO THE GERMAN FLEET OF JUNE 14, 1900.

We, Wilhelm, by the grace of God, German Emperor,
King of Prussia, etc., order in the name of the Empire, with
the consent of the Federal Council and of the Reichstag, what
follows :

I. SHIP ESTABLISHMENT.

Clause 1.

There shall consist :

1. The Battle Fleet of—

2 fleet flagships,
4 squadrons of 8 battleships each,
8 large cruisers ⎱ as scouts.
24 small cruisers ⎰

2. The Foreign Service Fleet of—

3 large cruisers,
10 small cruisers.

3. The Material Reserve of—

> 4 battleships,
> 3 large cruisers,
> 4 small cruisers.

To this prescribed establishment are to be reckoned at the promulgation of this Law the ships specified in Schedule A.

Clause 2.

Except in the case of losses of ships there shall be replaced:

> Battleships after 25 years,
> Cruisers after 20 years.

The periods run from the year of the granting of the first instalment for the ship to be replaced to the granting of the first instalment of the replacing ship.

For the period from 1901 to 1917 the replacement building will be regulated according to Schedule B.

II. Maintenance in Commission.

Clause 3.

With regard to the maintenance in commission of the Battle Fleet the following principles obtain:

1. The First and Second Squadron form the active Battle Fleet, the Third and Fourth Squadrons the Reserve Battle Fleet.
2. Of the Active Battle Fleet all, of the Reserve Battle Fleet half of the battleships and cruisers shall be kept permanently in commission.
3. For manœuvres some ships of the Reserve Battle Fleet which are out of commission shall be temporarily placed in commission.

III. Personal Establishment.

Clause 4.

Of warrant officers, petty officers, and men of the seamen's divisions and of the dockyard and torpedo sections there shall be:

1. Full complements for the ships belonging to the Active Battle Fleet, half of the torpedo-boats, the school-ships, and the special service ships.

2. Nucleus crews (engine-room personnel $\frac{2}{3}$, remaining personnel $\frac{1}{2}$ of the full complements) for the ships belonging to the Reserve Battle Fleet, as well as for the second half of the torpedo-boats.
3. $1\frac{1}{2}$ crews for the ships on foreign service.
4. The necessary shore requirements.
5. An addition of 5 per cent. to the total requirements.

IV. COST.

Clause 5.

The provision of means for the carrying out of this **Law** is subject to annual determination by the Imperial Budget.

Clause 6.

In so far as from the financial year 1901 the additional requirements of recurrent and non-recurrent expenditure in the ordinary estimates of the naval administration exceed the additional yield of the Imperial stamp duties to the sum of M. 53,708,000, and the deficit is not covered from other sources of the Empire's revenue, the deficit shall not be raised by augmenting or adding to indirect Imperial taxes on articles consumed by the masses.

V. FINAL PROVISION.

This Law comes into force simultaneously with the Laws with regard to the Amendment of the Imperial Stamp Law of April 27, 1894, and with regard to the Amendment of the Customs Tariff Law.

The Law with regard to the German Fleet of April 10, 1898, is repealed.

Legally attested under our own signature and Imperial seal.

Given at Castle Saalburg, near Homburg vor der Höhe, June 14, 1900.

WILHELM.

FÜRST ZU HOHENLOHE.

SCHEDULE A.

ENUMERATION OF THE SHIPS TO BE RECKONED TO THE FIXED
ESTABLISHMENT ON THE PROMULGATION OF THIS LAW.

Battleships.	Large Cruisers.	Small Cruisers.
1. Bayern	1. König Wilhelm	1. Zieten
2. Sachsen	2. Kaiser	2. Blitz
3. Württemberg	3. Deutschland	3. Pfeil
4. Baden	4. Kaiserin Augusta	4. Arkona
5. Oldenburg	5. Hertha	5. Alexandrine
6. Brandenburg	6. Victoria Louise	6. Greif
7. Kurfürst Friedrich Wilhelm	7. Freya	7. Irene
	8. Hansa	8. Prinzess Wilhelm
8. Weissenburg	9. Vineta	9. Schwalbe
9. Wörth	10. Fürst Bismarck	10. Wacht
10. Kaiser Friedrich III.	11. Prinz Heinrich	11. Jagd
11. Kaiser Wilhelm II.	12. B	12. Sperber
		13. Bussard
12. Kaiser Wilhelm der Grosse		14. Meteor
13. Kaiser Barbarossa		15. Falke
14. Kaiser Karl der Grosse		16. Komet
		17. Kormoran
15. C		18. Kondor
16. D		19. Seeadler
17. E		20. Gefion
18. F		21. Geier
19. G		22. Hela
20. Siegfried		23. Gazelle
21. Beowulf		24. Niobe
22. Frithjof		25. Nymphe
23. Hildebrand		26. C
24. Heimdall		27. D
25. Hagen		28. E
26. Ægir		29. F
27. Odin		

SCHEDULE B.

DISTRIBUTION AMONG THE INDIVIDUAL YEARS OF THE *REPLACEMENT*
SHIPS TO BE BUILT IN THE YEARS 1901 TO 1917 INCLUSIVE.

Replacement Year.			Battleships.	Large Cruisers.	Small Cruisers.
1901	...	...	—	1	—
1902	...	...	—	1	1
1903	...	...	—	1	1
1904	...	...	—	—	2
1905	...	...	—	—	2
1906	...	...	2	—	2
1907	...	...	2	—	2
1908	...	...	2	—	2
1909	...	...	2	—	2
1910	...	...	1	1	2
1911	...	...	1	1	2
1912	...	...	1	1	2
1913	...	...	1	1	2
1914	...	...	1	1	2
1915	...	...	1	1	2
1916	...	...	1	1	2
1917	...	...	2	—	1
Totals ...	...		17	10	29

ACT OF JUNE 5, 1906, AMENDING THE LAW RELATING TO THE GERMAN FLEET OF JUNE 14, 1900.

We, Wilhelm, by the grace of God German Emperor, King of Prussia, etc., order, in the name of the Empire, with the consent of the Federal Council and of the Reichstag, what follows:

Single Paragraph.

The ship establishment fixed in Clause 1 of the Law relating to the German Fleet of June 14, 1900, is increased:

1. In the case of the Foreign Service Fleet by 5 large cruisers;
2. In the case of the material reserve by 1 large cruiser.

Legally attested under our own signature and Imperial seal. Given at the Neues Palais, June 5, 1906.

WILHELM.
FÜRST VON BÜLOW.

ACT OF APRIL 6, 1908, AMENDING CLAUSE 2 OF THE LAW RELATING TO THE GERMAN FLEET OF JUNE 14, 1900.

We, Wilhelm, by the grace of God German Emperor, King of Prussia, etc., order in the name of the Empire, with the consent of the Federal Council and of the Reichstag, what follows:

Single Clause.

The following takes the place of Clause 2 of the Law relating to the German Fleet, June 14, 1900:

Clause 2.

Except in the case of the loss of ships, battleships and cruisers will be replaced at the end of 20 years.

The periods run from the year of the granting of the first instalment of the ship to be replaced to the granting of the first instalment for the replacing ship.

For the period from 1908 to 1917 the replacement building will be regulated according to Schedule B.

Legally attested under our own signature and Imperial seal.

Given at Palermo on board M.Y. *Hohenzollern*, April 6, 1908.

WILHELM.

FÜRST VON BÜLOW.

SCHEDULE B.

DISTRIBUTION AMONG THE INDIVIDUAL YEARS OF THE *REPLACEMENT* SHIPS TO BE BUILT IN THE YEARS 1908 TO 1917 INCLUSIVE.*

Replacement Year.	Battleships.	Large Cruisers.	Small Cruisers.
1908	3	—	2
1909	3	—	2
1910	3	—	2
1911	2	—	2
1912	1	1	2
1913	1	1	2
1914	1	1	2
1915	1	1	2
1916	1	1	2
1917	1	1	1
Totals	17	6	19

* The programme of shipbuilding, including replacement and additional ships, 1897-1917, is shown in Appendix V.

ACT OF JUNE 14, 1912, AMENDING THE LAWS RELATING TO THE GERMAN FLEET OF JUNE 14, 1900, AND JUNE 5, 1906.

We, Wilhelm, by the grace of God German Emperor, King of Prussia, etc., order in the name of the Empire, with the consent of the Federal Council and of the Reichstag, what follows :

Clause 1.

The following Clause 1 replaces Clause 1 of the Law concerning the German Fleet of June 14, 1900, and the amendment of this Law of June 5, 1906.

There shall consist :

1. The Battle Fleet of—

    1 fleet flagship,
    5 squadrons of 8 battleships each,
    12 large cruisers ⎫
    30 small cruisers ⎬ as scouts.

2. The Foreign Service Fleet of—

    8 large cruisers,
    10 small cruisers.

Clause 2.

The following paragraphs replace paragraphs 1 and 2 of Clause 3 of the Law concerning the German Fleet of June 14, 1900 :

1.   1 fleet flagship,
    3 squadrons of battleships,
    8 large cruisers, and
    18 small cruisers
        form the Active Battle Fleet ;
    2 squadrons of battleships,
    4 large cruisers, and
    12 small cruisers
        form the Reserve Battle Fleet.

2. The whole of the battleships and cruisers of the Active Battle Fleet and a quarter of those of the Reserve Battle Fleet are to be kept permanently in commission.

Clause 3.

The following paragraphs are to replace the opening sentence and paragraphs 1 and 2 of Clause 4 of the Law concerning the German Fleet of June 14, 1900:

The following proportions of warrant officers, petty officers, and men of the Seamen, Dockyard, and Torpedo Divisions, as well as the Submarine Sections, shall be available:

1. Full crews for the ships belonging to the Active Battle Fleet, for the whole of the torpedo boats and submarines with exception of the Material Reserve of both these classes of boats, for the school ships and for the special ships.

2. Nucleus crews (one-half of the engine-room personnel, one-quarter of the remaining personnel of the full crew) for the ships belonging to the Reserve Battle Fleet.

Clause 4.

The Imperial Chancellor is empowered to publish the text of the Law concerning the German Fleet of June 14, 1900, with such alterations as result from the Laws of June 5, 1906, April, 1908, and the present Law. Given at the New Palace, June 14, 1912.

WILHELM.

VON BETHMANN HOLLWEG.

———

MEMORANDUM APPENDED TO THE GERMAN NAVY BILL, 1912.

The organization of the Fleet still suffers from two serious defects:

The one defect consists in the fact that in the autumn of every year the time-expired men—*i.e.*, almost one-third of the crew in all ships of the Battle Fleet—are discharged, and replaced mainly by recruits from the *inland population*. Owing to this, the readiness of the Battle Fleet for war is considerably impaired for a prolonged period.

The second defect consists in the fact that at the present time, with an establishment of fifty-eight capital ships, only twenty-one ships are available at first, if the Reserve Fleet cannot be made ready *in proper time*. Since the Fleet Law was drawn up, this latter has become more and more unlikely, as the moment at which the Reserve Fleet can be ready for

war gets more and more deferred. This is a consequence of
the ever-growing complexity of modern ships, and of the
steadily growing difficulty in training large organizations. At
the present day, therefore, the Reserve Fleet only comes into
consideration as a *second fighting line* ; but in view of our great
numerical strength in reserve men, it still maintains its great
importance.

Both these defects are to be removed, or at any rate considerably ameliorated, by the gradual formation of a third
active squadron.

The requisite *ships* for this third active squadron are to be
derived :

(*a*) By dispensing with the Reserve Fleet Flagship.

(*b*) By dispensing with the present existing Material Reserve
—4 battleships, 4 large, and 4 small cruisers.

(*c*) By newly constructing 3 battleships and 2 small cruisers.

As the *maintenance in commission* of ships in the Reserve
Fleet can be reduced by one-half in consequence of the increase
of active organizations, the formation of a third active squadron
only renders the additional maintenance in commission of three
battleships, three large and three small cruisers necessary
beyond those to be maintained in commission already provided
for in the Fleet Law. This involves a corresponding increase
in personnel.

A further increase in personnel is necessary as the complements of all classes of ships, including torpedo boats, have
had to be augmented.

Moreover, an increase in submarines and the acquisition of
some airships is contemplated. The submarines, which are
still at the present moment without organization, are to be
organized—as regards manning—after the manner of the
torpedo-boats.

APPENDICES.

1. Comparison of the Amendment with the Fleet Laws.
2. Programme of Construction.
3. Increased requirements of Personnel.
4. Calculation of Cost.

APPENDIX 1.

Comparison of the Amendment with the Fleet Laws.

PROVISIONS OF THE FLEET LAW.

I. *Establishment of Ships.*

Section 1.

There shall be (1) the Battle Fleet, consisting of—2 fleet flagships, 4 squadrons of 8 battleships each, 8 large cruisers, and 24 small cruisers as scouts. (2) The Foreign Service Fleet, consisting of—8 large cruisers and 10 small cruisers. (3) The Material Reserve, consisting of—4 battleships, 4 large cruisers, and 4 small cruisers.

ALTERATIONS OF THE AMENDMENT.

I. *Establishment of Ships.*

Section 1.

There shall be (1) the Battle Fleet, consisting of—1 fleet flagship, 5 squadrons of 8 battleships each, 12 large cruisers, and 30 small cruisers as scouts. (2) The Foreign Service Fleet, consisting of—8 large cruisers and 10 small cruisers.

PROVISIONS OF THE FLEET LAW.

II. *Maintenance in Commission.*

Section 3.

The following principles obtain regarding the maintenance in commission of the Battle Fleet: (1) The First and Second Squadrons form the Active Battle Fleet, the Third and Fourth Squadrons the Reserve Battle Fleet.

(2) The whole of the battleships and cruisers of the Active Battle Fleet, and one-half of those of the Reserve Battle Fleet, are to be kept permanently in commission.

ALTERATIONS OF THE AMENDMENT.

II. *Maintenance in Commission.*

Section 3.

The following principles obtain regarding the maintenance in commission of the Battle Fleet : (1) 1 fleet flagship, 3 squadrons of battleships, 8 large cruisers, and 18 small cruisers form the Active Battle Fleet, 2 squadrons of battleships, 4 large cruisers, and 12 small cruisers form the Reserve Battle Fleet.

(2) The whole of the battleships and cruisers of the Active Battle Fleet and *one quarter* of those of the Reserve Battle Fleet are to be kept permanently in commission.

PROVISIONS OF THE FLEET LAW.

III. *Establishment of Personnel.*

Section 4.

The following proportions of warrant officers, petty officers, and men of the Seamen, Dockyard, and Torpedo Divisions shall be available :

(1) Full crews for the ships belonging to the Active Battle Fleet, *for half* of the torpedo-boats, for the school-ships, and for the special ships.

(2) Nucleus crews (two-thirds of the engine-room personnel, one-half of the remaining personnel of the full crews) for the ships belonging to the Reserve Battle Fleet, as well as *for the second half* of the torpedo-boats.

ALTERATIONS OF THE AMENDMENT.

III. *Establishment of Personnel.*

Section 4.

The following proportions of warrant officers, petty officers, and men of the Seamen, Dockyard, and Torpedo Divisions, *as well as of the Submarine Sections*, shall be available :

(1) Full crews for the ships belonging to the Active Battle Fleet, *for the whole of the torpedo - boats and submarines with exception of the Material Reserve of both these classes of boats, for the school-ships and for the special ships.*

(2) Nucleus crews (one-third of the engine-room personnel,

one-quarter of the remaining personnel of the full crews) for the ships belonging to the Reserve Battle Fleet.

The remaining provisions of the Fleet Laws remain unaltered.

EXPLANATIONS.

With regard to Section 1.

The legal establishment of ships experiences *an increase of three battleships and two small cruisers* through the Amendment:

	Previous Establishment.	Future Establishment.	Increase.
Battleships	38	41	+ 3
Large cruisers... ...	20	20	—
Small cruisers	38	40	+ 2

With regard to Section 3.

Of the legal establishment of ships, there are to be in commission:

	Battleships.		Large Cruisers.		Small Cruisers.	
	Previously.	In Future.	Previously.	In Future.	Previously.	In Future.
In the *Active* Battle Fleet	17	25	4	8	12	18
In the *Reserve* Battle Fleet	9	4	2	1	6	3
Totals	26	29	6	9	18	21

Consequently, additionally in commission in future:

3 battleships, 3 large cruisers, 3 small cruisers.

With regard to Section 4.

1. In accordance with the Memorandum to the Estimates of 1906 there are to be:

Altogether—144 torpedo boats.

Of which ready for use—99 with full active service crews.

As Material Reserve—45 without crews.

Nothing is altered in this by the Amendment.

Section 4 of the *Fleet Law of* 1900 provided for 72 full crews, and 72 nucleus crews, making together a total of 116 full crews (compare footnote to Memorandum accompanying Estimates of 1906).

Only 99 are required, and the Fleet Law, therefore, demands 17 full crews too many.

Article 3 of the *Amendment* brings the number of crews legally to be held in readiness into line with actual requirements, *and therefore reduces the torpedo personnel demanded under the Fleet Law by seventeen boat's crews.*

2. It is proposed to demand 6 submarines every year. With a twelve years' life this gives an establishment of 72 boats. For 54 of these boats active service crews are estimated for; 18 form the Material Reserve without crews.

APPENDIX 2.
PROGRAMME OF CONSTRUCTION.
Previous Programme of Construction.

Year.			Battle-ships.	Large Cruisers.	Total Large Ships.	Small Cruisers.
1912 ...	...	...	1	1	2	2
1913 ...	...	...	1	1	2	2
1914 ...	...	...	1	1	2	2
1915 ...	...	...	1	1	2	2
1916 ...	...	...	1	1	2	2
1917 ...	...	...	1	1	2	2*

Future Programme of Construction.

Year.			Battle-ships.	Large Cruisers.	Total Large Ships.	Small Cruisers.
1912 ...	...	...	1	1	2	2
1913 ...	...	...	2†	1	3	2
1914 ...	...	...	1	1	2	2
1915 ...	...	...	1	1	2	2
1916 ...	...	...	2†	1	3	2
1917 ...	...	...	1	1	2	2*

* Including one additional ship outstanding from the Fleet Law.
† Including one additional ship under the Amendment.
The year of construction of one battleship and two small cruisers is reserved.

APPENDIX I

APPENDIX 3.

ADDITIONAL PERSONNEL REQUIRED.

(A.) Men of the Seamen, Dockyard, and Torpedo Divisions, as well as of the Submarine Sections—14,310; annual average 1,590.*

(B.) Executive Officers—433; annual average, 48.

(C.) Engineers—116; annual average, 13.

(D.) Medical Officers and Sick Birth Staff—175; annua average, 19.

(E.) Paymasters and Accountant Staff — 119; annual average, 13.

REMARK.

The requisite increase in personnel consists of—

(1) The personnel necessary for additional ships to be maintained in commission under the Amendment.

(2) The personnel to be held in readiness for the submarines.

(3) The personnel becoming necessary in consequence of alterations in complements and increased activity in training.

In regard to (3), the complements of torpedo-boats, and in part also of the ships, have experienced an increase which is not taken into account in the calculations for the requirements of personnel for the Fleet Law, as this could not be foreseen. The larger complements have become necessary owing to growth in size and speed of ships and torpedo-boats, as well as on account of the greater requirements of the guns in guns' crews.

The additional requirements of training personnel is a consequence of the increase in active naval fighting forces.

* Five hundred men are to be demanded in excess of the average annual increase in each of the three years 1912-1914. This increase is to be balanced by a corresponding decrease in the three years 1918-1920.

APPENDIX 4.
CALCULATION OF COST.

Description of Expenditure.	Expenditure.					
	1912. £	1913. £	1914. £	1915. £	1916. £	1917. £
A. Shipbuilding and armaments, including submarines and airships.	342,000	832,000	1,174,000	1,076,000	1,174,000	881,000
B. Other non-recurring expenditure: Increase in annual amount by	245,000	245,000	245,000	147,000	—	—
C. Recurring expenditure:* Augmentation of annual increase, foreseen in the sums required calculated in 1908, by £196,000 each on the average, graduated according to probable requirements	147,000	293,000	440,000	685,000	930,000	1,174,000
Totals, A to C	734,000	1,370,000	1,859,000	1,908,000	2,104,000	2,055,000
From which an increase in the demands on the ordinary revenue results, as compared with the previous year, of	+734,000	+636,000	+489,000	+49,000	+196,000	-49,000

NOTE.—The Navy Estimates for 1917, it is calculated, will amount to £22,651,000, including the additional sum required under the Amendment; that is to say, £98,000 *less* than the sum of £22,749,000 for the current year (1911) as calculated when the Law was amended in 1908 (which includes a further sum of £166,000 due to the increase of pay sanctioned in 1909).

* In consequence of the projected increase in the wages of the men, the sums quoted for recurring expenses will each be augmented by £49,000 from 1913 inclusive.

APPENDIX II

MEMORANDUM APPENDED TO THE GERMAN NAVY BILL, 1900

I. NECESSITY AND SCOPE OF THE INCREASE OF THE NAVY.

THE GERMAN EMPIRE NEEDS PEACE AT SEA.—For the German Empire of to-day the security of its economic development, and especially of its world-trade, is a life question. For this purpose the German Empire needs not only peace on land but also peace at sea—not, however, peace at any price, but peace with honour, which satisfies its just requirements.

A naval war for economic interests, particularly for commercial interests, will probably be of long duration, for the aim of a superior opponent will be all the more completely reached the longer the war lasts. To this must be added that a naval war which, after the destruction or shutting-up of the German sea fighting force, was confined to the blockade of the coasts and the capture of merchant ships, would cost the opponent little; indeed he would, on the contrary, amply cover the expenses of the war by the simultaneous improvement of his own trade.

An unsuccessful naval war of the duration of even only a year would destroy Germany's sea trade, and would thereby bring about the most disastrous conditions, first in her economic, and then, as an immediate consequence of that, in her social life.

Quite apart from the consequences of the possible peace conditions, the destruction of our sea trade during the war could not, even at the close of it, be made good within measurable time, and would thus add to the sacrifices of the war a serious economic depression.

NAVY LAW * DOES NOT YET MAKE ALLOWANCE FOR THE POS-
SIBILITY OF A NAVAL WAR WITH A GREAT SEA-POWER.—The
Navy Law does not make allowance for the possibility of a
naval war with a great naval Power, because, when it was
drafted in the summer of 1897, the first consideration was to
secure the carrying out in modern ship material of the 1873
plan for the founding of the fleet, limiting the increase to the
small number of battleships which was necessary to establish,
at least for a double squadron, the organization demanded by
tactical exigencies.

The Justificatory Memorandum to the Navy Law left no
doubt as to the military significance of the Battle Fleet. It is
therein expressly stated:

" Against greater sea-powers the Battle Fleet would have
importance merely as a sortie fleet."

That is to say, the fleet would have to withdraw into the
harbour and there wait for a favourable opportunity for making
a sortie. Even if it should obtain a success in such a sortie,
it would nevertheless, like the enemy, suffer considerable loss
of ships. The stronger enemy could make good his losses, we
could not. In war with a substantially superior sea-power,
the Battle Fleet provided for by the Navy Law would render
a blockade more difficult, especially in the first phase of the
war, but would never be able to prevent it. To subdue it, or,
after it had been considerably weakened, to confine it in its
own harbour would always be merely a question of time. So
soon as this had happened, no great State could be more easily
cut off than Germany from all sea intercourse worthy of the
name — of her own ships as also of the ships of neutral
Powers. To effect this it would not be necessary to control
long stretches of coast, but merely to blockade the few big
seaports.

In the same way as the traffic to the home ports, the German mercantile ships on all the seas of the world would be left
to the mercy of an enemy who was more powerful on the sea.
Hostile cruisers on the main trade-routes, in the Skager Rack,
in the English Channel, off the north of Scotland, in the Straits
of Gibraltar, at the entrance to the Suez Canal, and at the

* In this Memorandum "Navy Law" means the Navy Act
of 1898.

Cape of Good Hope, would render German shipping practically impossible.

Also with regard to this the Justificatory Memorandum to the Naval Law speaks unambiguously. In it is observed:

"Protection of sea trade on all the seas would occur principally in time of peace. In case of war it would be the task of the foreign service cruisers to afford their own mercantile ships the "utmost possible protection.""

That is to say, the ships would do the "utmost possible." What would be possible in this respect is clear when it is realized that the Navy Law provides altogether for forty-two cruisers, whilst the greatest Naval Power, for example, to-day already possesses 206 cruisers (finished or under construction), and, moreover, has as its disposal bases and coaling stations on all the chief trade-routes.

FOR THE PROTECTION OF SEA TRADE AND COLONIES THERE IS ONLY ONE MEANS—A STRONG BATTLE FLEET.—To protect Germany's sea trade and colonies in the existing circumstances there is only one means—Germany must have a battle fleet so strong that even for the adversary with the greatest sea-power a war against it would involve such dangers as to imperil his position in the world.

For this purpose it is not absolutely necessary that the German Battle Fleet should be as strong as that of the greatest naval Power, for a great naval Power will not, as a rule, be in a position to concentrate all its striking forces against us. But even if it should succeed in meeting us with considerable superiority of strength, the defeat of a strong German Fleet would so substantially weaken the enemy that, in spite of the victory he might have obtained, his own position in the world would no longer be secured by an adequate fleet.

In order to attain the goal which has been set, the protection of our sea trade and of our colonies by ensuring a peace with honour, Germany requires, according to the standard of the strength-relationships of the great Sea-Powers, and having regard to our tactical formations, two double squadrons of efficient battleships, with the necessary cruisers, torpedo-boats, and so on, pertaining thereto. As the Navy Law provides for only two squadrons, the building of a third and fourth squadron is contemplated. Of these four squadrons two will form a fleet. The second fleet is to be organized in its tactical composition in the same way as the first fleet provided for in the Navy Law.

For the scope of the maintenance in commission in time of peace the following consideration has been decisive : As the ship-establishment of the German Navy, even after the carrying out of the projected increase, will still be more or less inferior to the ship-establishments of some other great Powers, compensation must be sought in the training of the personnel and in tactical training in the larger combinations.

A trustworthy training of the separate ships' crews, as well as an adequate training in the larger tactical combinations, can be ensured only by permanent maintenance in commission in time of peace. To economize in commissioning in time of peace would mean to jeopardize the efficiency of the fleet for the event of war.

The minimum of commissioning is the permanent formation of that fleet which comprises the newest and best ships as an active combination—that is to say, a combination in which all battleships and cruisers are in commission. This fleet would form the school for tactical training in double squadron, and in case of war would bear the first shock. For the second fleet, which will comprise the older battleships, it must suffice if only half of the ships are permanently in commission. For training in the larger combination some further ships must then, it is true, be placed temporarily in commission during the manœuvres. In case of war this second fleet—the Reserve Battle Fleet—will have to make up its arrears in the training of the separate ships' crews and the deficiency of training in the larger combination behind the protection afforded by the Active Battle Fleet.

WITH FOUR LINE SQUADRONS, COAST SQUADRON IS LESS IMPORTANT.—If Germany possesses four squadrons of efficient battleships, a coast squadron composed of small armoured ships is less important.

INCREASE OF THE FOREIGN SERVICE SHIPS.—Besides the increase of the home battle fleet, an increase of the foreign service ships is also necessary. In consequence of the occupation of Kiauchow and the great enhancement of our oversea interests in the last two years, it has already become necessary, at the cost of the scouting ships of the Battle Fleet, to send abroad two large ships more than were provided for by

the plan of the Navy Law. Indeed, for an effective representation of our interests it would have been necessary to send
out even more ships, if such had only been available. In
order to form a judgment of the importance of an increase of
the foreign service ships, it must be realized that they are the
representatives abroad of the German defence forces, and that
the task often falls to them of gathering in the fruits which the
maritime potency created for the Empire by the home Battle
Fleet has permitted to ripen.

Moreover, an adequate representation on the spot, supported
on a strong home Battle Fleet, in many cases averts differences, and so contributes to maintain peace while fully upholding German honour and German interests.

A numerical demonstration of the additional requirements
cannot be given for a considerable time in advance in the
same manner as for the Battle Fleet, which rests upon an
organic foundation.

If the demand is made that the foreign service fleet shall be
in a position (1) energetically to uphold German interests
everywhere in time of peace, (2) to be adequate for warlike
conflicts with oversea States without navies deserving of the
name, an increase of at least five large and five small cruisers,
as well as of one large and two small cruisers as material
reserve, seems called for. The Navy Law foresees as ready for
use three large and ten small cruisers, and as material reserve
three large and four small cruisers.

A distribution of the foreign service fleet among the foreign
stations cannot be given, as this distribution depends upon
the political circumstances, and these can only be estimated
from case to case.

II. CARRYING OUT OF THE INCREASE—COST—
RAISING OF THE MEANS.

NECESSARY SEA-POWER SHOULD BE CREATED AS SOON AS
POSSIBLE.—If the necessity for Germany of so strong a fleet
is admitted, it will not be possible to contest, that the honour
and welfare of the Fatherland peremptorily demand, that the
home sea-power should be brought up to the requisite strength
as soon as possible.

THEREFORE THE INCREASE CANNOT BE DEFERRED TILL THE
EXPIRY OF THE SEXENNATE.—With the Budget for 1900 the

increase of the Navy provided for in the Navy Law is accomplished with the exception of one small cruiser. The additional ships will, after the passing of the Budget, stand on the slips in the summer of this year. For the further years it is only a question of building replacements. For the next three years the laying down of five large and seven small replacing ships is provided for in the building plan of the Navy Law. The small ships to be replaced are completely obsolete and absolutely useless for warfare. If the replacement of these is taken in hand first as especially urgent, there remain hardly any means over for the laying down of larger ships, since the sum provided in the building programme — M. 35,000,000—is almost absorbed by the rise in the price of the other ships and an increase in the supplies of ammunition which had become necessary. If it were desired to keep within the sum allowed by the Navy Law, no large ships could be laid down from 1901 to 1903.

In consequence of the urgency of a strengthening of the Navy on the one hand, and of the restriction in the building of big ships through the limitations of the Navy Law on the other, it was imperative that the demand for an increase of the ship establishment should not be postponed till the expiry of the sexennate but should be made now.

EXPOSITION OF THE BUILDING PROGRAMME.—The additional ships to be built have to fit as is expedient into the gaps left by the replacement buildings which fall due during the next few years, and the replacements of large ships, owing to their considerable cost, are the ones to be taken chiefly into account.

If the limitation of pecuniary means foreseen in the Navy Law is left out of consideration and regard paid only to the age of the ships, there will be due for replacement—

1. In the year 1901 : Seven large ships (four of the Sachsen class, König Wilhelm, Kaiser, Deutschland).

2. In the twelve years 1902 to 1913 : Three large ships (Oldenburg, Kaiserin Augusta, Siegfried).

3. In the four years 1914 to 1917 : Seventeen large ships (seven of the Siegfried class, four of the Brandenburg class, five of the Hertha class, Fürst Bismarck).

In consideration of the replacement construction, therefore, the necessary increase of the Navy should be carried out in the

years 1902 to 1913; but even then the yearly shipbuilding
activity would remain so irregular that it seems best to distribute the entire requirement of 46 large ships evenly over
sixteen years, and, as a rule, to lay down annually 3 large
ships. That such a rate of construction can be maintained
is, after the experience of recent years, in which also 3 large
ships were laid down annually, not to be doubted.

With regard to the small cruisers, it would be expedient to
choose a similar rate of construction. Within the next sixteen
years 29 ships have to be replaced: the increase amounts to
16 ships. Under a building programme extending over sixteen
years 3 keel-layings would, as the rule, fall to each year.

The construction of torpedo-boat divisions, gunboats, and
special service ships will run concurrently.

With regard to the age limit of the new large torpedo-boats,
experience is still lacking at the present time. If it is taken at
sixteen years, in every year there would become due the laying
down of 1 torpedo-boat division (4 additional divisions for the
new squadron, 12 replacement divisions for the 2 existing
squadrons and the coast squadron of armoured ships).

The additional and replacement construction of gunboats
and special service ships that will be necessary in the next
sixteen years cannot be foreseen.

ORDER OF CONSTRUCTION.—There remains for decision the
order in which the ships are to be built. In order to attain
with the utmost possible speed a greater military efficiency,
it is, in the first place, necessary to have ready a third squadron
of modern battleships with accessories. On its completion an
Active Battle Fleet of 17 ships of the line of the most modern
construction and a Reserve Battle Fleet of 17—with the exception of the Brandenburg class—inferior armoured ships (4 of the
Brandenburg class, 4 of the Sachsen class, 8 of the Siegfried
class, and the Oldenburg) can be formed. This will, it is true,
involve the putting back of the replacements of the Sachsen
class behind the additional construction to supplement the
Active Battle Fleet. This is a considerable drawback, but
seems permissible, since the Sachsen class underwent substantial reconstruction only in the last few years. True, that
has not transformed twenty-five-year-old coastal armoured
ships into fully efficient modern ships of the line; nevertheless
the ships are still seaworthy, and are in utility but little inferior

to those of the Siegfried class, which also belong to the Reserve Battle Fleet.

COST OF SHIP CONSTRUCTION AND ARMAMENT.—Under this building programme there would be required for ship construction, inclusive of the torpedo-boat divisions (additional and replacement construction), according to the price units of the Budget of 1900, altogether M. 1,306,000,000, or on an average M. 81,600,000 annually.

It will, however, be necessary to strengthen the heavy artillery on the battleships and large cruisers, and the equipment of ammunition on all classes of vessels. Accordingly, somewhat higher price units have been taken as the basis of the financial calculations, whereby an average annual requirement of M. 87,600,000 results. Still further expense arises:

1. From the building of gunboats and special service ships.

2. From the reconstruction of older ships, which is becoming necessary, in so far as the cost thereof cannot be met out of the means provided by the Budget for recurrent expenditure.

3. From the rise of prices in consequence of technical improvements.

4. From the rise in prices of materials and in wages.

The probable financial requirements for these purposes cannot be given. In the financial calculations M. 12,400,000 have been added to the average annual instalment of M. 87,600,000 mentioned above. That gives as the probable average requirement for shipbuilding and arming the sum of M. 100,000,000 annually.

INCREASE OF MILITARY PERSONNEL.—The increase in the establishment of ships renders necessary, up to the year 1920 (date of the readiness for war of the ships given out in the year 1916), an increase of the military personnel by 35,551, and in the following manner:

	Altogether.	Annual Average.
Naval officers	1,212	60
Marine engineers	283	14
Surgeons	188	9
Paymasters	122	6
Crews	33,746	1,687
Totals	35,551	1,776

It is in contemplation to demand, during the first ten years (period of the preparation of the Third Squadron and increase of the foreign service ships), an augmentation of the personnel higher than the average, and in the last ten years (period of the replacement of inferior armoured ships of the Fourth Squadron by fully efficient battleships) a correspondingly lower augmentation.

The obtaining of the professional personnel necessary for such an increase involves the annual enlistment of about 200 naval cadets and 1,000 ships' boys.

That enlistments of this magnitude will be practicable if the extension of the Navy is statutorily assured does not seem doubtful after the experiences of recent years.

OTHER NON-RECURRING EXPENDITURE.—The other non-recurring expenditure which will be rendered necessary by the increase of the fleet cannot be estimated. In order to cover the existing necessities out of the many possibilities, and to be able to choose what is right in the individual case, the working out of rival projects, and, consequently, long and expensive preliminary labours, are required. Accordingly, only general indications can be given.

EXTENSION OF THE SHIPYARD AND DOCK WORKS.—Of chief importance for the question of cost is the extension of the ship-yard basins and harbour works in order to provide mooring and equipment berths for the increased establishment of ships. This necessity principally affects Wilhelmshaven and Dantzig; Kiel less, since the spacious and protected harbour of Kiel can be utilized for berthing ships which are not under repair or in process of equipment. An extension of the shipyard works at Wilhelmshaven and Dantzig will probably present no special difficulties.

At Kiel and Wilhelmshaven the need for docks is temporarily covered by the docks which are either under construction or demanded for 1900, so that docking facilities are only to be increased at Dantzig.

An extension of the workshops is called for only by the increased requirements for the maintenance of the ships, as an enhancement of the building activity of the yards is not necessary.

Further, so far as the yards are concerned, consideration must be given to (a) increas of the working stock—tugs, praams, cranes, and so on; (*b*) increase of the materials for equipping ships—coal, lubricating material, and so on; (*c*) increase of the magazines.

COAST FORTIFICATIONS.—Larger outlay for coast fortifications is all the less necessary the more the Battle Fleet is strengthened. At the same time the existing coast fortifications must be maintained in a state of efficiency.

Moreover, in consequence of the extension of the harbour works, possible changes of channel, and so on, the construction of fresh detached batteries over a longish space of time will not be avoidable.

GARRISON ACCOMMODATION, ARTILLERY, TORPEDO, AND MINE WORKS.—The outlay for the extension of garrison accommodation (barracks, hospitals, and so on), as well as of the depots for artillery, torpedo, and mine material, will not, in view of the long period over which it will be distributed, and in comparison with the expenses for shipbuilding, require considerable sums.

ESTIMATE OF THE OTHER NON-RECURRING EXPENDITURE.— In order to obtain a serviceable standard for estimating the remaining non-recurring expenditure, it seems expedient to revert to the experiences of the past.

In the period of the greater development of the Navy, from 1873 to 1882, M. 9,000,000 was, on an average, absorbed by these expenses. This same average sum was contemplated for the first six years of the Navy Law.

In the coming period the expenses will not distribute themselves evenly over the individual years, but at the outset will exceed the average amount, because the great expenses for the extension of the yards will occur then.

If an average sum of M. 15,000,000 — that is to say, M. 6,000,000 more than the maximum of former longer periods of time—is taken as a basis, and M. 18,000,000 are put down for the first ten years, and for the next ten a gradual decline to M. 9,000,000—the hitherto highest amount—it will probably be found that an adequate allowance has been made.

INCREASE OF THE RECURRING EXPENDITURE.—For calculating the increase of the recurring expenditure, the best standard, as experience has shown, is afforded by the dimensions which the outlay for military personnel and commissioning will probably attain.

A calculation on this basis is given in the Annex IV.* It results in an average annual increase of M. 5,400,000. Nevertheless, the circumstance that the increase of personnel and the maintenance in commission must, as far as possible, keep pace with the increase of the ship establishment, makes it seem right to allow M. 6,000,000 in the first half, and M. 4,800,000 in the second half of the twenty-year period for the rise of recurring expenditure.

INCREASE OF THE TOTAL OUTLAY FOR NAVAL PURPOSES.— The following assumptions form the basis for the estimates of the financial requirements:

1. Annual quota for shipbuilding and armaments, M. 100,000,000; total requirements for sixteen years, M. 1,600,000,000, of which M. 603,000,000 are to be covered by annual loans, M. 997,000,000 from ordinary revenue.

Recourse to borrowed money to obtain additional ships is in accordance with the principles which have obtained hitherto. The loan amounts of the separate years have been adjusted in such a way that they gradually and evenly decline, and in the year 1920, after the last ship has been completed, reach nil, so that the normal renewal quota then falls upon the ordinary revenue.

2. Average quota for other non-recurring expenditure, M. 15,000,000; that is to say, in the first ten years M. 18,000,000, in the next ten years a gradual fall to M. 9,000,000; altogether for sixteen years M. 261,000,000. Of this sum M. 166,000,000 are, in accordance with the principles of the past, to be covered by loans, M. 95,000,000 from ordinary revenue. Here, too, the distribution of the loans over the separate years has been adjusted in such a way that the amounts of the loans gradually decline; while, on the other hand, the sums to be contributed by ordinary revenue correspondingly increase. In the year 1920 the loan amount is nil; the amount estimated to be covered out of ordinary revenue M. 9,000,000, which is the quota that is regarded as necessary for the maintenance of what would then be existing.

3. Average annual rise of recurring expenditure, M. 5,400,000, namely: In the first ten years, M. 6,000,000; in the last ten years, M. 4,800,000.

4. Increase of the pension fund to threefold its present dimensions.

* Not reprinted here.

5. The interest on past loans and those to be issued up to 1920 have been taken into consideration.

As is apparent from the calculation of the financial requirements, the total cost for the sixteen years will be :

1. Loans to the amount of M. 769,000,000.

2. An average annual rise of M. 11,000,000 in the naval expenditure covered out of ordinary revenue (inclusive of pensions and interest on debt).

The total annual outlay for the Navy (inclusive of pensions and interest on debt) would increase from M. 169,000,000 in the year 1900 to M. 323,000,000 in the year 1916, or, on an average, by M. 9,600,000 annually.*

This estimate of the financial requirements is intended to, and can, give only a survey of the total cost. The expenditure to be included in the annual Budgets, as well as its distribution between loans and ordinary revenue, are to remain subject to the annual determination of the legislative factors. If the method of the estimate of the financial requirements is taken as a basis, the amount computed in the table would in the individual years be allotted to the ordinary revenue, the balance in each case to loans.

RAISING OF THE MEANS.—The past development of the Imperial finances justifies the expectation that an annual increase of the claims on the ordinary revenue for naval purposes to the amount calculated above can be covered without fresh taxation.

Should this temporarily prove impossible to the necessary extent, it would only remain, if new sources of income cannot be opened out, to raise the amount of the loan in such years.

III. STATUTORY DETERMINATION OF THE INCREASE.

NECESSITY OF THE STATUTORY DETERMINATION OF THE STRENGTH AND ORGANIZATION OF THE NAVY IS ALREADY ADMITTED.—By the passing of the Navy Law, the necessity of placing the strength of the Navy and its organization on a

---

* That the average increase of the total expenditure—M. 9,600,000 —is smaller than the average increase of that portion of the naval outlay which falls on the ordinary revenue of the Empire— M. 11,100,000—is due to the annual diminution of the amount, contained in the former sum, which falls on the loans.

statutory basis was admitted. From this follows, of itself, that an increase of the Navy likewise requires statutory regulation. Though in this situation a further justification of the necessity of statutory determination is not necessary, the grounds on which the Federated Governments consider the statutory form indispensable shall nevertheless be once more explained in what follows.

ONLY IF THE ENTIRE INCREASE IS CARRIED OUT WILL ITS PURPOSE BE ATTAINED.—The Federated Governments are of the opinion, that an increase of the Navy can only fulfil the intended purpose, the securing of peace even against the most powerful naval opponent, if it is carried through in the proportions contemplated for it. Fractions of a squadron do not constitute a formation, and have, in a military sense, only the significance of a strengthened material reserve. Just as little would a limitation to three squadrons suffice, because thereby the aim of the increase would not be attained.

THEREFORE BEFORE A COMMENCEMENT IS MADE WITH ITS EXECUTION THE ENTIRE PLAN MUST BE ADOPTED.—It is, therefore, necessary, that before the execution of the plan is entered upon, the legislative factors should agree as to whether the entire plan is right and should be carried out. A decision on this question must be brought about, and it must be one of permanent validity. This can be only done by a law.

FURTHER REASONS FOR THE STATUTORY DETERMINATION.—Apart from this consideration the statutory determination of the increase is also necessary on the following grounds:

1. *Uncertainty as to whether the Entire Plan is to be Carried Through impedes its Execution.*

1. Only the statutory determination of the increase testifies the firm will to create the fleet. Unless this firm will is brought to indubitable expression, considerable difficulties, both of a personal and material nature, will oppose themselves to the execution of the great plan.

Only if a sure guarantee is given for the execution of the plan can the permanent participation of a large number of efficient undertakings in the building of the fleet be counted upon, as only then will the necessary capital be laid out on expensive works for the construction of warships. But healthy competition will only be rendered possible if the Navy is not restricted to a very few big undertakings. Only if a further development of the Navy is legally placed beyond question will there be adequate entries of naval cadets, ships' boys, and volunteers, that is to say of such persons as chose the naval service as their life profession.

Only under a statutory determination of the aim can the internal development of the Navy, and particularly the extension of the shipyard and harbour works, be properly adjusted from the outset to later requirements.

2. *Importance of the Statutory Determination for the Prestige of the German Name Abroad.*

2. The united decision of Federal Council and Reichstag to double the war fleet, as marked by a statutory determination of the increase, will be of the greatest importance for the prestige of the German name abroad, and so for the entire political and economic development of the German Empire.

OBJECTIONS TO A STATUTORY DETERMINATION.—Against a statutory determination of the increase it has been objected, that the time necessary for the execution of so great a plan is so long, that it is impossible to foresee whether, within this time, the technical, political, and financial conditions for such a statutory determination might not undergo a fundamental change.

The Federated Governments do not regard such radical alterations as probable. Should they, contrary to expectations, occur, the two legislative factors are at any time in a position to alter the Navy Law and the contemplated Amending Act.

That the Federated Governments will ever oppose a change of the Navy Law which becomes necessary in consequence of changes in the technical and military conditions of warfare no one can believe.

It is further objected that precisely the Navy Law has furnished proof that the strength which a fleet shall attain, that is to say, the goal of its development, is not adapted to statutory determination, and that, accordingly, the same mistake should not be committed again.

This objection can only be explained by an inaccurate view of the Navy Law. This consists of two parts—of one part of permanent validity, which in earlier Reichstag proceedings was described as "Aeternat," and of another part of only temporary significance, which received the name "Sexennat."

The first part is the essential one. It regulates the strength and organization of the fleet, the replacement construction, the maintenance in commission, and the personal establishment. In this essential part, the "Aeternat," the strength, and, as a necessary consequence, the provisions with regard to maintenance in commission, are to be extended. The remaining provisions of the Navy Law are not touched.

The second part of the Navy Law, the so-called "Sexennat," had merely the object of legislatively laying down a term for the attainment of the statutory ship establishment, and not for the carrying out of the replacement construction, for the building of replacement ships continues further in unbroken series beyond the Sexennat.

In the Reichstag proceedings with regard to the Navy Law, the statutory determination of a period within which the ship establishment was to be attained encountered by far the most difficulties, in consequence of misgivings in respect of Budget rights. The consequence of this was, that the essential feature of the Navy Law stepped into the background, and the statutory determination of a period for the attainment of the fixed establishment—that is to say, that part which after the passing of the Budget of 1900 was assured and therefore objectless, gave the Law among the public its character and the name of Sexennat.

DEMAND OF THE FEDERATED GOVERNMENT FOR THE BILL.— In consequence of the difficulties then encountered, and in recognition of the fact that it is somewhat questionable to lay down by statute a term for the completion of a plan for the carrying out of which so long a period is necessary, the Federrated Governments have considered that they should refrain therefrom, and have restricted themselves merely to the statutory determination of the goal. They are here guided by the confident expectation that the Reichstag, when it has accepted the goal of the development, will do its utmost, in the measure of the financial resources of the Empire, to bring this object to completion.

APPENDIX III

GERMANY'S SHIPBUILDING RESOURCES

THE growth of the war-shipbuilding industry in Germany has kept pace with every movement towards a higher standard of naval power. The remarkable character of this expansion of the country's resources was revealed by Count von Reventlow in an article which he contributed to the Marine Number of *Cassier's Magazine* published in December, 1911 ; and from the data which he then presented some conception can be formed of the phenomenal progress which has been made since. In 1890 German public opinion congratulated itself on the determination of their Government to rely no longer even on ships' plates manufactured in England, but to insist on German ships being built in the Fatherland of German materials.

The resources of the three Imperial yards, which have been greatly extended from time to time, are in keeping with the development which the navy has undergone in recent years.

The Imperial yard at Kiel has two large slips and a small one for torpedo-boats, six floating docks, and six dry docks. The yard at Wilhelmshaven has two large slipways, five floating docks, with four small ones for torpedo-boats, and seven dry docks. At Dantzig there is a comparatively small slipway, three horizontal slips, a docking-basin, and two floating docks. This yard is gradually being devoted to submarines. The Imperial yards are generally confined to repairs, yet they are designed on the principle that they shall possess a sufficient power of output so as to prevent private yards from being in a position to fix the prices at which war vessels should be built, and they have shown themselves equal to the occasion, and are by no means behind private establishments.

Count von Reventlow's descriptions of private establishments is the fullest and most authoritative which is available, and bears testimony to Germany's present capacity to build and equip the largest and most powerful men-of-war.

THE VULCAN COMPANY OF STETTIN.

The Vulcan was developed out of the shipyard which was founded in 1851 by Fruchtenich and Brock, in Bredow. This development took place in 1857. In the mercantile marine the Vulcan became the typical shipbuilding establishment for fast ships after the North German Lloyd, following the example of the Hamburg-America Line, had its ships built in German yards. The fact, also, that the North German Lloyd was bound to have its postal ships built in German yards was of great benefit to the Vulcan. On the other hand, the Vulcan was the first private shipbuilding yard to be in a position to build armoured vessels and to show that far-sighted policy—we had almost said boldness—of adapting itself to great undertakings. In 1868 the German naval authorities made the experiment of building an armoured corvette, the *Hansa*, in the State yard at Dantzig. The Vulcan Company received an order to build a sister-ship; the order hung back, however, for some considerable time, and it was only in 1873 that the *Preussen* was laid down at the Vulcan yard. The efficiency in the case of the Vulcan Company is all the more commendable, inasmuch as the Admiralty had warned the directors not to lay down an expensive plant for building armoured ships, as it was not certain that orders would be given. With the year 1873 came the oft-mentioned order of General Stosch that all warships belonging to Germany, and, as far as possible, all materials, should be constructed in Germany. This undoubtedly acted as a great stimulus to the Vulcan. The production of its yards may be seen from the following statistics: Since 1871 they have built 110 warships, among which a large number for the Chinese, Japanese, Russian and Greek Navies, respectively. Apart from torpedo-boats, the Vulcan has received more orders for vessels of war than any other yard, and has, dating from 1900, built a large number of torpedo-boats for the German Navy. The Vulcan has built over 159 screw-steamers, among them over a dozen mail steamers and about forty Atlantic freight and passenger ships. To these may be added fifty paddle-steamers and seven ice-breakers.

The area of the Vulcan yard is 283,400 square metres, of which 91,915 are covered with workshops. There are seven slips, of which two are over 200 metres, three between 150 and 200 metres, and two of 100 to 150 metres. There are two floating docks, one of 100 to 150 metres, and another under 100 metres. The Vulcan is in a position to build large warships and vessels for the mercantile marine, yet for years there has been an ever-increasing necessity to establish yards on the North Sea. On the one hand, now, was the question of locality, and on the other the draught of water in the Oder. The establishment at Bredow is of the most practical and modern. Round the slips lie the workshops and magazines; light railways facilitate transport between one part and another of the works. They have their own forges and armour-plate plant—in fact, everything associated with an up-to-date ship-yard. There are also engine and boiler works, and it may be mentioned that there are, in addition, locomotive and turbine building works.

The establishment on the Elbe dates from 1906. In that year a beginning was made with the construction of a yard on the island of Ross, within the boundary of the Hamburg Free Harbour. The yard has an area of 226,850 square metres, with a water front of 1,100 metres. The yard abuts on the Kaiser Wilhelm Harbour, and is connected with the State Railway. Up to the present there are two slips over 200 metres long and two large floating docks, while a third, of over 150 metres long with a lifting capacity of 25,000 tons, is in process of con-struction. By dredging in front of the slips, the depth of water has been so much increased that the largest ships may be launched and armed. Every mechanical device is at hand. The Vulcan will now be able to compete under far more favourable conditions with other shipbuilders, and it may be anticipated that the yards will pay, notwithstanding the enormous initial outlay. The capital of the Vulcan amounts to M. 15,000,000, and the last dividend was 11 per cent. The members of the staff and workmen were 12,000 in all. From the point of view of the Navy, it is of the utmost importance to possess so efficient a shipyard on the Elbe. In any war in the North Sea the Vulcan yards, and those of Blohm and Voss, would be immensely valuable for docking and repairing disabled vessels. That the company themselves consider this North Sea branch the most important, is shown by the fact that they have transferred their central bureau to Hamburg since October 1 of this year. Nevertheless, the yards at Bredow will retain much of their present importance, for the demands of ship-building are great and will continue to increase. The Vulcan is regarded in Germany, and with justice, as having grown up with the development of German shipping and the German naval power, as sharing in all their experiences, and as having always risen to the height of its demands.

THE SHIPYARD F. SCHICHAU, OF ELBING AND DANTZIG.

This is the unique and largest shipbuilding yard in Germany which is not a limited company, but remains in private hands. The Schichau works were founded in 1837 by Ferdinand Schichau at Elbing, and are now owned by his son-in-law, Geheimrath Zeiss. Ferdinand Schichau was a man whose abilities may not unjustly be compared with those of Alfred Krupp, founder of the works of that name. He started the works at Elbing for engine building in 1837, and ten years later obtained the first order for a marine engine. Hence-forward the works developed more and more in the direction of shipbuilding, and began with building dredges, which are to-day one of the specialities of the firm. In the early fifties the Prussian Government approached the Schichau works as to building the engines and boilers for the corvette *Dantzig*. I mention this otherwise unimportant fact to show the intimate connection which has existed between the firm of Schichau and the Prussian, later the German, Government—relations which have proved of the greatest importance, both in matters of shipbuilding and torpedo-boat construction. Later, the firm confined itself to its original engine building, until, in 1855, the iron ship *Borussia* was built in their newly-established shipyard. Shipbuilding now developed apace, and in the early seventies a second ship was constructed in partnership with the engineer Zeiss, the present owner. The Schichau engines proved them-selves as superior as the materials used in the construction of the torpedo-boats. In the seventies the Prussian Government gave an order for a spar-torpedo. The brilliant result of this boat and its successes laid the foundation of the firm's fame in this branch of their productions. In the eighties the German

Government turned to the torpedo, and Captain Tirpitz—as he was then—developed the type of boat and the general organization. The superiority of the Schichau-built boats lay chiefly in their light displacement, speed, large radius of operations, and seaworthiness, even in rough weather, large coal capacity and comfort. In open competition, in 1884, Schichau obtained the preference, and ever since, up to the beginning of the present century, has built almost all the German torpedo-boats. The reputation of these torpedo-boats brought them numerous orders from abroad. Great attention was drawn to them when a torpedo-boat of 140 tons, ordered by China, reached Foochow in sixty days, going under its own steam, without parent ship. As is well known, other builders besides "Vulcan" and "Weser" have entered into competition with Schichau in the domain of torpedo-boats, but the distinction of being the inventor of the German torpedo-boat belongs to Schichau. That is proved by the fact that our torpedo-boats of the present day preserve the type of the original Schichau boat.

At the end of the eighties the firm of Schichau acquired a yard at Dantzig, as they intended to devote themselves also to the construction of large vessels, and from 1890 onwards cruisers and battleships have been built for the German Navy, as also for other foreign navies. In addition, it must be noted that several large liners have been built for the North German Lloyd.

The works have grown with every demand made upon them, and would be more than equal to any extraordinary efforts which might be required of them in the matter of rapid shipbuilding by the German naval authorities. The ground covered by their yards at Elbing, Dantzig, and Pillau amounts to more than 87 hectares. The staff and workmen generally number 8,000.

The yard at Elbing has nineteen slips for torpedo-boats and two docks; that at Dantzig seven slips, of which four are adapted for ships of the largest tonnage. The slips are supplied with the most up-to-date appliances, such as electric cranes, etc. The present owner, like his predecessor, the founder, belongs to that band of great organizers of labour and distinguished experts.

Blohm and Voss Shipyard.

In 1877 the shipbuilding yard and engine works of Blohm and Voss were founded on the Island of Steinwerder in the Elbe, and were at first small and of little importance. The position of the enterprise to-day is most important. In 1911 the yards employed 7,500 men. The works cover 460,000 square metres, of which 300,000 have been built upon, and the water-front is 2,570 metres long. There are ten slips, of which four are over 200 metres long, five between 150 and 200 metres, and a small one of less than 150 metres. There are floating docks, the largest of which has a lifting capacity of 35,000 tons, and there are others of capacities of 17,500, 17,000, 4,700, and 3,000 tons. Two of these—the largest and the third—can be transported, and in case of war would be of great service to the fleet in the Elbe. In 1881 Blohm and Voss were turned into a limited liability company, with a capital of M. 6,000,000, and loan on mortgages of M. 8,000,000. A dividend of 6 per cent. was paid in 1910.

The yards are used for the construction of all kinds of ships, but a speciality is made of floating docks. In addition to shipbuilding, there are large works for the construction of steam-engines and turbines. There are two boiler-making establishments for cylindrical and water-tube boilers. Lately a foundry for bronze and steel has been added. In short, there is every modern requirement, both as regards machinery and equipment generally.

Shipbuilding of any importance for the German Navy dates back only a comparatively short time. This began in the eighties with the small cruiser *Kondor*, followed in the nineties by the battleship *Kaiser Karl der Grosse*, of about 11,000 tons, and from that date an uninterrupted series of armoured cruisers. Beginning with the cruiser *Freidrich Karl*, launched in 1902, there followed the *York*, *Scharnhorst*, *Von der Tann*, *Moltke*, *Goben*, and the cruiser "*J*"of the 1910 programme, not yet launched. The building of armoured cruisers has been specialized by Blohm and Voss, and the cruisers *Von der Tann* and *Moltke* have given them a reputation throughout the world. This was also the first German shipyard to make arrangements on a large scale for the construction of turbines, the cruiser *Von der Tann* having been the first large cruiser fitted with the turbine. Several years earlier the firm had received the second prize for the best plan of an armoured cruiser, and shortly afterwards the prize offered by the Russian Government for a new type of battleship. The works have in the last decade advanced enormously in the matter of battleship building, and can compete in this branch with any firm in the world. In war the position of the yard on the Elbe would be of great advantage as a repairing and refitting basis to Germany.

Messrs. Blohm and Voss have built a large number of steamers of all kinds for the mercantile marine, notably for the Hamburg - America and North German Lloyd Lines. Besides this they have built vessels for the Hamburg South American Line, for the Woermann, the German East African, and the Kosmos Lines. A considerable amount of the firm's activity is devoted to repairing vessels, as their position in Hamburg Harbour and their possessing manifold modern appliances stand them in great service. The number of workmen varies between 5,500 and 8,000. The yards of Blohm and Voss grow yearly in importance.

THE HOWALDT WORKS.

These works were started and opened as a shipyard in 1876 by their founder, Howaldt, and have only recently been turned into a limited liability company, up to which time they were the private property of the Howaldt family. The yards are in Kiel Harbour. In 1876 there were only 450 square metres covered with buildings, and a total ground area of 20,000 square metres. To-day there are 35,515 square metres covered with workshops, and the total area amounts to 735,695 square metres. The yards can, therefore, be very much enlarged. In these yards there is evidence—more, perhaps, than in any other—of the extraordinary growth of German shipbuilding. The old yard remains, but new and enlarged shipyards have been constructed. The original shipyard is principally utilized for the lighter and least important work, but the work is centralized. The Howaldt works have a water-front of fully two kilometres, one of which is arranged as a quay. This company has a capital of M. 7,750,000. They have had difficulties of recent years, and no dividend has been paid, but there is every ground for believing that this period of adversity is over. The shipyard has six slips, one of over 200 metres in length, two over 150, two over 100, and four less than 100 metres long. There is also a floating dock. The number of employees amounts to 3,500. A turbine manufactory is in process of construction.

Since 1876 Howaldts have built numerous ships of all sorts and sizes, more especially for abroad, among others, the Russian school ship *Okean*. Floating docks, floating cranes, and dredgers, form also part of their output. Modern naval construction by this firm is comparatively recent. Their first modern cruiser, the *Undine*, was begun there in 1901. There soon followed a battleship of 20,000 tons—namely, the *Helgoland*. It may be expected that the Howaldt yards will soon be in a position equal to that of any other German yards for building large men-of-war.

The Weser Limited Liability Company was founded in 1872, having been originally C. Waltjen and Co., established in 1843. The business was, from the beginning, remunerative, and the firm got many orders for mercantile ships, and also ships of war, though these were of comparatively small size. As ships grew larger with time the yards proved too small, and an extension on its original situation was impossible. In consequence, the whole establishment was transferred to Gropelingen, a suburb of Bremen, and the new works were gradually completed between 1901 and 1905. The shipyard as it now it, is entirely new and entirely up-to-date, having no old equipments. This is, naturally, a very favourable position to be in, but to accomplish this entailed a very heavy outlay. On the completion of these works the company became one of the important shipbuilding companies of Germany. They employ about 5,000 officials and workmen. There are five slipways, one over 200 metres long, another over 150 metres, one over 100 metres, and another less than 100 metres long. There is a floating dock of 100 to 150 metres long. The construction of two further slips has been begun. The dockyard harbour is 1,200 metres long, and the largest ships can easily be launched. The works cover an area of 600,000 square metres, and there is a waterfront of 1,200 metres long. Capital, M. 7,500,000. No dividend last year.

Mercantile ships were chiefly built for the North German

Lloyd. The latest were the *Göven* and the *Lützow*, and the transatlantic steamer *Berlin*, of 28,000 tons, the largest vessel built, up to that time, on the banks of the Weser. The company also built the first longitudinal-ribbed vessel in Germany. It will also be of particular interest to learn that the Hamburg-America Line has ordered this year a 6,500-ton cargo steamer, to be driven by oil-motors. The vessel will be 350 feet long, 50 feet beam, with a depth of 22 feet 6 inches. There will be two motors on the "Junkers" system, each capable of developing 800 effective horse-power. The speed is 10 knots. The auxiliary engines will be driven at sea by compressed air and electricity, and in harbour by steam.

The yard supplied the Navy with a considerable number of vessels, such as gunboats and small cruisers; but when the new yards were established at Gropelingen it was possible to take orders for battleships and armoured cruisers. In 1907 the order for the battleship *Westphalen*, of the Nassau class, of about 18,000 tons, was placed here, although no battleships had previously been built, but only cruisers and gunboats. The vessel was delivered in prompt time, and successfully underwent all the trials. This yard has, in a very short time, showed itself capable and efficient for building the largest class of vessel. They have introduced, also, a turbine on a system of their own, and known as the "Weser-Bergmann."

THE KRUPP GERMANIA YARD AT KIEL.

The Germania yard has a curious history, inasmuch as it had its beginning, not on the sea-coast, but inland. It derives its origin from a small foundry and workshop, which was founded by F. A. Egells, in 1822, in the neighbourhood of Berlin, and employed only ten men. The works were gradually enlarged, and frequently received orders for marine engines and boilers. In 1871 works were started at Tegel, near Berlin, and became the Markisch-Schleische Machinenbau- und Hutten-Aktiengesellschaft. The great industrial progress in Germany brought many orders for ships' engines and boilers. These became the specialities of the firm, and it was a natural consequence that they should turn to shipbuilding. In 1879 the company bought the Norddeutscher yard at Kiel, and in 1881 the two branches were united under the name of the Schiff- und

Maschinenbau-Aktiengesellschaft Germania. Under this designation the yard has produced much good work, and built a number of mercantile and naval vessels for home and abroad. As of interest in naval history, it ought to be mentioned that the cruiser *Kaiserin Augusta* was built in the Germania yard, the first German warship to be fitted with triple screws and to reach the then exceptional speed of twenty-two knots. The *Fürst Bismarck*, the first German armoured cruiser, launched in 1897, was built by the Germania. In 1896 Friedrich Krupp, of Essen, took over the yard on a twenty-five years' lease. By the terms of the contract the firm of Krupp stipulated that they might make any alterations in the situation they might deem necessary. They also reserved the right to acquire the yard for themselves. The moment for this occurred in 1902. On April 1 of that year this yard became the possession of Krupp, under the name of Friedrich Krupp Aktiengesellschaft Germania-werft. It then entered upon a new period of development. Many millions were invested in the new plant, and nothing was spared in making the establishment one of the biggest and best-equipped in Germany. This has happened, and the Germania is now equal to the greatest possible demands which may be made, either for the construction of naval or mercantile ships. The area covered by the works is 235,000 square metres. There are four slips of between 150 and 200 metres, three of between 100 and 150 metres, and six under 100 metres. The Germania does not possess a dock. There are 4,000 workmen employed. The capital belongs to the Krupp, Essen Company. The Germania stands alone in Germany in so far that it produces its own guns and armour. The purchase of the Germania yards would appear to have been a favourite idea of the late Herr Krupp, and it is well to draw attention to this, as its development is being pushed forward by every possible means. The first German shipbuilding works to be covered in were constructed, and a passing visit will show that no expense has been spared. Battleships, cruisers, torpedo-boats, and, as a speciality, submarines, are built. For many years Germania has built torpedoes for foreign Governments, and at the beginning of the present century begun to build regularly for the German torpedo flotilla, with excellent results. Experiments were also made with submarines, and in 1902 the first submarine, the

Forel, was delivered to Russia, to be succeeded by others. A few years later the first submarine for the German Navy was built, and proved in every respect a satisfactory type.

Mercantile vessels are also built, and a large number have been supplied to the orders of the North German Lloyd and Hamburg-American Lines, as well as large numbers of tugboats, railway steamers, dredgers, and freight steamers.

The Germania has also taken up the turbine, and alone produces the water-tube boilers on the system Schultz. Furthermore, she builds oil-motors and all engines and boilers installed in ships of her building.

The Krupp Germania has this difference as compared with all the other German yards, that she has not gradually developed, but has been made at one stroke, by means of the Krupp millions, a great and modern yard. Her power of production, as that of most of the German yards, is far superior to the present demands likely to be made upon it.

Yards.	Area in Square Metres.	Slips.			
		Up to 100 Metres Long.	From 100 to 150 Metres Long.	From 150 to 200 Metres Long.	Over 200 Metre Long.
Vulcan Works, Hamburg [1] ...	227,180	—	—	—	2
Vulcan Works, Stettin ...	269,560	—	2	3	2
F. Schichau, Elbing, Dantzig	874,000	21	1	3	2
Blohm and Voss, Hamburg ...	460,000	—	1	5	4
Weser Company, Bremen [2] ...	604,400	1	1	1	3
Germania Yard, Kiel-Gaarden	225,000	6	3	4	—
Howaldt Works, Kiel ...	165,400	4	2	2	1
Bremer Vulcan Works, Vegesack ...	332,000	—	3	2	1
Joh. C. Tecklenborg, Geestemünde ...	210,000	1	2	1	2
Flensburger Shipbuilding Company, Flensburg ...	178,000	3	2	2	—
Reiherstieg Shipyard, Hamburg ...	68,300	—	2	—	—
Neptun Company, Rostock ...	107,000	1	2	2	—
G. Seebeck, Geestemünde ...	174,750	5	—	2 [3]	—
Stettin-Oder Works, Stettin ...	118,000	8	—	—	—
J. Frerichs and Co., Einswarden ...	161,390	1 [4]	3	— [5]	—
H. C. Stülcken and Son, Hamburg ...	18,020	7	—	—	—
Henry Koch, Lübeck ...	72,500	1	4	—	—
J. W. Klawitter, Dantzig ...	52,000	4	—	—	—
Heinr. Brandenburg, Hamburg ...	13,600	6	—	—	—
Rickmers Reismühlen Shipbuilding Company, Bremerhaven ...	94,000	2 [7]	2	—	—
Jos. L. Meyer, Papenburg ...	31,900	3	—	—	—
Rüscke and Co., Stettin ...	24,000	5	—	—	—
Stocks and Kolbe, Wellingdorf-Kiel ...	16,000	—	—	—	—
Stocks and Kolbe, Sonderburg Branch ...	60,000	6	—	—	—
J. H. N. Wichhorst, Hamburg	16,500	2	—	—	—
Shipyard and Machinery Works Company, Hamburg	8,900	4	—	—	—
C. Cassens, Emden ...	10,000	4	—	—	—
Johannsen and Co., Dantzig...	13,500	2	—	—	—
C. Lühring, Hammelwarden	6,200	5	—	—	—
Gustav Fechter, Königsberg	12,000	3	—	—	—
G. H. Thyen, Brake ...	15,000	2	—	—	—
Eider Shipbuilding Company, Tönning [8] ...	60,000	—	4	—	—
North Sea Works, Emden ...	280,000	—	—	—	1 [4]
Bremen State Docks ...	—	—	—	—	—
North German Lloyd ...	—	—	—	—	—
Totals ...	—	107	34	27	18
			186		
The three Imperial yards ...	7,850,000		5		
Grand totals ...	—		191		

Dry Docks		Floating Docks			Number of Officials and Workmen Employed	Remarks
Up to 100 Metres Long	Over 100 Metres Long	Up to 100 Metres Long	From 100 to 150 Metres Long	Over 150 Metres Long		
—	—	—	1	1	13,000	
—	—	1	1	—	8,000	
—	—	4	—	3	9,000	
—	—	1	1	—	5,000	
—	—	2	1	—	5,600	
—	—	1	—	—	3,500	
—	—	—	—	—	3,500	
1	1	—	—	—	2,600	
—	—	1	—	—	2,800	
—	—	—	2	—	2,000	
—	—	1	—	—	1,700	
3	4	—	—	—	1,100	
—	—	2	—	—	1,000	
—	—	—	—	—	750	
—	—	3[6]	1[6]	—	700	
—	—	2	—	—	750	
—	—	1	—	—	600	
—	—	—	1	—	500	
—	—	—	—	—	500	
—	—	—	—	—	450	
—	—	2	—	—	400	
—	—	—	—	—	300	
—	—	—	—	—	50	
—	1	—	—	—	300	
—	—	—	—	—	340	
—	—	—	—	—	150	
—	—	—	—	—	130	
1	—	—	—	—	120	
—	—	—	—	—	120	
1	—	—	—	—	110	
—	—	—	—	—	—	
—	1[9]	1	—	—	400	
—	2[9]	—	—	—	—	
6	9	22	8	4	65,470	
15		34				
12		13[10]			24,000	
27		47			89,470	

Remarks:

[1] In addition to one floating dock over 150 metres long and of 25,000 tons lifting capacity, and one floating dock of 17,500 tons lifting capacity under construction for Hamburg.

[2] The Germania yard belongs to the Krupp firm.

[3] Building dock.

[4] Transverse slip.

[5] One slip projected.

[6] Dock A, two sections, altogether 86 metres long; Dock B, one section, 53·5 metres long; Dock C, two sections, altogether 93 metres long; B and C docks, combined in three sections, have a length of 146·5 metres.

[7] Including one transverse slip.

[8] This yard is not working.

[9] In Bremerhaven. An additional dry dock of 260 metres, belonging to the Bremen State, is also under construction at Bremerhaven.

[10] Four dock pontoons for torpedo craft. One floating dock contemplated.

BRITISH AND GERMAN SHIPBUILDING PROGRAMMES

THE following tables show the British and German ships laid down between 1897 and 1913, and the programmes of subsequent years—the British figures being based on the Admiralty forecast, and the German on the latest German Fleet Law:

		Great Britain.				Germany.			
	Battleships.	Armoured Cruisers.	Protected Cruisers.	Destroyers.	Torpedo Boats.	Battleships.	Armoured Cruisers.	Protected Cruisers.	Destroyers.
Mixed armament period									
1897-1898 ...	4	4	3	6	—	1	—	—	—
1898-1899 ...	7	8	1	12	—	2	1	2	6
1899-1900 ...	2	2	1	—	2	3	—	2	6
1900-1901 ...	2	6	1	5	2	2	—	2	6
1901-1902 ...	3	6	2	10	5	2	1	3	6
1902-1903 ...	2	2	6[1]	9	4	2	1	3	6
1903-1904 ...	5	4	4[1]	15	—	2	1	2	6
1904-1905 ...	2	3	—	—	—	2	1	3	6
1905-1906 ...	—	—	—	—	—	2	1	3	6
Totals	27	35	18	57	13	18	6	20	48
Dreadnought period									
1905-1906 ...	4	—	—	6	12[3]	—	—	—	—
1906-1907 ...	3	—	—	2	12[3]	2	1	2	12
1907-1908 ...	3	—	1	5	12[3]	3	—	2	12
1908-1909 ...	2	—	6	16	—	4	—	2	12
1909-1910 ...	8	—	6	20	—	4	—	2	12
1910-1911 ...	5	—	5	20	—	4	—	2	12
1911-1912 ...	5	—	4	20	—	4	—	2	12
1912-1913 ...	4	—	8[2]	20	—	2	—	2	12
1913-1914 ...	5	—	8	16	—	3	—	2	12
1914-1915 ...	4	—	—[5]	—[5]	—[5]	2	—	2	12
1915-1916 ...	4	—	—[5]	—[5]	—[5]	2	—	2	12
1916-1917 ...	4	—	—[5]	—[5]	—[5]	3	—	2	12
1917-1918 ...	4	—	—[5]	—[5]	—[5]	2	—	2	12
Totals authorized (1905-1913) (Dreadnought period) ...	39	—	38	125	36	26	1	16	96
Grand totals, including additional ships of German Fleet Law	82[4]	35	56	182	49	53[4]	7	44	192

[1] Included in these two figures are eight scouts—small cruisers—which were laid down in 1902 and 1903.

[2] The cruisers of 1912-13 were designated "light armoured cruisers."

[3] These thirty-six craft are small destroyers, and were built as such.

[4] These totals include battle cruisers.

[5] No programme of British cruisers or torpedo craft announced.

The thirty-nine British battleships exclude the two Colonial vessels—*Australia* and *New Zealand*—and the battleship given by the Federated Malay States, and ordered early in 1913.

APPENDIX VI

GUN AND TORPEDO ARMAMENT OF THE BRITISH AND GERMAN FLEETS, MARCH, 1918

BRITISH FLEET

	13·5-in.	12-in.	10-in.	9·2-in.	7·5-in.	6-in.	4·7-in.	4-in.	3-in.	Torpedo Tubes. Under Water.	Above Water.
Battleships * ...	66	284	8	52	28	428	—	316	590	223	9
Armoured cruisers ...	—	—	—	68	70	318	—	—	222	83	—
Protected cruisers ...	—	—	—	2	—	352	62	236	314	86	64
Coast-defence ships ...	—	—	—	—	—	—	—	—	—	—	—
Totals ...	66	284	8	122	98	1,098	62	552	1,126	392	73

GERMAN FLEET

	13·5-in.	12-in.	11-in.	9·4-in.	8·2-in.	6·7-in.	5·9-in.	4-in.	8·4-in.	Torpedo Tubes. Under Water.	Above Water.
Battleships * ...	—	68	106	40	—	140	330	—	438	195	—
Armoured cruisers ...	—	—	—	6	44	—	82	—	152	36	2
Protected cruisers ...	—	—	—	9	10	—	30	328	70	78	2
Coast-defence ships ...	—	—	—	—	—	—	—	—	30	9	3
Totals ...	—	68	106	55	54	140	442	328	690	318	7

* Battle-cruisers are included.

APPENDIX VII

NAVAL EXPENDITURE, ETC., OF GREAT BRITAIN AND GERMANY IN EACH OF THE YEARS 1901-02 TO 1913-14

GREAT BRITAIN

(FINANCIAL YEAR : APRIL 1 TO MARCH 31)

Year.	Total Naval Expenditure.*	Amount Voted for New Construction, including Armament (Expenditure shown in *Italics*).	Amount of New Construction. †	Numbers of Personnel.
	£	£	Tons.	
1901-02	34,872,299	10,420,256 (*10,341,780*)	139,940	117,116
1902-03	35,227,837	10,436,520 (*9,782,217*)	89,465	121,870
1903-04	40,001,865	11,473,030 (*12,398,133*)	155,225	125,948
1904-05	41,062,075	13,508,176 (*13,184,419*)	85,880	130,490
1905-06	37,159,235	11,291,002 (*11,368,744*)	116,570	127,667
1906-07	34,599,541	10,859,500 (*10,486,397*)	83,260	127,431
1907-08	32,735,767	9,227,000 (*8,849,589*)	119,937	127,228
1908-09	33,511,719	8,660,202 (*8,521,930*)	77,202	127,909
1909-10	36,059,652	11,227,194 (*11,076,551*)	92,957	127,968
1910-11	41,118,668	14,957,430 (*14,755,289*)	176,582	130,817
1911-12	43,061,589	17,566,877 (*15,148,171*)	183,045	132,792
1912-13 (estimated)‡	45,616,540	17,271,317 (*16,323,926*)	113,089	137,500
1913-14 (estimated)	47,021,636	16,101,884	236,406	146,000§

* The gross total of naval expenditure excludes the annuity in repayment of loans under the Naval Works Acts, and includes (*a*) the expenditure out of loans under those Acts, and (*b*) appropriations in aid.

† Tonnage, when completed, of vessels launched.

‡ Including Supplementary Estimate.　　　　　　§ Maximum numbers.

376

GERMANY

(FINANCIAL YEAR : APRIL TO MARCH)

Year.	Total Naval Expenditure.	Amount to be met from Loans.*	Amount Voted for New Construction, including Armament.	Amount of New Construction.†	Numbers of Personnel.
	£	£	£	Tons.	
1901-02 ...	9,530,000	2,701,712	4,653,423	62,640	31,157
1902-03 ...	10,045,000	2,463,111	4,662,769	30,119	33,542
1903-04 ...	10,400,000	2,307,975	4,388,748	64,340	35,834
1904-05 ...	10,105,000	2,256,115	4,275,489	44,072	38,128
1905-06 ...	11,300,000	2,295,939	4,720,206	45,729	40,843
1906-07 ...	12,005,000	2,486,056	5,167,319	53,180	43,654
1907-08 ...	14,225,000	2,806,764	5,910,959	33,985	46,936
1908-09 ...	16,490,000	4,214,048	7,795,499	104,971†	50,531
1909-10 ...	20,090,000	5,371,161	10,177,062	83,184†	53,946
1910-11 ...	20,845,000	5,515,287	11,392,856	101,830†	57,373
1911-12‡ ...	22,031,788	5,328,274	11,710,859	122,630†	60,805
1912-13‡ ...	22,609,540	4,039,628	11,491,187§	—	66,783
1913-14‖ ...	22,876,675	2,502,446	10,864,112¶	—	73,176

* Interest on loans and annuities in repayment of loans do not appear in Navy Estimates.

† Submarines not included.

‡ Estimates as voted.

§ Includes £97,847 for airships and experiments with airships.

‖ Estimates as proposed. Supplementary Estimate of £146,771 for Aeronautics not included.

¶ Including £144,325 for airships and aviation, but not the Supplementary Estimate for Aeronautics.

APPENDIX VIII
EXTENT OF BRITISH AND GERMAN EMPIRES

BRITISH EMPIRE

	Area.	Population.
United Kingdom	121,391	45,365,599
India	1,773,088	314,955,240
Europe	119	248,038
Asia (except India)	165,879	8,324,050
Australia and Pacific Islands ...	3,190,168	6,147,974
Africa	2,187,275	34,999,986
America	4,010,034	9,360,484
Totals	11,447,954	419,401,371

GERMAN EMPIRE

	Area.	Population.
Europe	208,780	65,400,000
Africa	931,460	13,419,500
Asia	200	168,900
Pacific	96,160	357,800
Totals	1,236,600	79,346,200

INDEX

7